The Hot Stove League

"Baseball is a serious thing in this country, and if that reveals our immaturity, I suppose there is little we can do about it until we grow up."

Laraine Day
A Day with the Giants

The Hot Stove League

Lee Allen

A. S. Barnes and Company   New York

for John and Jess Tattersall

For information about permission to reproduce selections from this book, please write to:
Permissions
Total/*SPORTS ILLUSTRATED*
100 Enterprise Drive
Kingston, NY 12401

Cover design: Chad Lawrence
Interior design: Donna Harris
Typesetting: North Market Street Graphics

ISBN: 1-892129-44-2
Library of Congress Catalog Card Number: 00-100101

Printed in United States of America by RR Donnelley & Sons
10 9 8 7 6 5 4 3 2 1

Contents

Foreword

No one knows when baseball followers first began to gather in winter around the hot stove of a barber shop or country store. Obviously, there has been talk about baseball as long as the game has existed. The phrase, "hot stove league," is of uncertain origin. Ernest J. Lanigan, historian at the game's Hall of Fame at Cooperstown, New York, thinks it was almost certainly coined by a sports writer around the turn of the century, perhaps by Ren Mulford, who covered baseball in Cincinnati and wrote long winter columns about the sport. A glossary of baseball terms published in 1897 does not include it.

This is a book about professional players, mostly major league players, and I have tried to show something of their life, where they come from, how long they last, what becomes of them, and what sort of people they are. I have tried to avoid well-known anecdotes, particularly the often repeated stories about such characters as Dizzy Dean, Vernon Gomez and Babe Herman, even though such stories are admirable and perhaps worth repeating.

Although this is a discursive book, there are a lot of facts about baseball that somehow did not get into the manuscript. For example, I could find no way of inserting the information that the mother-in-law of Frank Chance, famed manager of the Cubs, was Mrs. Priscilla Pancake; or that in an International League game one day, Richmond beat Grant; or that a player haggling over salary once wired his club, "Blinded by your offer, but am studying braille, so suggest you raise the figures."

The first story in this book, the little episode involving Bill Dickey and Joe Gantenbein, first appeared in the syndicated column of that refreshing wit, Red Smith. It later appeared in a New Zealand publication and was attributed to a baseball writer in Washington, D.C. I mention this to indicate how such stories get around and how difficult it is always to properly credit original sources.

I should like to extend thanks for valuable aid to John C. Tattersall, of Drexel Hill, Pa.; J. G. Taylor Spink, St. Louis, Mo.; Frank G. Marcellus,

Philadelphia; S. C. Thompson, Long Beach, Calif.; Karl Wingler, Ft. Wayne, Ind.; Ernest J. Lanigan, Cooperstown, N.Y.; and Hy Turkin, Forest Hills, L.I. Also owed a great debt is the staff of the Historical and Philosophical Society of Ohio: Virginius C. Hall, Director; Mrs. Alice P. Hook, Librarian; and Miss Lillian C. Wuest, Assistant Librarian.

Also I should like to thank various librarians in cities I shall not name who permitted me to smoke while doing the research, in violation of all known fire regulations.

Lee Allen
Cincinnati, Ohio.

I
Start with a Martini

Bill Dickey, the noted catcher for the New York Yankees, stood outside the Chase Hotel in St. Louis waiting for a taxi. He had hit a home run that afternoon, winning the fifth and deciding game of the 1943 World Series, and now he was anxious to make his train. Standing beside him was an Army corporal who looked familiar, and Dickey studied him.

"Don't I know you?" Bill asked.

"Sure," replied the corporal.

"I thought so," Dickey said, "although I don't know your name. But didn't I used to pitch you high and outside?"

"That's right," the corporal laughed. "My name's Joe Gantenbein. I was with the Athletics three or four years ago."

Ballplayers, even in the exclusive air of the major leagues, come and go so fast that they can scarcely remember each other's names. In the case of Gantenbein the important thing for Dickey to recall was how to pitch to him and he remembered that. Fans, who seldom know or care how to pitch to the thousands of batters who have stepped up to the plate throughout the years, content themselves with remembering the names. In season, when the games are on, they shout the magic names of the players from grandstand and bleachers. But in the long winters that interrupt the pennant races, when the only active league is around the old hot stove, they affectionately recall the names of their favorites: the long names and short names, the strange names and common names, the endless names of the endless players who have hit or caught or pitched a baseball in the seasons that have fled.

It is curious, in view of the universal interest in these names, how much confusion has arisen around even the famous ones. It would seem, for example, that the name of Joe DiMaggio was important enough to know and remember, yet it took several years after Joe began professional play to determine what his name actually was.

DiMaggio played his first game in organized baseball for the San Francisco Seals of the Pacific Coast League on October 1, 1932. He appeared in the box score of that game as Demaggio.

Joe was a shortstop that afternoon, but the following year he was shifted to the outfield. When he launched a consecutive batting streak that was to extend through sixty-one games, a Pacific Coast record, early in 1933, his name was still something of a mystery. "Joe Demaggio, the seventeen-year-old outfielder signed by the San Francisco Seals, is creating quite a furore," proclaimed *The Sporting News*, baseball weekly, in its issue of May 25, 1933. "This hard-hitting kid seems to have no weakness at the plate and in addition to his prowess with the bat he knows how to play the outfield much better than some experienced fly-chasers."

A few weeks later the same publication printed his name as De Maggio, and not until its issue of August 5, 1933, did it list him properly as DiMaggio. This was certainly not the fault of *The Sporting News*, which was relying on its San Francisco correspondent for word of the new player, but for several seasons newspapers everywhere printed the name as Demaggio, De Maggio and DiMaggio. When the late Charlie Graham, president of the San Francisco club, wished to present Joe with a loving cup by way of remembering his 1933 work, he had to ask the player how his name was spelled so it might be correctly engraved.

A pal of DiMaggio's on the Yankees, second baseman Tony Lazzeri, had previously been the source of similar confusion. When Lazzeri was in the process of hitting sixty home runs for Salt Lake City of the Pacific Coast League in 1925, newspapers referred to him as La Zerre, Lizzeria and Lizerri. Bill Lane, an official of the Salt Lake team, always made out his paychecks as Li Zerri.

Even the simple and wonderful name of Babe Ruth was once in doubt. Ed Barrow, one of Ruth's managers at Boston, once recalled that the Babe had signed his first Red Sox contract as Ehrhardt. Later Ruth told Tom Meany, a New York baseball writer, that his real name was Erhardt, omitting the first "h." But still later, when Ruth was fretting in retirement, he decided that his name had always been Ruth and that the Ehrhardt-Erhardt business was fiction.

Robert (Lefty) Grove, one of the very greatest of lefthanded pitchers and a Cooperstown immortal, often saw his name spelled as Groves in box scores, and the venerable Connie Mack refers to him as Groves to this day; the Killefer brothers, Bill and Wade, for years permitted their name to be spelled Killifer; and Hank Severeid, who probably caught more games, major and minor, than any other receiver in history, often appeared in scores as Severoid.

The late William Wrigley, president of the Chicago Cubs and founder of an industrial empire welded with chewing gum, spent six million dollars annually advertising his name to Americans, and yet, on one occasion, he had to spell it out three times for a Chicago traffic cop who was issuing him a tag.

Mike Donlin was a star outfielder for years for the New York Giants. But before that, as a youngster, he decided to join other adventurers and head for the gold fields of Alaska. While loafing around one day in Burbank, California, he noticed a beer truck that bore a sign advertising a forthcoming semipro game. Donlin raced out to the park and managed to get a job on the team. When he hit a triple in his first appearance at bat, a reporter edged onto the players' bench and called to him, "What's your name?" Donlin, by this time hurrying to take his position in the field, shouted over his shoulder, "Wait!" In the Burbank papers the next morning his name appeared in the box score as Waitt.

Players with exceptionally long names have frequently changed them for box score purposes. So it was that Herman Schultenhenrich became Herman Schulte, Casimir Kwietniewski became Cass Michaels, Leopold Hoernschemeyer became Lee Magee and Aloysius Szymanski became Al Simmons. Al used his correct surname until the spring of 1922 when he wrote to Connie Mack for a trial with the Athletics. Feeling that no one named Szymanski would ever be looked over carefully, he adopted the name Simmons, which sounded something like his own, and which was a name he had seen in Wisconsin on billboards advertising hardware.

Because players with difficult names often change them, no name longer than thirteen letters has ever appeared in a major league box score. There have been less than a dozen that long, and Ken Raffensberger, the veteran Cincinnati pitcher, was the last. Baseball was spared what would have been its longest and most improbable name in 1880 when teams ignored signing a French-Canadian player who advertised for a job in the old New York *Clipper*, a sporting publication, and who signed himself Peter Zaucquewinketonuxaronoic.

Strange names fascinated early writers of the game. The Cincinnati *Commercial-Gazette* observed in its issue of July 13, 1883: "Vandeboncoeur of the Port Hurons has been released. And now the Port Huron papers will have space for market reports as well as baseball. Let Reipschlager beware!" The Reipschlager in question was a catcher for an early New York team, the Metropolitans. When a pitcher named Jake Aÿdelotte signed with Indianapolis in 1884, the *Commercial-Gazette* scoffed, "We doubt that he will Aydelotte to the team."

Just as there has never been a player in the majors with a name longer than thirteen letters, there has never been one with less than three, although Chattanooga of the Southern Association, operated by that master showman, Joe Engel, about twenty years ago employed a Chinese first baseman named George Ho. When the Boston Braves in 1925 came up with a pitcher named Joe Ogrodowski, Burt Whitman, a Boston writer, used to refer to him in stories as Joe Og, but the other scribes laboriously spelled out his full name. A two-letter player may yet make it, for in 1952 the Cincinnati Reds signed an infielder for their minor league chain named Charles Re.

Jake Atz was an infielder who played for the Chicago White Sox and Washington Senators in the early days of the century and later he was a prominent manager in the Texas League. A favorite of the winter banquet circuit, he delighted in telling hot stove league audiences a story about his name.

"My real handle is Zimmerman," Atz would say, "but when I was a kid starting out in the minors, I happened to connect with a ball club that paid off its players alphabetically. On the first payday I got into line, but recent attendance hadn't been good so by the time they got to Zimmerman all the money was gone. I made up my mind right there and then that Zimmerman wasn't the right name to have, and on the next payday I was the first in line. 'From now on my name is Jakey Atz' I told them."

It spoils a good story, but Jake's widow reveals that her husband's name was never Zimmerman, never, in fact, anything but Atz.

Most players, like people in all walks of life, have a first and middle name, but some have middle initials that do not stand for anything and still others lack even middle initials. The St. Louis Cardinals in 1914 exhibited an infielder who had six names, but the situation was clarified when Christian Frederick Albert John Henry David Betzel told the other players to refer to him merely as Bruno.

In certain sections of Texas and Oklahoma some parents delight in not naming their children at all, giving them initials only. Such a player is J. W. Porter, who reached the majors as a catcher-outfielder with the St. Louis Browns in 1952. Others were D. C. (Dee) Moore, J. T. (Jake) Mooty, V. T. (Tommy) Tatum and L. D. (Luke) Hamlin. Strangely, Moore, Mooty and Tatum all played for the Reds and Moore, Tatum and Hamlin saw service with the Dodgers.

Players used to be extremely secretive about their middle names, fearing ridicule from enemy dugouts, and even today a few players will not reveal them. Baseball historians have never been able to find out the middle names of Sylvester W. Johnson, who pitched in the big leagues for nineteen years starting in 1922, and Herschel E. Lyons, another pitcher who appeared in one game for the Cardinals in 1941.

The Joe Beggs case is typical. Beggs is an extremely intelligent man of Croatian ancestry who became a noted relief pitcher with the Reds in 1940. At that time he was usually listed in rosters as Joseph N. Beggs. Asked what the "N" stood for, he would smile mysteriously and reply, "For nothing. Literally for nothing. When I was with the Norfolk team of the Piedmont League, I was given a questionnaire to fill out. Where it said 'middle name' I wrote in 'None.' Later someone made a list of players, showing their first names and middle initials. I had written Joseph None Beggs, so my listing became Joseph N. Beggs."

Years later, after months of prodding, Beggs at last revealed that his middle name was actually Stanley, a common enough name, and why he was so furtive about it for so long is a complete mystery.

Tristram E. Speaker, one of the greatest of outfielders, is one of the brigade of players whose initials stand for nothing. A similar case is that of Harry H. Davis, who lasted twenty-two years as a first baseman and spent most of his time with the Athletics. Davis gave himself the middle initial to distinguish himself from the other Harry Davises in the Philadelphia phone book. And the star Cincinnati outfielder, Edd J. Roush, acquired his middle initial because of a parental compromise. Roush's two grandfathers were named James and Joseph, and when Edd was born, his parents gave him the initial "J" in the belief that it would be acceptable to both grandfathers.

"Pepper" Martin, hero of the 1931 World's Series, is usually shown in the records as John Leonard Martin, but his correct Christian name is Johnny. When his manager at St. Louis, Frank Frisch, used to say, "John, come here!" Martin would always reply, "It's Johnny, Frank, not John. Remember?"

A similar case was that of Joe Gregg Moore, one of the best lead-off men and first ball hitters in the business when he played for the Giants of Bill Terry, and whose correct first name was not Joseph. And it will probably come as a surprise to followers of the Yankees that shortstop Phil Rizzuto's given name is not Philip but Fiero. At least that's the way he signed his driver's license—Fiero Rizzuto.

American Indians have been responsible for some of the most interesting names in baseball. Some Pittsburgh fans still chuckle when they recall that the Pirates brought up a pitcher named Moses Yellowhorse in 1921. Yellowhorse was around for several seasons and was extremely popular because of his odd name. Even today there are fans at Forbes Field who will yell derisively, "Put in Yellowhorse!" whenever the Pittsburgh pitcher is taking a bad drubbing.

Before Yellowhorse there was a National League pitcher named James Bluejacket. Actually, his name was James Smith, which is hardly unusual. He had been discharged from the Navy because of bad eyes, and when he reported to the Bartlesville, Oklahoma, team in 1908, the only clothing he had was his old Navy uniform. This he wore when he pitched his first game, and a local sports writer, too disinterested perhaps to find out what his name actually was, listed him in the box score as Bluejacket. The pitcher liked the new name and kept it throughout his career.

At about the same time Cincinnati had an outfielder named Frank Jude, who came from the White Earth reservation in Minnesota and whose mother was the daughter of an Ojibway chief. When Jude reached the age of twenty-one and came into an inheritance, he was startled to learn from court records that his actual name was Gay-Bay-Aush.

You could easily pick an all-star team of players named for United States presidents, and with Grover Cleveland Alexander pitching you would not lose many games. It is entirely understandable why George Washington Harper, an outfielder in the National League, was so named because he was a twentieth child and his parents had run out of names by the time he was born. More mysterious is the naming of Ulysses Simpson Grant (Lil) Stoner, a pitcher for the Tigers who was born in normally Democratic Texas. Even unsuccessful presidential candidates have given their names to players: Samuel James Tilden Sheckard roamed the Cub outfield for years; Stephen Arnold Douglas Houck was a well-known shortstop in the game's early days; and there have been few better second basemen than William Jennings Bryan Herman.

Sports writers in the major leagues used to enjoy playing a little press-box game in which they mentioned players whose names suggested certain occupations. Roy Stockton of the St. Louis *Post-Dispatch* was probably responsible for more inspired creations of this kind than any of his contemporaries, and some of them are still remembered. "Rogers Hornsby, an orchestra leader," Stockton would propose. "Stanley Bordagaray, an interior decorator; Baxter Jordan, a stagecoach driver; Gordon Slade, a Mississippi showboat gambler; Red Lucas, Jim Bivin and Hank Leiber, three cowboys."

Many players adopt pseudonyms in attempts to hide their true identities. It was for this reason that Eddie Collins, one of the finest of second basemen, was listed as Sullivan when he began his career with the Athletics. Collins was attending Columbia University at the time and wanted to preserve his amateur standing. For the same reason Lou Gehrig, a student at the same institution, began his professional baseball life at Hartford under the name of Lewis.

Art Shires, a first baseman remembered more for his pugilistic tendencies than his playing ability, is probably the champion of the pseudonym department. Shires used at least four names while playing football at five colleges. He started out under his real name at Wesley College, Greeneville, Texas in 1922; bobbed up as Dana Prince at Marshall College, Huntington, West Virginia in 1924; then entered Canisius at Buffalo, New York, as Bill French in 1926; and finally used the name of Robert Lowe while playing for Geneva College, Beaver Falls, Pennsylvania and Westminster at Wilmington, Delaware. Inability to collect his salary regularly inspired his frequent meanderings, and Harry Simmons, secretary of the International League, recalls reading that Shires is supposed to have left one of the colleges because he could not remember the name under which he had enrolled.

The average player, of course, does not have an exceptionally long name, or an exceptionally short one; he uses the name he was born with and is not secretive about it. The most common name in baseball, as might be expected, is the most common name in general use throughout the United States, Smith.

Here is how the frequency of names in major league baseball compares with the population at large:

Frequency of Surnames In the United States	Frequency of Surnames In Baseball
1. Smith	1. Smith
2. Johnson	2. Miller
3. Brown	3. Brown
4. Williams	4. Johnson
5. Miller	5. Jones
6. Jones	6. Williams
7. Davis	7. Wilson
8. Anderson	8. Sullivan
9. Wilson	9. Moore
10. Taylor	10. Murphy

It will be observed that the seven most common names in baseball are among the ten most common in the entire nation. Only Sullivan, Moore and Murphy, names famous in baseball, do not occur as frequently in the country at large. That they are met with so often in baseball is explained by the early domination of the game by the Irish.

It is still difficult at times to determine what a player's correct name actually is. When at the height of his pitching fame, Dizzy Dean used to supply a name and place of birth to suit every occasion, but he was usually listed as Jerome Herman Dean or Jay Hanna Dean, born either at Holdenville, Oklahoma or Lucas, Arkansas.

Hy Turkin, one of the authors of *The Official Encyclopedia of Baseball,* finally got to the bottom of the Dean case after Diz had abandoned the playing field for a microphone. "Look, Diz," Turkin said. "You've had a lot of fun giving out different names and birthplaces. It's been good for a lot of laughs, and we've all enjoyed it. But I want your correct name and place of birth for the official records. This is not just a story but history. How about it?"

"Okay," Dean replied. "My name is honestly Jay Hanna Dean, and I was born at Lucas, Arkansas, January 16, 1911."

Complicated though the Dean case is, it is not half so confusing as the still unsolved matter of a pitcher named Martini. Back in 1935 when Connie Mack was trying unsuccessfully to avoid a cellar finish for his Athletics, he employed, within a week, three obscure pitchers later identified in the official averages as Guido Martini, Earl Huckleberry and Woodrow Upchurch. Like so many of Connie's discoveries they appeared only briefly.

Years later, while compiling a history of the American League, Karl Wingler, a scholar of the game at Fort Wayne, Indiana, sought to obtain their correct names and vital statistics. Huckleberry and Upchurch yielded their data promptly, but Martini was a different proposition.

Wingler obtained the pitcher's address and sent him a questionnaire. Martini filled it out and promptly returned it, saying that his full name was Wedo Southern Martini, that he had been born on July 1, 1914 at Birmingham, Alabama, and that he had attended the Cunningham Grammar School in that city.

Wingler was suspicious, thinking that the middle name of Southern was strange indeed, so he wrote to the Cunningham Grammar School. Records there showed that the player's name was not Martini at all but Martine, that he had no middle name, and that he was born not on July 1, 1914, but either on May 28, 1913 or July 1, 1913.

Meanwhile, the Heilbroner Baseball Bureau, a national clearing house for records of all professional players, showed that Martini or Martine, whose first name was Guido or Wedo and who had no middle name, had attended Overbrook High School, Overbrook, Pennsylvania, graduating in 1931. But a letter from Wingler to that institution brought this reply: "There is no record of Martini ever having attended the Overbrook High School."

Drawing a deep breath, Wingler again wrote to the player, pointing out the contradictory statistics. Martini, in replying, said that his name was Guido Martine.

At the present time it is believed that Guido or Wedo Martini or Martine, who may or may not have a middle name, was born at Birmingham, Alabama, on July 1, 1913, May 28, 1913 or July 1, 1914. Absolutely certain though is the fact that he pitched in three games for the Athletics of 1935, winning none and losing two.

Names make news, of course. But for the student of baseball they also frequently make trouble.

II
Red, Lefty and a Few Animals

Benny Fields, a talented song and dance man with a long memory who, with his wife, Blossom Seeley, has toured the night club circuit for years, is an apparently incurable baseball fan whose greatest pleasure is to lounge with acquaintances in the press room of some major league team and dissect the game from every angle. Invariably, in such company, he will propose playing a little game he enjoys. "Name for me," he will say, "an all-star team consisting of major league players whose names or nicknames are the names of animals and insects." Then he will sit back and smile as others suggest the names he is waiting for: Rabbit Maranville, Moose McCormick, Ox Eckhardt, Flea Clifton, Spider Jorgensen, Harry (The Cat) Brecheen, Goose Goslin, Ducky Medwick and Hippo Jim Vaughn. Perhaps he will then add a few that were missed: Turkey Tyson, Mule Haas and Bullfrog Dietrich.

Most of these men were players whose nicknames reflected their size. Hippo Jim Vaughn was a Cub pitcher of enormous proportions; Ox Eckhardt's bulk made him as durable as his nickname would imply; and Rabbit Maranville was as agile as the rodent for which he was named.

But the size of a player is only one of numerous characteristics that can determine a nickname. A player can inherit such a name from his father (as Smoky Burgess of the current Phillies did), he can have it as a hangover from his childhood (as Bubba Church, now a pitcher for the Cubs, did), he can give it to himself (as Babe Herman did, patterning himself after Babe Ruth) or he can get it because of some quirk of his physical appearance, age, temperament, or from some mannerism or some buried incident in his life. Often the incident that caused the nickname is forgotten by the player in question. Frank (Noodles) Hahn, a fine southpaw at the turn of the century, never could account for his nickname. "All I know is they always called me Noodles," he will say. But a friend of Hahn's recalls the origin quite well. "When Hahn was a boy in Nashville," the man explained, "he always had to carry his father's lunch to him. His father worked in a piano factory, and the lunch was always noodle soup. You never saw the boy without the noodle soup, so the nickname was a natural."

A few nicknames, however, are absolutely unaccountable. One day in 1924 a young pitcher with the Cubs, John Fred Blake, was sitting around in a Chicago hotel room talking with his cronies. As easily might have happened in such a place and at such a time, the talk turned to Prohibition, bootleggers and revenue officers. In the course of the fanning bee one of the men began to refer to Blake as Sheriff, though for no observable reason. The name stuck, and so well known did it become that by the time Blake retired as a pitcher in 1937 few were aware that his real first name was John. What percentage of present-day fans know that the given name of the Yankee catcher, Yogi Berra, is Lawrence, or that Brooklyn's flashy second baseman, Junior Gilliam, answers to the name of James?

A colorful nickname can endear a player to his followers, but there has been a striking lack of originality shown in selecting most of them. The two most common nicknames are the equally obvious Red and Lefty, and there are others almost as tiresome.

Cy, one of the common or garden variety of nicknames, is an abbreviation of Cyclone and usually is reserved for a pitcher gifted with extraordinary speed. The similarly sounding Si is an abbreviation of Silas and, like Rube, is usually given to show that a player is of rural origin.

Players endowed with great physical strength are apt to be called Moose, Buck, Zeke (short for physique), Hack (after the great wrestler, Hackenschmidt) and Ox. Athletes who are small of stature or light of weight may be called Flea, Bitsy, Tiny, Bunny, Imp, Rabbit, Shorty, Skeeter, Peanuts and Jigger (incorrect for Chigger).

The best of nicknames are those that indicate some distinctive manner-ism the player has. It was Jimmy Cannon the New York baseball writer, who first referred to Luke Hamlin, the Dodger pitcher, as Hot Potato because of the way he juggled the ball in his glove while readying his pitch. Similarly, after watching the players in action, any fan could understand the origin of the nicknames assigned to Fidgety Phil Collins, Pretzels Pezzullo, Twitchy Dick Porter, Jumping Jack Jones and Herky Jerky Horton.

Nicknames can show a player's place of origin (Dixie Walker, Texas Jack Kraus, Rebel Oakes, Broadway Jones), they can indicate his skill (Cannon-ball Crane, Smoky Joe Wood, Scooter Rizzuto, Deerfoot Harry Bay, Harry the Cat Brecheen), they can commemorate his home town (Pea Ridge Day, Vinegar Bend Mizell), they can call attention to his temperament (Jittery Joe Berry, Sad Sam Jones, Sunny Jim Bottomley, Bugs Raymond, Scrappy Bill Joyce, Mysterious Walker, Smiling Mickey Welch) and they can even hint at his eating habits (Sweetbreads Bailey, Oyster Burns, Spud Krist).

A few nicknames, however, are so complicated in origin and so related to the deep past that they can be explained only in the form of anecdotes. A few samples:

Pongo Joe Cantillon was a major and minor league player and manager who was in uniform for forty-five years, from 1879 through 1924, and for all those seasons his strange nickname followed him around, though few play-ers or fans were aware of its origin. Early in his career Cantillon played for San Francisco at a time when Charlie Dryden, later more famous as a base-ball writer and wit in Chicago and Philadelphia, was with one of that city's papers. A reader wrote to Dryden one day, asking Cantillon's nationality, and the printed reply, written with the Dryden tongue in cheek, stated: "Cantillon's real name is Pelipe Pongo Cantiliono. He is an Italian noble-man who fled to America to escape an idle life of social ease." The Italian residents of the Bay area were delighted and immediately made the Irish Cantillon their favorite. The cry of "Pongo, Pongo" reverberated through the stands each day, but whenever rooters approached Pongo Joe and spoke to him in Italian, he would draw back fiercely and reply in tones so guttural and threatening that his listeners would hurry off in astonishment.

Honest John Kelly was another of the game's early figures whose nick-name was universally applied. He was a famed National League umpire of the previous century, such a good one that he is listed on the Honor Roll of the game's immortals at the Hall of Fame in Cooperstown, New York. One bleak winter day Kelly and a friend had dinner at a roadhouse just outside of Akron, Ohio. Hurrying back to town in the darkness over bad roads, their horse lost his footing in a snowdrift and bolted, but Kelly and his companion escaped injury by jumping out. After walking three miles to a farmhouse, Kelly knocked at the door and was soon greeted by a bewhiskered old man holding a lantern.

"My name is John Kelly, and I want to hire a conveyance to get to town," the umpire said.

"I ain't never heard of ye, but ye look honest to me, John Kelly, and I'll give ye a lift," replied the farmer.

Harnessing up the farmer's mare to a buckboard, Kelly gave his benefactor two dollars and promised to return the rig the next day. He reached Akron safely, but the mare died during the night, and the following day Kelly had to return to the farmhouse with the buckboard hitched on behind his stylish buggy. The farmer's face fell when he saw the mare was missing, but Kelly explained the circumstances, paid the farmer twenty dollars and was glad to escape so easily. "You're honest, John Kelly," the farmer said with satisfaction. Thereafter he *was* Honest John Kelly, an admirable name and an appropriate one for an umpire.

Equally picturesque was the manner in which Frank Schulte, hard-hitting outfielder of the Cubs from 1904 through 1916, acquired his nickname of Wildfire. Schulte was a great admirer of that heroine of the theatrical world, Lillian Russell, an affection that she reciprocated. She thought his Pennsylvania Dutch twang was lovely and always made it a point to attend games in which he played. One Spring when Lillian was touring in the play, *Wildfire,* she made an appearance in Vicksburg, Mississippi, where the Cubs were also scheduled for an exhibition game. She staged a big party for the players, and Schulte, who owned trotting horses, gratefully named his best one Wildfire, racing it successfully around Syracuse, New York. Fans followed the course of these events in the newspapers and began calling the player Wildfire Schulte.

Although it would be impossible for followers of the game, without knowing the circumstances, to figure out how Pongo Joe Cantillon, Honest John

Kelly and Wildfire Schulte got their names, most such designations are more obvious. But even so there can be confusion because sometimes nicknames mean exactly the opposite of what they seem to indicate. Tiny Osborne, for instance, stood six feet four inches in height when he reported to the Cubs as a pitcher in 1922. On that same team a rookie catcher named Charles Leo Hartnett was nicknamed Gabby because he never said anything at all. Hartnett, of course, overcame that timid start to become a star, and in later years when he was positively garrulous few fans knew him as anything but Gabby, although fellow players usually called him Leo. Jumping Joe Dugan was not so named because of the way he leaped to spear line drives at third base but because, as a sensitive youngster with the Athletics, he was so troubled by the hooting of the fans that he often jumped the club. And Peach Pie Jack O'Connor, the old catcher for and later the manager of the Browns, did not receive his nickname because of an inordinate fondness for a particular pastry but because, as an amateur player, he had performed for a St. Louis street team known as the Peach Pies. By referring to him always as Peach Pie Jack O'Connor, newspapermen and fans avoided confusing him with another Jack O'Connor prominent in the game, just as Spartanburg Mike Kelly has always been called that to distinguish him from Minneapolis Mike Kelly.

Not all players are known in the dugouts as they are in the newspapers. Babe Ruth's intimates on the Yankees usually referred to him as Jidge, a nickname that never caught on with the public. Honus Lobert, called that because of his physical resemblance to that greatest of Honuses, Wagner, prefers to be called John, his correct given name.

When Dazzy Vance was blazing his fast ball past National League hitters, those who watched the Brooklyn pitcher assumed that his nickname was derived from the way he dazzled the batters. Actually, Vance was known as Dazzy by the time he was eleven. As a child in Nebraska, he knew a cowboy who used to look down at his pistol, pat it, and say affectionately, "Ain't it a dazzy?" under the impression that he was saying "daisy." Vance picked it up and later, when he began pitching, he started to refer not to his fast ball but to his change of pace as a "dazzy" because it was such a thing of tantalizing beauty.

College is usually a fertile breeding ground of nicknames, and several big league players picked up good ones in such surroundings. Charles (Spades)

Wood was a southpaw who saw brief service with the Pirates in 1930 and 1931. Wood attended Wofford College in Spartanburg, South Carolina, and one Sunday morning he passed up the compulsory religious services for a friendly game of bridge. When one deal provided him with thirteen spades, a local newspaper publicized what seemed to be his good fortune, but college authorities expelled him. Thereafter he was Spades Wood. Gordon Slade, a shortstop who came up with the Dodgers at about the same time, brought with him his old University of Oregon nickname, Oskie, given to him because his Alma Mater had a cheer that went, "Oskie, Wah Wah!"

Players do not always care for their nicknames, and some are so sensitive about them that few people are rash enough to utter them in their presence. The most extreme case of this kind was John McGraw's revulsion for his nickname, Muggsy. It was originally given to him because he resembled physically a corrupt Baltimore politician who was called that. McGraw's hatred for the name was so well known that players only whispered it. Umpire Bill Klem was similarly, although not quite so acutely, sensitive about being called Catfish, and many were the players who were thrown out of games for calling him that. But George (Catfish) Metkovich, the first baseman and outfielder of the present day, never minded the nickname despite the fact that he acquired it painfully, as he was actually bitten by a catfish in one of those strange, off-the-field injuries that ballplayers are susceptible to. Johnny (Grandma) Murphy, finest of Yankee relief pitchers, was another player who never particularly cared for his nickname. It was given him by Pat Malone, his crony of the bullpen, because he was so sedate and reserved. It is understandable too that Walter (Duster) Mails never cared for his nickname, a souvenir of beaning a player named Coltrin at Seattle in 1915.

Other players with nicknames that might be interpreted as derogatory do not seem to mind them. Lynn (Line Drive) Nelson, so called because of the ringing glee with which batters greeted his delivery on certain occasions, has never objected to being called that, and Walter (Boom Boom) Beck, named for similar reasons, was always amused by the designation. A splendid fellow and one of the few players who could recite "Casey at the Bat" in its entirety, Beck acquired the nickname one day at old Baker Bowl in Philadelphia, when ball after ball boomed off his delivery and hit the tin of the right field fence. "I don't mind being called Boom Boom," Beck used to say. "Why, even my wife calls me Boom!"

Some unfortunate players, through the years, have borne real names or nicknames that were the names of girls. One of the first of these was Arthur Shafer, a pink-cheeked, quiet and respectable young man who reported to the Giants in 1909. When John McGraw introduced him to the players in the clubhouse by saying, "Men, I want you to meet Arthur Shafer, our new third baseman," one of the veterans of the team, Cy Seymour, ran over to Shafer, kissed the startled recruit on both cheeks and screamed, "Hello, Tillie! How are you?" After that it was Tillie Shafer to players and fans alike. A natural ballplayer but ridden unmercifully, Shafer became depressed and quit the game, entering the haberdashery business in Los Angeles.

Russell Blackburne, a shortstop and later manager of the White Sox, was another in the feminine brigade, picking up his nickname as a rookie at Worcester, Massachusetts. Sent there by the Athletics in 1908, he was known as Lean, Slivers and Slats because of his thin frame. On Decoration Day a morning game was scheduled with Brockton, and on that club was an outfielder named Cora Donovan. When Blackburne returned to the bench after making an inning-closing play so brilliant the fans arose to cheer, one noisy rooter, seated directly behind the Worcester dugout, yelled, "Oh, you Lena! Are you any relation of Cora Donovan?" It was Lena Blackburne after that.

Charles (Lady) Baldwin, a great southpaw of the previous century who won forty-two games for Detroit of the National League in 1886, acquired his nickname because he did not smoke or swear and never joined his fellows in the drinking bouts that were customary in that era. He would probably be known as Deacon today. The most unfortunate experience of all must have been that of Florence Sullivan, who pitched for Pittsburgh in 1884, for that was his actual name.

When the batteries were announced one day at Reading in an International League game with Rochester, tittering fans thought they heard the names of four girls. Bell and Florence were announced for the visiting team, Francis and Grace for the home club. At about the same time Pittsburgh had a battery, Meine and Susce, that was dangerously close to Minnie and Susie.

A player's nationality has often inspired his nickname. Irish Meusel, Frenchy Bordagaray, Dutch Schesler, Scotty Robb and Shanty Hogan serve as examples. But this practice can be deceiving. Dominic (Mike) Ryba was a utility player who first reported to the Cardinals when Bill McKechnie managed the team. All through Spring training McKechnie called him Mike, and Ryba, frankly puzzled, asked why. "My name's not Mike," he insisted. "I'm a Pole, not an Irishman" . . . "From now on your name is Mike," McKechnie told him. "I don't go for that Dominic."

Even the comic sections of newspapers have been the source of nicknames. The Reds had a catcher in 1935, Hank Erickson, who was so good at contorting his face in imitation of the comic strip hero, Popeye, that he was often called that by other members of the team, and Edmund (Bing) Miller, who batted in the winning run of the deciding game of the 1929 World's Series for the Athletics, was given his name as a child by his brother, Eugene, because of his fondness for following the doings of a character called "Uncle George Washington Bing, the Village Story Teller," who appeared in the Vinton, Iowa, *Eagle*. Wellington Quinn, a pitcher who arrived with the Cubs in 1941, was gleefully dubbed Wimpy after the cartoon character, J. Wellington Wimpy.

Hollis (Sloppy) Thurston was the most immaculate of players. Thurston inherited his nickname from his father, who ran a high class restaurant at Tombstone, Arizona, that became known as Sloppy Thurston's place because of the proprietor's habit of feeding soup to tramps at the back door. Later, Sloppy, Jr., while a pitcher for the Dodgers, opened a bar and grill on the Pacific Coast that he called First Base. Dropping in one night for a snack and a chat, Earl Sheely, a teammate of Thurston's on the White Sox years before, said to the proprietor, "Why do you call your place First Base, Sloppy? Nobody ever stopped at first when you were pitching!" And at the same time there was in Chicago a saloon called Third Base, and in the window was a sign that read, "Always stop at Third Base on your way home."

Like Thurston, Herold (Muddy) Ruel, the battery mate of Walter Johnson at Washington, was not unkempt, but obtained his nickname after falling into a mud puddle as a child.

Two of the most appropriate nicknames of all time were Big Poison and Little Poison, as applied to Pittsburgh's famous outfield brothers, Paul and

Lloyd Waner. But they were not referred to that way because they constituted a lethal dose for enemy pitchers. The name is a corruption of "person," and came into being when a baseball writer overheard an Ebbets Field fan continually say, in Brooklynese, as the Waners came to bat, "Here comes that big poison" or "Here comes that little poison."

The greatest of players acquire soubriquets in addition to nicknames. So it was that Ty Cobb was called the Georgia Peach, Tris Speaker the Gray Eagle, Honus Wagner the Flying Dutchman, Walter Johnson the Big Train and Amos Rusie the Hoosier Thunderbolt. Attempts to bestow soubriquets on lesser players usually fail. Ed Heusser, a pitcher for the Cardinals, among other teams, was called the Wild Elk of the Wasatch because he hailed from the Wasatch mountain region of Utah, and although it was a vivid designation, the fans never really picked it up.

But nicknames come inevitably to almost all players. Any performer named Collins or Rhodes or Young or O'Neill knows in advance and usually to his disgust what his baseball nickname is going to be. Because in baseball every Collins is Rip, every Rhodes is Dusty, every Young is Pep and every O'Neill is Tip. The first players in the game to bear such surnames have passed along their nicknames to their descendants.

III
Strains in the Melting Pot

The Irish player rages on the field,
Fights with the umpire, frequently is canned,
Is worshipped by the bleachers, and, quite oft,
Spends all his salary with lavish hand.
The slow, methodic German seldom kicks,
Counts it "a business," works for those who pay
His salary—works earnestly, and it's a cinch—
Plants heaps of shekels for a rainy day.
The Indian, sad, morose, receives applause
Without a smile upon his Sphinx-like face,
And, inwardly, thinks he gets even when
He draws big wampum from the pale-skinned race!
                                        W. A. Phelon

The author of the above verse, William A. Phelon, was an eccentric of the press box who covered baseball for many years for the Cincinnati *Times-Star* and whose fondness for practical jokes, some of them extremely cruel, is believed to have inspired the character that Ring Lardner made famous in his brilliantly biting short story, "Haircut." Phelon sometimes kept lizards in his pocket, he liked to float alligators in hotel bathtubs and he enjoyed the company of monkeys and squirrels, but he also found amusement in the antics of the human race. It seemed to him that baseball supplied, in miniature, the same melting pot experiment that the United States provided, and he was constantly pleased to observe and describe the racial characteristics of ballplayers.

Baseball really has served as such a crucible, a practical demonstration of democracy. Although a player's racial background in theory should be of no consequence, there have been times when it mattered very much.

One afternoon in 1931 a young outfielder named Wally Moses, who was then starting his career as a professional with Augusta, Georgia, of the Palmetto League, was visited by a scout for the New York Giants. "You look good to me, young fellow," the scout told him. "You can run, hit and throw. Don't be surprised if you hear that the Giants bought you." Then he added, almost apologetically, "By the way, Moses, you're Jewish, aren't you?" Moses smiled. "No, I'm not Jewish. What's the difference?"

There was a difference, for at that time John McGraw, manager of the Giants, was on the prowl for a Jewish player who could pack the Polo Grounds. Moses, who was passed up because he could not fill the bill, reached the majors instead with the Athletics and subsequently enjoyed an illustrious career.

McGraw's quest for a Jewish player began with the opening of Yankee Stadium, across the Harlem River, in 1923. Anxious to compete for attendance with the Yankees in the heavily Jewish residential areas of upper Manhattan and the Bronx, the Giant manager felt that a colorful Jewish player might very well counteract the drawing power of the Yankees' Babe Ruth. The first one signed was Moses Solomon, an outfielder and a native of New York who was released after appearing in only two games.

Andy Cohen, an infielder, came closer than any other player to supplying the need. Replacing Rogers Hornsby at second base for the Giants at the start of the 1928 season, Cohen was carried off the field by a grateful and jubilant crowd of admirers after he had scored two runs, batted in two more and fielded sensationally in his debut. But although he remained with the team as a regular for two years, Andy never quite lived up to expectations. His football career at the University of Alabama had apparently sapped the juice from his legs.

McGraw passed up Moe Berg, whom he saw as a sandlot shortstop, thinking him too slow for that position. Berg reached the majors as an infielder with the Dodgers, but found his niche later as a catcher for the White Sox, assuming that post when all the regular receivers were crippled.

Hank Greenberg, one of the greatest sluggers of all time, might have become the answer to the search. Hank sought a tryout with the Giants, but was thumbed down by the club secretary, Jim Tierney. Contrary to legend, McGraw never saw Greenberg work out with the team.

Eventually the Giants found their Jewish stars, Hank Danning and Sid Gordon, but by that time McGraw was dead. He lived to see Danning break in as a catcher in 1933, but never saw Gordon.

This search for a Jewish player involved an exceptional situation because ordinarily, when a scout is out looking for talent, he confines himself to considering the player's skill, age and habits. A player's racial strain is usually of interest only to those bench jockeys with a penchant for not particularly clever barbs. But just about every imaginable race has been represented in the game.

Apparently the best ballplayers are second generation Americans. The earliest professionals were, for the most part, the sons of Irish and German immigrants. They dominated the rosters to such an extent that in early times, on St. Patrick's Day, teams in training used to arrange intrasquad exhibition games between the Germans and Irish.

Cincinnati and St. Louis, both charter members of the National League, were the centers of heaviest German culture. In 1896 the old St. Louis Browns, then a National League member, had Christian Frederick Wilhelm Von der Ahe as president, Harry Diddlebock as manager, Benjamin Stewart Muckenfuss as secretary and Herman Fenske as groundskeeper. The Browns also produced the famed "pretzel battery" of Ted Breitenstein and Heinie Peitz.

Being Irish was considered such an esteemed privilege that Roger Bresnahan on the Giants, one of the most famous of catchers, was known as the Duke of Tralee because he enjoyed telling people he had been born at Tralee, Ireland. His actual place of birth was Toledo, Ohio.

Today's second generation Americans are largely Italian and Polish, and players of those nationalities now dominate the game, though not to the same degree that the early Irish and Germans did. There was one player of Polish descent, Oscar Bielaski, on the scene with the Chicago White Stockings when the National League was formed in 1876, but many years passed before there was another one. Apparently the first Italian was Edward J.

Abbaticchio, who came up as a second baseman with the Phillies in 1897 and who is still enjoying life at Fort Lauderdale, Florida.

Although Italians are now extremely common in baseball, for years there was not a single first class player of that strain who was a pitcher. Mario Russo of the Yankees would have been a good one had he not hurt his arm, but Manuel Salvo, Italo Chelini, Lou Polli and Julio Bonetti were of little moment. Then came Vic Raschi of the Yankees and Sal Maglie of the Giants, Italians and pitchers of real class, to end the drought.

There is a peculiar situation regarding Greeks in baseball. Dana Fillingim, a pitcher who came up with the Athletics in 1915 and then put in a half dozen seasons with the Boston Braves, was invariably referred to as a Greek by sports writers. But Fillingim, who is now an investigator for the Alabama Beverage Control Board, is of French and German extraction.

When the Reds brought up a second baseman named Alex Kampouris in 1934, the press hailed him as "the first Greek in baseball since Dana Fillingim." But the fact of the matter is Kampouris, though adopted by a Greek family, is French. The major leagues, though, have seen real Greeks in Charlie George, a catcher introduced by Cleveland in 1935, Gus Niarhos, another catcher first shown by the Yankees in 1946, and Gus Triandos, who did not know whether he was a catcher or first baseman when the Yankees presented him in 1953.

Major league baseball has not yet produced a Chinese or Japanese, although several have performed in the Pacific Coast League. The Japanese are enthusiastic about the game, but do not hit well enough to attain stardom as professionals. Sacramento signed a Japanese pitcher, Kenso Nushida, who stood exactly five feet in height and weighed a sparkling 95 in 1932. He won two and lost four and did not return. There have been several Hawaiians, notably Henry (Prince) Oana, who played the outfield for the Phillies in 1934 and returned as a pitcher for the Tigers a decade later.

For a time during the summer of 1883 it appeared that there might be an entire team of Chinese. Baseball that season reached the epidemic stage, and teams of every description were formed in all sections of the country. There were teams of amputees, teams of men over seventy and teams of Negro girls. In Philadelphia a man named John Lang organized a team of Chinese. Rigorous practice was scheduled and a tour arranged. But when the left fielder, a man named Ah Sin, suffered a broken nose, the players demanded twenty dollars a week and Lang abandoned the experiment.

The only major league player who was born in Alaska was Tommy Sullivan, a catcher who was a native of Nome and who appeared in one game for the Reds in 1925. But from the very earliest times Canada was a center of baseball interest, and the Maple Leaves of Guelph, Ontario, constituted one of the finest professional nines of the 1870's. Canada's greatest player was perhaps James Edward (Tip) O'Neill, who was born at Woodstock, Quebec, in 1858. O'Neill starred as an outfielder with the Browns in the 1880's, and his name is etched indelibly in the record books because his batting average in 1887 was a startling .492. O'Neill was aided by a rule, in force only in that year, that credited a base on balls as a hit, but even without the rule Tip's batting figure would have been .442 according to John C. Tattersall, a Philadelphia historian who waded through the box scores and found that Tip walked fifty-one times during the season. O'Neill's true average then is four points higher than the next best mark of .438 attained by Hugh Duffy of the Boston Nationals in 1894.

Players have come to baseball from almost everywhere. Joe Quinn, a well known second baseman of the previous century's Browns, was born at Sydney, Australia; Alexander (Rube) Schauer, who pitched for the Giants for four years starting in 1913, was born at Odessa, Russia; Arndt Jorgens, a catcher who rusted on the Yankee bench for a decade while Bill Dickey was doing most of the work, was born at Modum, Norway; Alex Campanis, a second baseman who had a trial with the Dodgers in 1943, was born at Cos in the Dodecanese Islands; Heinz Becker, a first baseman with the Cubs during World War II, was born in Berlin, Germany; Elmer Valo, currently playing the outfield for the Athletics was born at Ribnik, Czechoslovakia; and Bobby Thomson, whose home run off Ralph Branca decided the National League pennant race in favor of the Giants in 1951 was born at Glasgow, Scotland.

Because ridicule, no matter how banal, is used as a weapon in baseball, players with exotic racial backgrounds have frequently been subjected to abuse. Ed Pinnance was an American Indian and a pitcher who joined the Athletics in 1903. One of his catchers was Irish. A newspaperman approached the catcher one day and said, "What about Pinnance? What sort of a pitcher is he?" . . . "I don't know about letting these foreigners into the game," the catcher replied. "Personally I'm agin' it."

Cubans have been playing baseball nearly as long as United States citizens, but their fight for equality has been a long and painful one. The first Cuban in the majors was Vincent (Sandy) Nava, who caught for Providence of the National League in 1882, but there were no more for years.

Then, in 1910, Dan O'Neil, owner of the New Britain franchise of the Connecticut League, introduced four at once. With his team reclining in the cellar two months before the close of the season, he called in Armando Marsans, an outfielder; Rafael Almeida and Alfredo Cabrera, infielders; and Padrone, first name unknown, a pitcher. The four Cubans enabled New Britain to drive to a third place finish, missing the pennant by only two games, but there was considerable criticism of O'Neil for "crossing the color line," although none of the players was a Negro. Almeida and Marsans were purchased by Cincinnati, and Cabrera later saw service with the Cardinals.

Catcher Mike Gonzalez and pitcher Adolfo Luque were the next Cubans to arrive, going on to stardom after starting with the Braves, and since their advent the supply of Latin Americans in the game has been plentiful.

The signing of acknowledged Negroes has been an entirely different matter. Moses Walker, a catcher, and his brother, Welday, an outfielder, appeared briefly for Toledo of the American Association, then a major league, in 1884. There were other fine Negro players throughout the minors in that era, notably George Stovey, a pitcher at Newark, and Bud Fowler, a second baseman who played almost everywhere in the United States at one time or another. The door to the big leagues was shut in their faces by Adrian (Cap) Anson, manager of the Chicago White Stockings, who refused to take the field against Stovey in an exhibition game. It was this action of Anson's that established the unwritten law barring Negroes from organized ball, a policy that became traditional and was not defied until Branch Rickey signed Jackie Robinson for the Montreal team prior to the season of 1946.

Bud Fowler was one of the most interesting players of all time. For years he played in the mining camps of the Far West, where drunken fans wagered gold dust on the results of games; he played with lumbermen in the pine forests of the Northwest, and with farmers on the Nebraska plains. Originally from Findlay, Ohio, Fowler began his career at Hudson, New York, in

1866. For more than thirty years, until he was well over fifty, he annually began the pilgrimage that led him wherever Negro players were accepted.

At the conclusion of each season Fowler, in his later years, used to visit with his friend, Harry Weldon, the great baseball editor of the Cincinnati *Enquirer*, who always liked to print his observations on the game.

"It was hard picking for a colored player this year," Fowler told Weldon in September, 1895. "I didn't pick up a living; I just existed. I was down in the lower Illinois country and in Missouri, cross-roading with teams in the little towns. The election excitement was too much for the little country leagues.

"My skin is against me," Bud said. "If I had been not quite so black, I might have caught on as a Spaniard or something of that kind. The race prejudice is so strong that my black skin barred me. There are three or four professional players—some of them have been in the leagues—who are colored men. They are whiter than I am and always passed for white. But if you had seen their people as I have, you would know they are colored. I am not going to say who they are."

A few years after Fowler retired, another Negro second baseman, Charlie Grant, became the central figure in a strange story. Grant was from Cincinnati and each spring he used to go to Hot Springs, Arkansas, where he worked as a bellhop at the Eastland Hotel. John McGraw managed Baltimore of the American League in 1901 and took his team to Hot Springs to train. There he first saw Grant, performing at second base on a team of hotel employees, and marveled at his skill. The more he watched the more he realized he was looking at a player of genuine major league ability, barred only because of his color.

In an office just off the hotel lobby there was a big wall map of the Southeastern United States. Studying it one day, McGraw was seized with an inspiration. He immediately sought out Grant and said, "Look, Charlie! You have the features of an Indian. I've just been looking at a map, and I've found a Creek called the Tokohoma. That's your name from now on, Charlie Tokohoma. You're a Cherokee, Charlie, and you're going North with us, the second baseman of the Orioles."

That night it was announced that McGraw had signed an Indian infielder, Charlie Tokohoma, but even before the season opened the scheme was exposed. Charlie Comiskey, president of the White Sox, angrily called in reporters. "I'm not going to stand for McGraw ringing in an Indian on the Baltimore team," Comiskey shouted. "If Muggsy really keeps this Indian I will get a Chinaman of my acquaintance and put him on third. Somebody told me that the Cherokee of McGraw's is really Grant, the crack Negro second baseman from Cincinnati, fixed up with war paint and a bunch of feathers."

Tokohoma, by this time referred to in the papers as Indian Grant, indignantly denied Comiskey's charge. "My mother is a Cherokee and my father a white man," Grant told Baltimore newspapermen. "My mother lives at Lawrence, Kansas, and it would be easy to prove she is an Indian."

But Comiskey's blast put an abortive end to Tokohoma's career in the majors, and Charlie, uncomfortable in his Baltimore uniform, left the team on its northward trek and went to Chicago, where he played for the Columbian Giants, a Negro team.

In later years, whenever the New York Giants visited Cincinnati, a pass was always left at the gate for Charlie Grant, who would visit McGraw on the bench and talk about the Tokohoma Creek and the unfortunate experiment of 1901. Finally, one sweltering July afternoon in 1932, Grant was seated on the stoop in front of the Somerset Apartments at Reading Road and Blair Avenue in Cincinnati. He was the janitor of the building and often sat there, hoping that a breeze might enable him to escape the heat. An automobile turned the corner, blew a tire, climbed the curb, struck Grant and killed him instantly. You can find him now in an unmarked grave, Section 68, Lot 417 in Spring Grove Cemetery, a few hundred yards from the grave of another Cincinnati second baseman, Miller Huggins, who had the foresight to be born white.

Thanks to Branch Rickey and Jackie Robinson the shameful put-out credited to Cap Anson and the assist provided by Charlie Comiskey have been erased from the game's scorebook. There are still a few bigots at large who would bar the Negro, and some of them own ball clubs, but their cause is hopeless and they know it. The melting pot now properly contains all strains, and baseball is American at last.

IV
Psychiatrist Needed at Wilkes-Barre

A course in mental hygiene might have accomplished wonders for an out-fielder with the Wilkes-Barre club of the Eastern League in 1907. Normally this player was a righthanded hitter, but it was observed that on certain days he faced the pitcher from a lefthanded stance. H. G. Merrill, a sports writer, cornered him one day and asked what it was all about.

"Well, I'll tell you," the player began, "I bat lefthanded only on days when I get a letter from home. It all started several months ago when I heard from an old friend back there. He bawled me out for something I had done, something personal that I don't want to tell you about. And he ended up the letter by saying, 'Now turn around and bat hard against it.' A few days after that I got a letter from my brother bawling me out about something else. And he said in his letter, 'You'll make a failure if you don't change right about face and take a firmer grip on the bat.' Somehow these letters affected me. It was funny they both told me to turn around. Of course they didn't mean turn around at the plate, but the next time I got a chance I did switch around and hit left, and got four hits including a triple. If you don't believe me, you can look it up in your scorebook. I always bat lefthanded now if there's a letter for me at the park. I never open the letters any more until the next day because I don't want to know what's in them, but I don't worry any more. The letters are always all right. No bad news. But I bat lefthanded on the days they come just to be sure."

Most players, unlike the Wilkes-Barre outfielder, have no compulsion to change their batting styles on certain days, although of course there are a few switch hitters who bat righthanded against lefthanded pitchers and left-handed against righthanders. The theory is that a southpaw's natural curve ball breaks away from a lefthanded hitter. The same thing naturally applies when a righthanded hitter faces a righthander. Obviously it is easier to hit a ball when it breaks in towards the bat. Christy Mathewson's famous fade-away pitch was effective because it broke away from lefthanded hitters. Matty was the only pitcher of his time to employ such a delivery and it made him the top righthander in the game. Carl Hubbell, a southpaw, later came along with his screwball. Breaking away from righthanded hitters, it was the same pitch as the fadeaway. Today numerous pitchers have added the screwball to their equipment so that the presumed mastery of a southpaw over a lefthanded batter is little more than a myth.

A survey of the 2,744 players who entered the major leagues from 1929 through 1953, a period of twenty-five years, discloses these facts: a total of 1,858 players (67 per cent) batted righthanded, 779 (29 percent) batted left-handed and only 107 (4 per cent) were switch hitters.

When a similar inquiry was made in regard to throwing, righthanders predominated even more. A study of the same group of players showed that 2,233 (81 per cent) threw righthanded and 511 (19 per cent), lefthanded.

There are six possible ways a player can bat and throw. He can bat and throw righthanded, bat left and throw right, bat both ways and throw right, bat left and throw left, bat right and throw left and bat both ways and throw left. Theoretically, he could also bat both ways and throw both ways, although the major leagues have not contained such a creature in this century.

Here is a chart showing the number of men who entered the major leagues, year by year, during the period studied, indicating how they batted and threw:

Year	New Players	Bat R Throw R	Bat L Throw R	Bat Both Throw R	Bat L Throw L	Bat R Throw L	Bat Both Throw L
1929	109	60	24	4	19	0	2
1930	98	66	14	3	9	5	1
1931	102	70	14	5	10	2	1

Year	New Players	Bat R Throw R	Bat L Throw R	Bat Both Throw R	Bat L Throw L	Bat R Throw L	Bat Both Throw L
1932	93	62	15	4	7	3	2
1933	70	40	13	3	9	4	1
1934	113	71	10	5	23	2	2
1935	115	81	14	2	14	4	0
1936	100	59	14	3	22	1	1
1937	110	75	11	4	15	4	1
1938	109	75	13	4	13	4	0
1939	127	86	18	5	13	4	1
1940	104	65	12	3	19	3	2
1941	120	83	10	3	20	2	2
1942	110	71	19	5	12	2	1
1943	147	102	16	4	20	5	0
1944	153	101	15	1	26	6	4
1945	124	76	22	4	17	3	2
1946	107	69	16	2	14	3	3
1947	98	56	15	1	23	3	0
1948	114	65	22	2	22	2	1
1949	92	57	14	0	17	4	0
1950	105	73	12	2	16	2	0
1951	110	71	12	4	19	3	1
1952	114	76	16	1	20	1	0
1953	100	75	8	5	11	1	0
Totals	2744	1785	369	79	410	73	28

Looking at it another way, here is how the players of the period in question batted and threw:

> 64½ per cent batted and threw righthanded
> 14 per cent batted left and threw right
> 3 per cent batted both and threw right
> 15 per cent batted and threw lefthanded
> 2½ per cent batted right and threw left
> 1 per cent batted both and threw left

Because he is several steps closer to first base, the lefthanded hitter has an advantage that is really decisive. Lou (The Clocker) Miller, a sports writer and student of the game who has made a specialty of clocking runners, discovered in 1952 that when Mickey Mantle, the switch-hitting outfielder of the Yankees, batted lefthanded he could reach first base 3.2 seconds after hitting the ball, but that when he batted righthanded the time required was 3.5 seconds. This difference of three tenths of a second would often be the difference between being safe or out. Since Mantle travels to first base at about nine yards per second, he loses about eight feet when batting righthanded. Although Mantle is the speediest runner in the game, or at least in the majors, any player, regardless of his speed, would notice the same difference.

Switch hitting was introduced professionally by Robert V. Ferguson, captain of the Atlantics of Brooklyn, when that team sent the famous old Cincinnati Red Stockings down to their first defeat on June 14, 1870. Coming to bat in the eleventh inning, Ferguson, normally a righthanded hitter, wanted desperately to avoid batting the ball to the Cincinnati shortstop, George Wright, who covered his position like a London fog. So he went up to the plate lefthanded and singled in the tying run. The rally was kept alive and the Atlantics were able to send the Red Stockings to their first defeat in almost two seasons of play.

So far the greatest switch hitter in the game has been Frankie Frisch of the Giants and Cardinals, although Mantle has an excellent chance of surpassing him. Mantle seems to have more power from both sides of the plate than Frisch did and also he is still improving. Frisch employed two different stances, depending on whether he was hitting right or left, spreading his feet much further apart when batting righthanded.

The practice of switch hitting has supplied baseball with several anecdotes. Clyde Milan, the fine Washington outfielder, had a younger brother, Horace, who once obtained an apartment as a result of switching. Depressed because he could not find a suitable place to live during his first summer as a professional, he tried batting lefthanded, thinking he would be so bad that he would draw his unconditional release and could then return home. But, strangely, his work at the plate began to improve, he won a regular job and was flooded with offers of places to live.

Pete Reiser, a startlingly good hitter in his prime, never seemed to be able to make up his mind which way to bat. He was a natural righthander, but after playing professionally three years, he began to switch, and his batting average of .343 was good enough to lead the National League in 1941.

Later he batted lefthanded exclusively. Moving to the Braves in 1949, Pete still swung from the left side in games but began batting righthanded in practice. He explained this to Bob Holbrook of the Boston *Daily Globe* by saying, "I just want to see how it feels to bat righthanded again. The reason I do it now and then is because it makes me feel more confident when I get up there in a game."

Even more mixed up than Reiser was Lee Grissom, a Cincinnati pitcher who sometimes switched during the course of a single time at bat. He often took two strikes righthanded and then swung at the third one lefthanded, a grotesque performance that provided the home fans with a painful sort of amusement.

Much more rare than switch hitters, as the chart accompanying this chapter shows, are players who bat right and throw left, and most of those who have appeared were pitchers whose batting style made little difference. The only players of real class who threw lefthanded but batted in the orthodox fashion were Jimmy Ryan, outfielder who played for eighteen years, mostly with the Chicago White Stockings, starting in 1885; the extraordinary Hal Chase, a fielding genius at first base but a good hitter as well; Johnny Cooney, originally a pitcher but later a fine outfielder for the Braves and Dodgers; and Rube Bressler, who also began as a pitcher for the Athletics but who became a formidable hitter and outfielder for four National League teams.

An even more obscure group includes those few who batted both ways but threw lefthanded. Of the twenty-eight players in this category all but three were pitchers. Only one of the three was a star, James (Rip) Collins, who succeeded Jim Bottomley as the regular first baseman of the Cardinals. The other two were Chuck Stevens, a first baseman who played regularly with the Browns in 1946 and who also had trials in 1941 and 1948, and Joe Mack, still another first baseman with the Braves in 1945.

It is seldom that a player can learn to bat in any style that is not natural to him. Leo Durocher, a poor hitter as a youngster, soon abandoned one brief experiment in hitting lefthanded, but afterward improved greatly at the plate. Leo today is inclined to belittle whatever hitting he did, but he was tough in a pinch, and his average of .286 in 1936 was impressive enough to warrant respect.

In the early days managers cared little whether their players batted right or left. Charlie Comiskey, a good first baseman and manager before he became a club owner, piloted the St. Louis Browns to four consecutive American Association pennants starting in 1885 without a single lefthanded hitter in the lineup. It was Ned Hanlon, manager of the Baltimore Orioles in the nineties, who began the practice of using lefthanded hitters against righthanded pitchers and vice versa. John McGraw, schooled under Hanlon before becoming a manager, then revolutionized hitting by carefully spacing the lefthanded hitters in his batting order.

Today the practice that Hanlon introduced is greatly overworked. The platoon system prevents a player from enjoying the regular chores that would enable him to learn to hit any type of pitcher. It may appear to be percentage to use righthanded hitters against southpaws, but teamwork is greatly improved if the same eight players, exclusive of the pitchers, are called on daily, and only by appearing regularly can a player build up a fan following of any proportions. Youngsters who follow baseball tend to identify themselves with some local hero. Identification becomes impossible if the manager changes his lineup with almost every game.

Casey Stengel has enjoyed conspicuous success with the platoon system while managing the Yankees, but he would be the first to say he does not consider it an ideal arrangement.

In the early days of baseball the rules permitted substitutions only in the event that a player was injured or ill. If a pitcher in that era received a bad pounding, he could shift to some other position but he had to remain in the game. The rule was not changed until 1892. The change made possible for the first time the use of pinch hitters, and the first one employed by a National League team was Jack Doyle, who stepped into a game for Cleveland on June 7, 1892, and singled.

The manner in which a player throws is of much less consequence than his method of batting, although early in the game it was recognized that players who threw lefthanded could not do their best work at certain positions. That is why, in the major leagues today, you do not see southpaws catching, or playing second base, third base or shortstop. Branch Rickey, ever the experimenter, considered making a catcher out of a lefthanded first baseman, Dale Long, at Pittsburgh in 1951, but the player never went behind the bat in a championship game. The last lefthanded catcher in the big show was Joe Wall, who last appeared for the Dodgers in 1902. That same season John (Jiggs) Donohue caught a few games for the Browns, though later he was more famous as a first baseman for the White Sox. To find a really good lefthanded catcher you have to go back to the previous century and examine the record of John T. Clements, who worked regularly for the Phillies from 1884 to 1897.

Lefthanded infielders, exclusive of first basemen, have been equally scarce. Hal Chase appeared in sixteen games at second base for the Reds in 1916, but only because of an emergency. Billy Hulen of the Phillies was the last and best of the lefthanded shortstops, appearing for the last time at that position with Washington in 1899. At third base the most skillful southpaw was Warren (Hick) Carpenter, with the Reds from 1882 to 1889. The great Willie Keeler, normally an outfielder and a Cooperstown immortal, played some third base for the Dodgers in 1893.

When you consider the split timing required to make a double play, it is easy to see why a lefthanded thrower is not comfortable at second or short. Getting in position to throw after the pivot would simply be too awkward. But it makes no difference whether pitchers, first basemen and outfielders throw left or right. First basemen are included because they rarely have to throw to first base, and when they do they merely make a beanbag toss to the covering pitcher.

Not since players adopted gloves has any major leaguer thrown both righthanded and lefthanded, and for a long time there was doubt that such a stunt had been accomplished, even in the barehanded days. However, evidence has recently been unearthed that would seem to indicate that Tony Mullane occasionally performed the trick. Mullane's supposed ambidexterity has long been a legend, but pinning down the exact date and place of such activity has been difficult.

Tom Brown, an outfielder with Columbus and Pittsburgh of the American Association in the eighties, once said that Mullane, while pitching for Cincinnati, on one occasion threw him two strikes righthanded, then turned southpaw and made him hit a pop fly to the third baseman, Hick Carpenter. Brown, of course, did not remember the date of this event.

Mullane was asked about his ambidexterity in October, 1899, when he visited Washington to seek a job as a National League umpire. In an interview with the Washington *Post* he said:

I was ambidextrous, but as a rule I never called on my left hand unless we were playing an exhibition game, or in practice for the amusement of a few friends. But my two-handed trick got me into trouble when I was pitching for the Baltimore team early in the eighties. We were up against it in the last inning, and the old Eclipse team of Louisville had us on the run. One hand was out, second and third were occupied, and the next man up was Pete Browning. I slung three hot incurves close to Pete's shirt and he fanned. Chicken Wolf came to the bat, and he was about due for a hit. In a reckless moment I shifted the ball to the left hand, pitched him a slow curve, and I guess the ball is still on the run. He pasted it over the left field fence, and I went to the dressing room and clubbed myself in the shins with a baseball bat and was fined twenty-five dollars for being fresh. It was the first slow curve that Wolf ever hit off me; as the slow teaser was his weakness.

That would seem to prove once and for all that Mullane actually threw both ways in the same game. The trouble is Tony did not pitch for Baltimore until 1893, when Wolf had retired. The only pitching that he did against the old Eclipse team was during the time he spent with St. Louis in 1883, Toledo in 1884, and Cincinnati from 1886 through 1889.

Ed Head, Paul Richards and Clyde (Pea Ridge) Day, all of whom were with the Dodgers in recent years, claimed to be ambidextrous, but all threw strictly righthanded in championship games. Head was a promising south-paw as a youngster, but after his arm was badly mangled in an automobile accident, he learned to throw righthanded. As a righthander he posted a no-hit game against the Braves in 1946, but his victories totaled only twenty-seven in his five years at Brooklyn.

More important than the manner in which players throw is the strength with which they throw, the speed with which they get their throws away and the accuracy of their heaves.

Throwing for distance is a stunt that has interested various players throughout the years, although few modern players would care to risk per-manent injury by participating in such exhibitions. The world's record for long throws has been stepped up only about thirty-four feet in eighty years.

John V. Hatfield, one of the earliest professionals, first established the record at 400 feet, 1 inch, with a heave at Brooklyn in 1872. That mark stood for a dozen years, or until Ed (Cannonball) Crane, a pitcher for Boston of the Union Association, threw a ball 406 feet, ½ inch at Cincinnati on October 12, 1884.

Honus Wagner, the game's greatest shortstop, tried to beat Crane's mark at Louisville on October 16, 1898, but fell just a few feet short, his best throw landing 403 feet, 8 inches away. Crane's mark was broken, though, and decisively, on October 12, 1910, in a field meet at Cincinnati by Sheldon Lejeune, an outfielder then with Evansville of the Central League, whose distance was measured at 426 feet, 9½ inches.

After his retirement, Lejeune lived in Grand Rapids, Michigan, and then at Detroit, where he found employment as a ticket seller at the Fair Grounds race track. The record throw was his proudest memory. "I could always throw," he once told Sam Greene of the Detroit *News*. "When I was a player for the White Sox, I used to give exhibitions in which I'd throw the ball out of the park. I did the same thing in the minors many times, and I've never had a sore arm in my life."

Lejeune's throw stood as the official record until only recently when Hugh McMullen, a collegian without professional experience, threw one 427 feet, ¼ inch at the University of Arizona, July 9, 1952.

Don Grate, an outfielder with Chattanooga and a former star athlete at Ohio State University who had several trials with the Phillies as a pitcher, read about McMullen's feat and determined to surpass it. In a special exhibition before a Southern Association game at Engel Stadium, Chattanooga, on September 7, 1952, Grate upped the record to 434 feet, 1 inch. Grate threw from a marked line in center field toward the grandstand. He made twelve tries, and the one that set the new mark hit atop the Chattanooga dugout.

Bob Meusel, slugging left fielder of the Yankees during the Ruth era, is usually considered to have had the strongest and most accurate arm in the game's annals. Clarence (Tillie) Walker, another outfielder with the Athletics just prior to Meusel's arrival, was another whose throwing was celebrated. Since Meusel, perhaps the best arm was that of Ronnie Northey of the Phillies, or possibly that of Carl Furillo of the Dodgers.

By a peculiar circumstance Bob Meusel's brother, Emil (Irish) Meusel, had one of the poorest arms ever seen. On one occasion, while playing in right field, Irish picked up a ball, started to throw to the plate, and saw the ball slip over his fingers and land high in the right field stands.

One night when he was a member of the Giants, Irish and his manager, John McGraw, were standing out in front of their hotel during a Western trip. A skid row bum, reeking with wine, approached the pair, looked at Irish and began his spiel.

"Pardon me, sir," the panhandler began. "I had the misfortune to lose my arm and———"

"On your way," McGraw barked. "Irish ain't got it!"

V
Mr. Gaedel and Mr. Gee

Branch Rickey was sitting on the bench one day in Orange, Texas, in the Spring of 1921. He had just begun to build the Cardinal farm system that was destined to become a mighty baseball empire. Before him, on the field, dozens of hopeful players were working out under the unrelenting sun, shagging flies, throwing the ball around the infield, sliding in the pits and playing pepper games along the sidelines. Suddenly Rickey jumped to his feet and shouted, "Get that bat boy out of the shortstop's position!"

"That's not a bat boy, Mr. Rickey," said one of his aides.

"Oh, it isn't? Well, who is he?"

"That's Earl Adams."

"Judas Priest," Rickey exploded. "Do you mean that is the man we paid seven hundred and fifty dollars for?"

Rickey's bewilderment was understandable, for Adams, a product of the mining country of Pennsylvania, stood exactly five feet four inches in height, one-half inch shorter than Rabbit Maranville, the smallest player in the majors at that time. But although he lacked stature, he had the eye and the arm and the nerve that were to make him a big league star. Rebuffed in that first trial with the Cardinals, Adams made the grade with the Cubs two seasons later. Eventually he was sold back to Rickey's Cardinals and appeared in two World's Series for them more than a decade after being mistaken for a bat boy on the field at Orange.

When Adams joined the Cubs as a second baseman late in the 1922 season, he was nicknamed Rabbit on account of his size. But when the veteran Maranville joined the Chicago team, he said to Adams, "Look here! We can have only one rabbit on this team and it's going to be me. You're a spark plug, so we'll call you Sparky." For the next thirteen seasons the National League grandstands he delighted knew him as Sparky Adams.

Adams is the shortest man who ever played regularly in the National League in modern times, although trials were given to several others who were exactly the same height. One was Nick Tremark, an Italian boy from Yonkers, New York, who went to the Dodgers as an outfielder in 1934. Tremark, a lefthanded hitter, cocked his right leg in the manner of Mel Ott while batting, but he never won a regular job. But his lack of stature caught the eyes of the fans, and although he broke into only thirty-five contests in three seasons, he is still affectionately recalled in Hot Stove League sessions. Another short performer was Pat Ankenman, a shortstop introduced by the Cardinals in 1936 who also had a couple of trials with the Dodgers. Pat also matched Adams's height exactly.

A new record for pygmies who played regularly was set by the American League in 1953 when Washington introduced Pompeyo Antonio Davalillo, a stunted citizen of Caracas, Venezuela. Although scouting reports listed him at five feet seven, Davalillo, when measured, proved to be exactly five feet three and one-quarter inches tall. Nicknamed Yo-Yo by Bob Wolff, play-by-play broadcaster of the Senators, Davalillo won the regular shortstop job and became an immediate favorite of the fans. Hardly able to speak English, he communicated with his mates by emitting an unearthly whistle that spurred them on to greater effort.

There is no reason why an infielder, except a first baseman, should worry about lack of stature. Walter (Doc) Gautreau, a second baseman with the Braves in the middle twenties who was about the same size as Adams, used to say, "I think it is an advantage to be small at second base. A quick start is what counts and a little man can get under way much sooner than a big fellow. Besides, he's closer to the ground and can scoop up the low ones better."

Miller Huggins, later famous as manager of the Yankees, broke in as a second baseman at Cincinnati and proved to be a graceful fielder despite his light frame. But all his life Huggins was sensitive because of his size. As a young man he had a suppressed desire to be a drum major, and he yearned for the glittering baton and the tall hat. Even after he made the grade in the majors, Huggins used to imitate the strut of a drum major in the offices of his club president, Garry Herrmann, demonstrating his prowess with an umbrella.

Another player who stood only five feet four was, surprisingly, a pitcher, Denny Gearin of the 1923 Giants. A kid from Providence, Rhode Island, who learned to throw by tossing potatoes at cats in the yard behind his father's grocery, Gearin remained with the team for two seasons but won only two games.

When Bobby Shantz was electrifying American League audiences by his great pitching for the Athletics in 1952, his mates, suspecting that he was the shortest pitcher of all time, made him submit to measurement in a club-house ceremony. It was discovered that he was five feet six, or two inches taller than Gearin.

But the shortest player of all time was none of these men. That distinction, such as it is, must go to Eddie Gaedel, Bill Veeck's famous midget on the Browns of 1951. Gaedel, a baseball *cause célèbre* if there ever was one, stood exactly three feet seven and weighed sixty-five pounds. Those who insist that baseball is a serious business dismiss Gaedel with a derogatory wave of the hand, implying that he was not a ballplayer at all, but the fact remains that he appeared in a championship American League game, even though his name was not included in the official averages.

Veeck, whose sense of humor is exceeded only by his sense of box office, got the inspiration for the Gaedel incident after reading James Thurber's hilarious short story, "You Could Look It Up," a tale about a midget signed by a minor league team that was in a slump and ready to try anything. Veeck decided to use Gaedel as part of the show when the Browns celebrated the fiftieth anniversary of the founding of the American League.

Gaedel was a twenty-six-year-old resident of Chicago and an office worker for Drover's *Daily Journal* in that city. Veeck obtained him through a theatrical agency, and signed him to a legitimate contract. His salary was fixed at one hundred dollars a game.

On the day of the celebration, August 19, the Browns met the Tigers in a double-header before an enthusiastic gathering of 18,369, a remarkable attendance for the lacklustre Browns. Veeck provided the fans with free ice cream and cake, souvenir salt and pepper shakers, circus acts, band music and a parade of early automobiles and Gay Nineties bicycles. Between games a huge cake was wheeled out to home plate. When it was cut, out popped Gaedel, and his signing was then announced over the public address system.

Frank Saucier, an outfielder, was scheduled to lead off for the Browns in the first inning of the second game. Instead, and to the delight of the crowd, Gaedel was sent up to hit for him, swinging three miniature bats and wearing the number ⅛ on the back of his uniform. Umpires Ed Hurley and Art Passarella called time and were about to put a stop to the nonsense when Zack Taylor, the manager of the Browns, rushed out of the dugout and showed them Gaedel's contract. They examined it with all the thoroughness of Soviet customs inspectors, failed to find anything out of order and instructed Bob Cain, the Detroit pitcher, to begin his delivery. Gaedel kept his bat stationary under instructions from Veeck and stood as erectly as possible, watching four straight balls sail over his head. After the second pitch, Cain and his catcher, Bob Swift, called a conference and decided on the strategy of throwing straight fast balls. But each pitch was high, and Gaedel trotted down to first while the crowd howled. A player of normal proportions, Jim Delsing, was then immediately substituted as a runner.

That night from the austere offices of the dignified American League, President William Harridge issued a communique that said: "The American League office does not approve the contract submitted by the St. Louis American League club for the services of Edward Gaedel on the basis that his participation in American League championship games in our judgment is not in the best interests of baseball."

Gaedel then emitted a yelp not unlike the speech of a character in one of the plays by William Saroyan. "This is a conspiracy against all short guys," he whined. "This is a strike-out against the little people."

Harridge, pressed for further comment, said solemnly, "I feel that his participation in American League championship games comes under the heading of conduct detrimental to baseball."

Veeck, by this time resigned to his fate, made a tongue-in-cheek reply that was not without merit. "I suppose Gaedel's height would have given the

Browns an unfair advantage over their opponents," he said. "If that's the case, I want to protest that visiting clubs that play such men as Ted Williams have an unfair advantage over us. In fact, more so than we did when we played our midget against Detroit. For Gaedel drew a base on balls good for one base, while Williams hits home runs against us. How tall do you have to be to play in the American League? This has never come up before."

Veeck was unable to appeal Harridge's decision because at the time baseball was operating without a commissioner. The club owners, who had earlier removed Happy Chandler as their czar, were enjoying a period of anarchy. But it is not likely that any commissioner would have sanctioned the continued use of a midget, rule or no rule.

Harridge's decision also prevented Veeck from signing a man who was Gaedel's antithesis, Ted Evans, a giant from England who claimed that he was nine feet three and one-half inches in height and who offered his dubious services to the Browns.

But Gaedel, even though black-listed, had not yet suffered the final humiliation. Two weeks after his career had been nipped in the bud by the *opéra bouffe* at Sportsman's Park, he visited Cincinnati with a traveling rodeo. Late at night he was sauntering along the downtown streets. Two police officers who were on the prowl in a patrol car thought he must be a wandering urchin.

"Hey, little boy!" one of them called. "Aren't you up kinda late?"

According to the officers, Gaedel then wheeled around and turned loose a torrent of profanity. They then tossed him into the car and took him to police headquarters where he was booked on a charge of disorderly conduct. Shortly afterward he was released on a twenty-five dollars' bond.

Two days after that Gaedel bobbed up as a pinch hitter in a sandlot game at Sycamore, Illinois. This time his lack of stature failed to unnerve the pitcher, and he promptly struck out. As he turned away from the plate, he shouted over his shoulder, "You are the worst umpire I ever want to see." It was probably his last appearance on the diamond.

But despite the unparalleled "career" of Eddie Gaedel and the occasional advent of normal players who are short of stature, major leaguers, as a class, are growing. The average player of 1953 was more than an inch taller than the average of 1929, as the following chart demonstrates:

Year	New Players	Total Height in Inches	Average Height in Inches
1929	109	7,742	71.0
1930	98	7,018	71.6
1931	102	7,252	71.1
1932	93	6,682	71.8
1933	70	5,025	71.7
1934	113	8,108	70.9
1935	115	8,257	71.8
1936	100	7,176	71.7
1937	110	7,881	71.6
1938	109	7,809	71.6
1939	127	9,179	72.2
1940	104	7,546	72.5
1941	120	8,696	72.4
1942	110	7,924	72.0
1943	147	10,581	71.9
1944	153	10,977	71.7
1945	124	8,899	71.7
1946	107	7,742	72.3
1947	98	7,059	72.0
1948	114	8,249	72.3
1949	92	6,655	72.3
1950	105	7,556	72.6
1951	110	7,926	72.0
1952	114	8,275	72.5
1953	100	7,238	72.4
			71.9

It can be seen that the average recruit each season has averaged six feet in height each year since 1946, and the average player for the entire period studied just misses that figure by one tenth of an inch. Baseball today is assuredly a game for six-footers.

There are two reasons why players are getting bigger. For one thing the average man in the United States today is taller than he was a century ago; we all seem to be growing. But there is also a second factor. Ever since Babe Ruth made home runs popular, scouts have been instructed to look for the big fellows who can hit the ball out of the park. The game that was prevalent in the first two decades of this century with its accent on defense no longer exists. With the notable exception of such players as Phil Rizzuto, clubs are almost entirely interested in big men who hit with authority.

But unlike basketball, which offers opportunity to the ectomorphs, those gangling specimens of manhood with faulty pituitary glands, baseball does not attract the abnormally tall athlete. Most extremely tall players have led a miserable existence, badgered by the fans and heckled from the dugouts. The slim string beans are usually not happy in the game.

There was nothing abnormal, though, about Eppa Rixey, except his strange name and his height. A graduate of the University of Virginia who reported to the Phillies in 1912, Eppa was still on the job pitching for the Reds in 1933, and he would have played even longer had he been able to persuade his boss at Cincinnati, Larry MacPhail, that he needed to work oftener. Obtaining no guarantee that he would be pitched in turn at the age of forty-three, Rixey quit the game and is now a prosperous insurance executive. Known as the Eiffel Tower of Culpeper, Virginia, Eppa stands six feet six. He was the tallest pitcher who ever won with any real degree of regularity and he boasted 266 National League victories when he called it a career. He seems to represent the limit in height that a pitcher can attain without sacrificing co-ordination and grace.

Ewell Blackwell, also a pitcher with the Reds and Yankees, was the same height as Rixey. For a time it appeared that he would be an even greater pitcher. Uncoiling like a snake, he appeared to throw at righthanded batters from the vicinity of third base, and he was virtually unhittable during the season of 1947, when he won twenty-two and lost eight for the Reds, won sixteen straight games and authored a no-hitter. But Blackwell, like so many of the big fellows, was visited by misfortune. An operation for the removal of a kidney destroyed his effectiveness, and he was a winning pitcher in only three of his nine seasons.

The tallest player of all time was Johnny Gee (pronounced with a hard "g") who stood six feet nine and one-half inches tall and weighed 212. Gee, a pitcher, jumped from the University of Michigan to Syracuse of the International League in June, 1937. He made the grade instantly, winning seventeen and losing eleven in his first full season, 1938, and then rolled up a twenty and nine mark in 1939. The Reds had a working agreement with Syracuse then and could have selected Gee for a nominal fee under its terms, but Warren Giles, the Cincinnati general manager, permitted Jack Corbett, the Syracuse chieftain, to sell Johnny on the open market.

The Pirates then laid down seventy-five thousand dollars and four players for the gangling southpaw in the biggest deal made in the International League since Baltimore peddled Lefty Grove to the Athletics in 1925. But Gee became visited by a hex, and thereafter his career reads like something from the Book of Job. When he made his debut as a Pirate pitcher on September 17, 1939, his mates committed eight errors, booting away the game, 7 to 3. In his next start Johnny struck out eleven Braves and earned his first major league victory, 6 to 4, but it was to be his only triumph in two years. In 1940 he injured his arm at the Pirate training camp and did not appear in a single game all year, spending the summer at Charlotte, Vermont, in consultation with his old college coach, Ray Fisher.

After that his life was a series of sore arms and comeback attempts. Despite their heavy investment in him, the Pirates sold him to the Giants in 1944 for a fraction of the price they had paid Syracuse. He remained at the Polo Grounds for more than two seasons, trying in vain to work the kinks out of his arm. During batting practice he could be seen bare to the waist, sitting in the outfield, hopeful that the sun might bake his arm and restore its magic. But the arm never came around, and when he finally retired after the 1946 season, he had seven wins and twelve defeats to show for eight years of effort.

During the years when Gee was struggling with fate, the Indians exhibited a pitcher named Mike Naymick who stood six feet eight. Rejected by the Army, Navy and Marines because he was too tall, Naymick occupied two adjoining berths on the train, sleeping diagonally, whenever the Tribe took to the road. When dressing, he had to put his trousers on before getting into his size seventeen shoes because he found it impossible to pull his pants over them.

A pleasant, easy-going kid, Naymick eventually developed an inferiority complex because of his height, and for that reason he never realized his early promise. He felt that people were constantly staring at him. After four years that produced only five victories, he was shunted by the Indians to the

Cardinals, and they, in turn, released him after one game in 1944, his last season in the majors.

But despite the jinx that hovers over players of high altitude, the Milwaukee Braves are hopeful that Gene Conley, the game's latest giant who first joined them in 1952, will develop into a great star. Conley stands six feet eight and appears to be more agile than either Gee or Naymick.

VI
A Study in Suet

During the nation's great depression when attendance dwindled and even major league teams faced an uncertain future, life was particularly burdensome for the two clubs in Philadelphia. Shibe Park, the home of the Athletics, and Baker Bowl, the shabby resting place of the Phillies, were seldom filled to capacity. One dreary afternoon Dave Driscoll, business manager of the Dodgers, was walking in Philadelphia and chanced to pass Baker Bowl. The Phillies were on the road, but in spite of that a pathetic vendor of peanuts was hawking his wares before an imaginary crowd near the entrance to the bleachers.

"There won't be a crowd here today," Driscoll told him. "Why don't you go to Shibe Park?"

"I've been to Shibe Park," the vendor replied. "There's nobody there either."

It was this situation that helped explain a remark made at one time by Joe McCarthy, the great manager of the Yankees. McCarthy had a pitcher at New York by the name of Walter Brown, a mammoth righthander. Although possessed of a great number of physical assets, Brown was used sparingly. When he did work, it was usually in Philadelphia against the Athletics.

"Why is it you pitch Brown only in Philadelphia?" McCarthy was asked one day.

"It's the only way I know to fill Shibe Park," Joe quipped.

McCarthy's reasoning was impeccable, for Walter, at 265 pounds, was the heaviest player who had ever appeared on the major league scene. Strangely, he owed his start to one of the lightest men the game has ever known, Rabbit Maranville. During the season of 1925 Maranville managed the Cubs for about a month, and it was at that time that Brown, a sandlotter who had been pitching around Brockton, Massachusetts, reported to him. Walter was so heavy that he found traveling uncomfortable, but he was to do plenty of it during his career. The trail that began in Chicago led to Sarasota, New Orleans, Cleveland, Omaha, Oklahoma City, New York, Jersey City, Newark, Cincinnati and New York again before he wound up his career in 1941. He is now the proprietor of a sporting goods store at Freeport, Long Island.

The peculiar thing about Brown's weight was that he put on sixty-eight of his 265 pounds during a single winter. He belonged to Cleveland at the time and weighed only 197 at the close of the 1927 season. But after an operation for the removal of his tonsils, he shot up to 265, and despite working out five hours a day at the Y.M.C.A. gymnasium, he was never able to shed the excess suet.

But Brown was no clown. He pitched big league ball for twelve years and won more games than he lost. He was also a particular favorite at Newark, where he won twenty and lost six in 1934 and led the International League in earned run percentage. Hy Goldberg of the Newark *Evening News* was asked one day what sort of stuff Brown threw. "He throws a fast ball, curve and the biggest shadow in baseball," Goldberg sallied.

Players as fat as Brown usually delight the galleries. When a player can overcome the handicap of excess weight, it is usually because he has other assets that more than make up for his bulk. Cy Young, winner of more games than any pitcher in major league history, reached his greatest peak of popularity towards the end of his career, when a bulging paunch made it almost impossible for him to field bunts. Ernie Lombardi, who sometimes weighed close to 240, was the most popular performer that Cincinnati ever had.

Bob Fothergill was another of the game's famed fatties who obtained a tremendous degree of popularity. A stroke cut him down at the age of thirty-nine in 1938, but he is still recalled with sweet nostalgia in Detroit, where the fans worshipped him and where he simply pulverized the ball from 1922 through 1929.

Waite Hoyt, one of the finest of Yankee pitchers and now a Cincinnati broadcaster, still shudders whenever he thinks about pitching to Fothergill and his mates. "It was awful," Hoyt has frequently said. "The Yankees would go into Detroit for a series in August and find that the entire Tiger outfield would be hitting nearly .400. Ty Cobb and Harry Heilmann were bad enough, but in some ways Fothergill was the most frightening of all. He was murder!"

Fothergill weighed about 235 pounds when he was in shape, but he was surprisingly light on his feet. Once, thinking he had been thrown at by George Earnshaw of the Athletics, he smashed a majestic home run and then climaxed his tour of the bases with a somersault that saw him land on home plate with both feet.

His full name was Robert Roy Fothergill, and he carried a handsome suitcase around the American League that had his initials, R.R.F., in big letters. When asked what they stood for, he would always reply, "For Runs Responsible For."

Fothergill really belonged in a previous age. He was one of the last of those rare spirits who appeared to play for the fun of it, and he seemed able to extract the fullest amount of pleasure from life. After the game you could find him with a thick porterhouse steak and a seidel of beer, and he would chuckle to himself and mumble out of the side of his mouth, "Imagine getting paid for a life like this!"

Finally Detroit sold him to the White Sox, but before leaving the team he made fifty-one separate bets with friends that he would get a safe hit the first time up in his new uniform. Several days later all fifty-one received identical telegrams: "Pay up. I singled to left."

Frank (Shanty) Hogan was a catcher whose dietary requirements startled John McGraw, led to frequent finings and were responsible for some of the game's most repeated stories. Hogan weighed about 240 when in his best form, and it is probable that at certain times he weighed almost as much as Walter Brown. This would be difficult to prove for, unlike Brown and Fothergill, Hogan was reluctant to get on the scales. Chief Bender, the veteran scout of the Athletics, recalls that when he was a coach for the Giants in 1931, Hogan bet four or five players five dollars each that he would weigh 230 or less when the season began, but that when the campaign did start, they could not induce him to settle the argument.

Hogan may have been fat, but he had plenty of courage. One day, after being hit on the jawbone by a fast ball from the hand of Guy Bush of the Cubs, he trotted to first base without even rubbing his chin.

Still another leading heavyweight was Garland Buckeye, a big bird from Heron Lake, Minnesota, who had trials with the Senators, Indians and Giants for a decade starting in 1918. Buckeye was a southpaw pitcher and his weight was officially listed at 238. He was also a good batter, but was far too portly to be used at any other position. His weight put him on the defensive, and he used to say, "I'm not fat really. Now just feel that leg. You can see I'm just big-boned." Buckeye did his last professional pitching at Milwaukee. One day he attempted to field a bunt, fell on his stomach and was helped to his feet by two infielders. That was enough to teach him it was time to quit the game.

Players in the major leagues today are getting heavier just as they are getting taller. The average major league recruit of 1953 weighed 184.6 pounds, and the average for the quarter century studied is 180.6. Here, year by year, is how they have grown:

Year	New Players	Total Weight in Pounds	Average Weight in Pounds
1929	109	18,967	174.0
1930	98	17,377	177.3
1931	102	18,011	176.5
1932	93	16,409	176.4
1933	70	12,641	180.5
1934	113	20,322	179.8
1935	115	20,454	177.8
1936	100	18,025	180.2
1937	110	19,773	179.7
1938	109	19,439	178.3
1939	127	22,906	180.3
1940	104	18,970	182.4
1941	120	22,031	183.5
1942	110	20,086	182.6
1943	147	26,721	181.7
1944	153	27,603	180.4

Year	New Players	Total Weight in Pounds	Average Weight in Pounds
1945	124	22,314	179.9
1946	107	19,608	183.2
1947	98	17,855	182.1
1948	114	20,920	183.5
1949	92	16,884	183.5
1950	105	19,080	183.4
1951	110	19,851	180.4
1952	114	20,980	184.0
1953	100	18,463	184.6
			180.6

Thus, about ten tons of ballplayers are annually deposited on the major league shores, and the 1953 crew was the heaviest in history.

Thanks to a rare book called simply *Baseball* and published in 1902 at San Francisco by S. R. Church, who was also the author, it is possible to get a fairly good line on how big players were in the old days. Apparently Church intended to produce numerous volumes that would supply statistical data on all the players of major league history, a dream that has bemused numerous historians of the game. Unfortunately, the only volume that Church published covered only the National Association of 1871 to 1875, the first major league. But of the 120 players who were in that circuit in 1871, Church has provided height and weight data on about half, and from other sources statistics have been obtained on some others. It can now be shown that the player of 1871, big league baseball's first season, averaged 68.54 inches in height and 156 pounds in weight. Ballplayers, then, have grown 3.4 inches and put on twenty-eight pounds in eighty-two years.

The game had a few big men in the old days. Pop Anson, first baseman and manager of the Chicago White Stockings, listed his weight at 227 pounds, and one of his leading pitchers, Jim McCormick, was only one pound lighter. Two early hitting stars, Dan Brouthers and Roger Connor, weighed in at 207 and 220 respectively.

Players with excess poundage became a subject of mirth very early in the game's development. In April, 1877, Louis Meacham, baseball editor of the Chicago *Tribune*, the first paper in that city to give adequate coverage to the game, printed this comment about a Cincinnati catcher, Nat Hicks:

An Eastern paper prints the Cincinnati *Enquirer*'s description of the training undergone by the Red Stockings and gently scoffs at the idea of Hicks doing anything of the kind. By the way it is so rare that one gets a chance to describe a ballplayer right out of the Bible that such an opportunity must not be missed. The picture of Jeshurun fits Hicks so exactly it must be quoted: "But Jeshurun waxed fat and kicked; thou art waxen fat; thou are grown thick; thou art covered with fatness."—Deuteronomy XXXII—15.

The *Enquirer* wasted no time in replying to this friendly libel, as O. P. Caylor, the baseball editor, wrote: "Get thee to a nunnery, friend Meacham. You don't know what you're talking about. Hicks, though fat, is one of the most earnest, good-natured workers in the Cincinnati nine."

The first player to quit the game because of overweight was Ned Williamson of the Chicago White Stockings, considered the greatest third baseman who ever lived and a fine shortstop, as well, at the time of his death. Williamson was a member of a band of players that toured the world following the season of 1888, and in a game at Paris, France, he was injured in a strange manner, cutting his knee on a rock that lay on the field while sliding into third. The enforced idleness following his injury caused him to gain an enormous amount of weight and he was never able to regain his old form, abandoning the game after the season of 1890. He then became a victim of dropsy and died at Hot Springs, Arkansas, where he had gone for treatment, March 3, 1894.

When Babe Ruth started spraying home runs around American League lawns in 1919 and finished with twenty-nine for the season writers were hard put to discover whose record he had surpassed. At first it was believed that John (Buck) Freeman of Washington had set the mark at twenty-five in 1899, but then Ernest J. Lanigan, one of the game's foremost authorities, made it known that Williamson had hit twenty-seven for the White Stockings in 1884.

Actually, Williamson's home run record is somewhat tainted. Prior to 1884 all fair balls hit over the short fences at Chicago were ruled two-base hits. The rule was changed that winter, and the result was something of a joke. The 1884 National League schedule called for only fifty-six contests in each park, and the White Stockings connected for 131 home runs in their home games and their opponents sixty-one more. When Williamson socked three over the beckoning barrier in right in the second game on Decoration Day, he became the first major leaguer to account for that many in the same game. Of his twenty-seven homers only two were smashed out on the road, both at Buffalo.

Williamson and Ruth were alike in many ways. Ned was childless but, like Ruth, genuinely devoted to children. He always carried candy and pennies for them, and when his funeral was held at his home in Chicago, the house was jammed with hundreds of urchins who looked as if their hearts would break.

Players who have attracted attention because they were underweight have been much more rare than those who had to struggle to get the pounds off. One of the first was Frederick (Bones) Ely, a shortstop who lasted from 1884 to 1902. Ely's nickname is self-explanatory, and when he batted he presented such a delicate picture that fans were afraid a pitched ball might splinter him.

Most of the extremely light players attained prominence in the nineteenth century. William (Candy) Cummings, now immortalized at Cooperstown because he is believed to have discovered the curve ball, actually weighed only 120 in his prime. Dave Birdsall, with Boston of the old National Association, was the lightest catcher, at 126 pounds. Bobby Mitchell, who became the major leagues' first southpaw when he joined Cincinnati in 1877, weighed in at 135. Mitchell's catcher, George Miller, weighed only 150, and when they joined the Reds from a team at Springfield, Ohio, that year, they were known as the Pony Battery.

Bill Veeck's midget, Eddie Gaedel, of course, was the lightest player of all time. It seems unlikely that any professional of the future will weigh less than his sixty-five pounds.

There are other physical characteristics, aside from weight, that have made certain players stand out. Slowness of foot, small feet, bowleggedness, baldness and the wearing of glasses or moustache have often marked players for ridicule.

The smallest feet in major league history were the property of Art Herring, a pitcher who spent most of his career with the Tigers and Dodgers. He wore a size three shoe. Myril Hoag, an outfielder with the Yankees, also had a peculiar pair of feet, wearing a size four shoe on one tootsy and a four and one-half on the other.

Lave Cross, a catcher and third baseman who played in the majors for twenty-one years, mostly with the Philadelphia teams, was the most bow-legged player of all time, although, in this department Honus Wagner was not far behind.

Most players of today do not affect moustaches, and when they do, they wear trim, businesslike ones. The last moustache of the handlebar variety adorned the lip of Silent John Titus, outfielder of the Phillies from 1903 to 1912. After returning to his home at St. Clair, Pennsylvania, as a young man following the Spanish-American War, Titus grew his moustache, along with friends who were members of the St. Clair Athletic Club, as a group project. When he joined the Phillies, he retained it, and it made him recognizable on the field in the days when players were not numbered.

Titus also invariably draped a toothpick in his mouth, both at bat and in the field, claiming it kept chewing tobacco off his teeth. Rival pitchers always tried to knock it out of his mouth but none succeeded, although Albert (Lefty) Leifield of the Pirates came closest, knocking off his cap one day. Titus always kept the toothpick at the side of his mouth until he decided to take a swing at the ball, and then he moved it in towards the center. Pitchers eventually discovered this mannerism and forced him to hit at bad pitches whenever they saw the toothpick change position, and began to whittle down his batting average.

Full beards, of course, have disappeared from American faces, and except on the chins of eccentrics have not been seen for years. In his excellent book, *Lost Men of American History*, Stewart Holbrook has traced the history of beards and moustaches in the United States, pointing out that not a single signer of the Declaration of Independence wore one, but that they came into favor about 1860. In baseball there was an old belief that hair on the face was an aid to eyesight, and though players were ashamed to wear glasses, they raised moustaches instead. The last player in the majors to wear a full beard on the field was Jack Remsen, an outfielder with Brooklyn who last played in 1884. Clark Griffith, owner of the Washington Senators, signed a bearded pitcher, Allen Benson, in 1934, but that was mostly a stunt and Benson, a House of David alumnus, disappeared after working in only two games.

Bald players have long been grateful for the custom of wearing caps. Tony Rensa, a catcher with the Tigers and Phillies in 1930, was so sensitive about his bald pate that he fastened his cap to his head with great wads of chewing gum. Every time he threw off his mask to chase a high foul his cap remained on his head, and he was spared the indignity of titters from the crowd.

Jimmy Ring, who pitched for the Phillies when Art Fletcher managed the team, always refused to work in the opening game of the season, and Fletcher believed it was because he would have to bare his head when "The Star-Spangled Banner" was played. It seems that early in his career Ring was warming up to pitch an opener when the band began to blare, and there was nothing for him to do but expose his head of skin. Fletcher claimed that he found the remarks from the stands so embarrassing that he vowed never again to pitch an opening game. Fortunately for Jimmy he did his pitching in the days before World War II. Since that time the national anthem has been standard procedure at most parks, not only for the opener but every day.

VII
Rookies Are from Everywhere

Ballplayers are born. If they are cut out for baseball, if they have the desire
and the ambition, they will make it. That's all there is to it.
Walter Johnson

It would be interesting to know what Ty Cobb was thinking about and what he
had to say on the evening of August 2, 1907. Ty was in Washington that night,
and a few hours earlier he had seen for the first time a kid who was pitching his
first big league game, a big, gangling country boy named Walter Johnson who
threw the ball faster than it ever had been thrown before. Cobb and the Tigers
beat Johnson and the Senators that day, 3 to 2, but they beat him by bunting and
were utterly unable to fathom his incomparable speed. Cobb, then in his third
year of American League play, went on to become the greatest player of history;
Johnson went on to become the greatest pitcher. At least that is the consensus.

The Senators discovered Johnson that summer pitching for a semipro
team at Weiser, Idaho. They were tipped off to him by a cigar salesman who
had previously recommended the boy to the Pirates and Tigers. Cliff
Blankenship, a Washington catcher who was out of the lineup because of
injuries, was sent out to Weiser to scout Walter, and he recognized immediately that the tobacco man knew a perfecto when he saw one.

Johnson was so much the busher that he had no idea where Washington
was. But he gladly accompanied Blankenship East after it was promised

that he would be given a railroad ticket home if he failed to make the grade. After breaking in by dropping that 3 to 2 decision to the Tigers, Walter was not even told there was a bus to carry the players downtown. Followed by a curious crowd, he walked down Pennsylvania Avenue in his baseball uniform. That night he was standing out on the sidewalk when a stranger approached and said to him, "You're famous already, kid. See, they've named a hotel for you."

Walter peered across the street where the man was pointing and saw a big illuminated sign that said, "Johnson Hotel."

"Do you know I actually believed the man?" Walter laughed years later. "They say rookies are supposed to be green. Well, I guess I was about the greenest one that ever was."

Johnson may not have known his geography or the ways of big cities, but he knew the exact location of home plate. His stunning control of his fast ball spared many a player from suffering a fractured skull.

Today, with major league scouts honeycombing the country, there would be slight chance of a player of Johnson's talents escaping notice. But in Walter's day rookies were plentiful and to the club owners they merely represented raw material or equipment. If they became injured or ill, they were easily discarded; plenty of others were ready to step in.

Big league clubs today get their players by staging tryout camps, by watching college games and high school games and American Legion games, and by following up all tips. No longer does an aspiring young player have to beg for a trial; the teams are looking for him.

There was a time when players actually resorted to the classified columns of newspapers to advertise their services. The following advertisement appeared in the March 21, 1903 issue of *The Sporting Life:*

OUTFIELDER—Frank Rehor, the fast outfielder, is open for engagements. Guarantees to bat above .300. Address, 29 Amos St., Cleveland, Ohio.

When Walter Johnson said that players were born and that they could attain their objective provided they had the desire and the ambition, he was, of course, assuming that first of all they had the ability. He merely wanted to indicate that if a young player were determined to make the grade, his early environment would make little difference. Johnson's own three sons never became professional players. This follows precedent because few famous players in baseball have had sons capable of following their footsteps, although a few have tried. Ed Walsh, the great spitball pitcher for the White Sox, had a son of the same name who won only eleven games in four years for the same team; Eddie Collins, Jr., in three years of trying, was never able to bat higher than .242 for the Athletics, the team for which his father starred at second base; and none of the sons of George Sisler has yet approached his record, although one of them, Dick, knew a moment of grandeur when his home run cinched the 1950 National League pennant for the Phillies.

Apparently it does not matter whether a youngster is encouraged by his parents to play the game or not. Tom Zachary, for years a prominent American League southpaw, was the son of a Quaker minister who sternly objected to his playing. Bill Zuber, who pitched for four American League teams over an eleven-year period, represents an even more extreme case. Zuber's family was a member of a communal religious sect, the Amana colony in Iowa, that originally absolutely forbade participation in any sports. The society was formed in Germany in 1714. In this country the group controlled twenty-five thousand acres of fertile Iowa farm land. By the time Bill was growing up the rules governing sports were relaxed, and the boys of the colony even formed teams. Zuber first pitched for the Middle Amana club, and did so well that he was soon lured to semipro ranks in Cedar Rapids, where Cleveland spotted him and brought him to the American League in 1936.

In Louisville years ago a wealthy man named Woodson Moss, delighted when he became the father of a son, announced to friends that a future major leaguer had been born. A few weeks later the boy, Malcolm Moss, received his first toy, a baseball. The senior Moss, who had been an infielder and manager in the Kitty and Blue Grass leagues, thought that a lefthanded player had a big advantage, so he trained Malcolm to be a southpaw. Every time the boy used his right hand he was corrected. Malcolm attended Bingham Military School at Asheville, North Carolina, then enrolled at Vanderbilt University, where he became a member of the scholastic elite in Phi Beta Kappa as well as a southpaw pitcher. He then followed his father's wishes and took up professional baseball. When the Cubs bought him from Louisville in 1930, it looked as though he might be on the threshold of a fine career, but he appeared in only nineteen innings and was neither given credit for a victory nor charged with a loss. He then pitched well for three seasons at Los Angeles but the majors never beckoned again.

Walter Mueller, possessed of the same ambition as Woodson Moss, had better luck. An outfielder with the Pirates from 1922 to 1926 but never a regular, Mueller prospered in the trucking business at St. Louis, earning the leisure to teach baseball to his two sons, Leroy and Don. Leroy's professional career was ended by malaria acquired in World War II, but Don, who spent the war in hazardous voyages with the Merchant Marine, nevertheless went right up the baseball ladder and reached the Giants, winning a regular job in right field.

It used to be that young players put in a long apprenticeship in the minors, but the process of polishing them has been enormously speeded. This was brought about largely because of a shortage of talent during World War II, but with each passing year good youngsters are becoming more plentiful.

One of the strangest cases of player development involved John Lloyd Powers, a pitcher who was farmed out to the majors from Class D. Powers was a high school boy in Hancock, Maryland, in 1926. His school principal got him a trial with the Martinsburg team of the Blue Ridge League, but when Pat Ragan, the manager of that Class D club, had to cut his squad to fourteen men, there was no room for the boy.

Lewis H. Thompson, a prominent businessman who owned the Martinsburg franchise, liked young Powers and called him into his office. "How would you like to pitch in the big leagues?" he asked.

"What is this, a joke?" the boy replied. "How could I pitch in the majors if I can't make your team?"

"Don't worry about that. You can learn to pitch up there. I've been corresponding with Connie Mack, and you're going to join the Athletics."

Powers reported to the A's and was used mostly as a batting-practice pitcher. But he stayed with the team all during the season of 1927, broke into eleven games—winning one and losing one—dressed in the same clubhouse with Ty Cobb, and ended up with a full share of second place money.

Millions of boys play baseball in America, and probably at least half of them would like to make a career of the game. The few with enough ability turn professional, but the major leagues have room for only four hundred each season.

They come from everywhere. All the states and the District of Columbia have served as the places of birth of these men, but the output in some localities has been exceedingly scarce. Nevada, for example, has not turned out a big leaguer since 1912 when Weiser (Wheezer) Dell, a native of Tuscarora in that state, began pitching for the Cardinals. And the only player in the past forty years produced by Wyoming is Bob Harris, another pitcher who started with the Tigers in 1938.

The earliest major league performers were born in and around the big cities in the East where the game was played: New York, Philadelphia, Boston and Baltimore. But the game followed the frontier on its westward course and by 1883 a total of twenty-four states had given birth to players.

Because it has served as a place of settlement for so many immigrants, Pennsylvania has been by far the most prolific source of major leaguers. But California, blessed with a climate that permits outdoor play throughout the year, has now surpassed Pennsylvania in this respect and provides the big leagues with more players than any other state.

A study has been made of the 2,744 men who broke into major league lineups during the quarter century starting in 1929, the same men examined in earlier chapters to determine their average height and weight and how they batted and threw. The places of birth of all but one of these men have been recorded, that one exception being William Gilbert Land, an obscure outfielder who appeared in one game for the Senators in 1929 and whose place of origin has so far escaped the game's historians. Ninety-six of the others were born outside the continental limits of the United States, leaving a working group of 2,647.

In the following table the first column shows the states in order of their population, the second shows what percentage of the nation's population each state contains; the third shows how the states rank in player production for the period studied; the fourth shows the number of players produced by each state; and the fifth shows what percentage of the total number of players each state has produced:

States Ranked By Population	Percentage of Total Population	States Ranked By Player Production	No. of Players	Percentage of Players
1. New York	9.84	California	249	9.4
2. California	7.02	Pennsylvania	238	9.0
3. Pennsylvania	6.96	Illinois	206	7.8
4. Illinois	5.78	New York	179	6.7
5. Ohio	5.27	Texas	141	5.3
6. Texas	5.11	North Carolina	140	5.3
7. Michigan	4.22	Ohio	138	5.3
8. New Jersey	3.20	Missouri	130	4.9
9. Massachusetts	3.11	Massachusetts	93	3.5
10. North Carolina	2.69	New Jersey	85	3.2
11. Missouri	2.62	Alabama	74	2.8
12. Indiana	2.60	Michigan	69	2.6
13. Georgia	2.28	Tennessee	66	2.5
14. Wisconsin	2.27	Oklahoma	64	2.4
15. Virginia	2.20	Georgia	62	2.4
16. Tennessee	2.18	Virginia	52	2.0
17. Alabama	2.03	Indiana	48	1.8
18. Minnesota	1.97	Louisiana	47	1.8
19. Kentucky	1.95	Arkansas	46	1.7
20. Florida	1.83	Wisconsin	46	1.7
21. Louisiana	1.78	Mississippi	42	1.6
22. Iowa	1.74	Maryland	41	1.6
23. Washington	1.57	Kansas	40	1.5
24. Maryland	1.55	South Carolina	40	1.5
25. Oklahoma	1.48	Iowa	39	1.5
26. Mississippi	1.44	Washington	34	1.3
27. South Carolina	1.40	Kentucky	33	1.2
28. Connecticut	1.33	West Virginia	21	.8
29. West Virginia	1.33	Nebraska	20	.7
30. Arkansas	1.26	Connecticut	19	.7
31. Kansas	1.26	Minnesota	19	.7
32. Oregon	1.00	Oregon	18	.7
33. Nebraska	.87	Florida	16	.6
34. Colorado	.87	Colorado	11	.4
35. Maine	.60	Dist. of Columbia	9	.3
36. Dist. of Columbia	.53	Arizona	9	.3
37. Rhode Island	.52	Utah	9	.3
38. Arizona	.49	New Hampshire	8	.3
39. Utah	.45	South Dakota	8	.3

States Ranked By Population	Percentage of Total Population	States Ranked By Player Production	No. of Players	Percentage of Players
40. New Mexico	.45	Rhode Island	7	.3
41. South Dakota	.43	New Mexico	6	.2
42. North Dakota	.41	Maine	6	.2
43. Montana	.39	Delaware	5	.2
44. Idaho	.39	North Dakota	5	.2
45. New Hampshire	.35	Vermont	4	.15
46. Vermont	.25	Idaho	3	.1
47. Delaware	.21	Montana	1	.04
48. Wyoming	.19	Wyoming	1	.04
49. Nevada	.10	Nevada	0	.00

A study of the foregoing table will show that nineteen states have produced players at a rate in excess of that which, considering population, might be viewed as normal. The group includes California, Pennsylvania, Illinois, Texas, North Carolina, Ohio, Missouri, Massachusetts, New Jersey, Alabama, Tennessee, Oklahoma, Georgia, Louisiana, Arkansas, Mississippi, Maryland, Kansas and South Carolina. Twelve of these are southern states, and that fact verifies the vague feeling of many fans that more players come from the South than any other region.

North Carolina stands particularly high, probably because that state has a happy balance between rural areas and the small cities and towns necessary for the formation of teams. Missouri also stands high for the same reason and has received an additional stimulus from well organized amateur baseball in St. Louis. Branch Rickey pioneered in the formation of Knothole League baseball in that area, and the movement has paid off.

The remarkable production of players in the South would be even more marked if the figures considered only white population, for the door has been opened to the Negro in baseball only in recent years. Harvey C. Lehman, a professor at Ohio University at Athens, Ohio, made a study of this subject before Negroes were admitted to organized baseball and published his findings in the *Journal of Educational Research.* He wisely considered only white population and although he used only 1,052 players in his sample, his findings were the same as those in this later and more inclusive survey.

But figures can be deceptive at times. Pennsylvania stands higher in the production of players than it normally would because the two Philadelphia teams, the Phillies and Athletics, chronic tailenders during most of the years under consideration, frequently filled out their rosters with local sand-lotters who otherwise would not have seen major league service. For of the 238 Pennsylvania players introduced eighty played for those two Pennsylvania teams, forty-four with the Phillies and thirty-six with the Athletics.

One of the sadder aspects of the study is the gradual but steady decline of baseball interest in New England, a fact brought home sharply to fans all over the country when it became necessary to transfer the Braves from Boston to Milwaukee. Other carefully planned shifts of franchises will continue if the game is to keep abreast of population trends.

It is probable that the invention of the automobile did more to help ruin baseball in New England than anything else. Before the auto that area was a nerve center of the baseball mania, not only in the professional ranks where the now defunct New England and Connecticut leagues flourished, but on the sandlots as well. Industrial baseball and town teams supplied unsophisticated but pleasant relaxation in the days of interurban transportation by rail, but today's New Englander thinks nothing of getting behind the wheel and driving to New York City for pleasures not connected with baseball. The automobile has also enabled people to participate in such competing sports as golf.

The same situation that exists in New England quite naturally applies, in varying degrees, to other sections of the country. Baseball's greatest popularity was reached in days when other sports and interests did not compete so keenly for their share of the people's leisure and dollars. But organized baseball is now alerted to the situation and for the first time in its history has taken steps to promote itself.

Because California is now supplying more major league players than any other state, 249 of them in the past twenty-five years, it is worth noting that twenty-seven of these men have been obtained by the Yankees, more than any other team has secured. It would seem to be more than coincidence that the club with the greatest record for winning games has found it profitable to concentrate on players developed in California. It is not likely that the Yankee scouts regret recommending Vernon Gomez, Frankie Crosetti, Joe

DiMaggio, Joe Gordon, Tiny Bonham, Jerry Priddy, Charlie Silvera, Gerry Coleman, Jackie Jensen, Bill Martin, Tom Morgan and Gil McDougald, not to mention Lyn Lary, Jimmy Reese, Myril Hoag, Art Schallock, Andy Carey, Bill Renna and Gus Triandos.

If a team were to reorganize its scouting staff as a result of this study, it might actually get by with only five scouts, one each in California, Pennsylvania, Illinois, Texas and North Carolina. Even with that slim staff the club could be assured of covering five states that turn out 36.8 per cent of the nation's players.

Actually, though, with such an arrangement in effect, there would still be numerous players missed, for good rookies come from everywhere. The St. Louis Browns found that out in the early twenties when they discovered a major league first baseman in a graveyard. Phil Todt grew up in St. Peter and St. Paul's Cemetery, 7030 Gravois Avenue, St. Louis, where his father, Anthony Todt, served as caretaker and lived on the grounds for years. The Browns lost title to his services because of a technicality, but Phil landed with the Red Sox and stayed in the American League for eight years.

VIII
Stars of All Ages

During the evening that followed the All-Star game of 1952, which was played at Shibe Park in Philadelphia with the National League winning, 3 to 2, in a contest limited to five innings by a driving rain, a group of baseball people lounged around the lobby of the host city's Warwick Hotel. A veteran baseball reporter who was present sidled up to Joe Boley, the old shortstop of the Athletics and by now a scout for the same team, and said gravely, "Joe, when you played for the A's, you roomed with Jack Quinn. Now, I know, of course, that Jack always made a mystery of his age, but he's been dead now six years and it shouldn't make any difference any more. How about it? How old was he anyway?"

Boley eyed his questioner carefully before replying; then said, "Well, I know how old he was all right, but I'm not going to tell you. I promised Jack I'd never tell anyone, and the fact that he's dead doesn't change it. If you want to know, ask his family. He's got a brother Mike, who's a barber up in Pottsville. If he wants to tell you, okay."

And so, even after his death, the question of Quinn's age remained shrouded in mystery. Jack's real name was John Quinn Picus, and although during his pitching career he was generally believed to be Welsh, he was in reality of Polish descent. He first appeared as a professional player in 1903, leaving the coal regions of Eastern Pennsylvania to join the Connellsville team of the Pennsylvania State Association. As early as 1909 he reached the majors with the New York Yankees, then also called the Highlanders. A spitball pitcher of moderate effectiveness, he remained on the scene for more years than he enjoyed recalling, and his trail led to the Braves, to Baltimore in the Federal League, to the White Sox, back to the Yankees, to the Red Sox and the Athletics, and finally to the National League where he ended up with the Dodgers and the Reds. Cincinnati cut him loose late during the summer of 1933, but he refused to quit. He reported to Hollywood of the Pacific Coast League in 1934 and, still bluffing the spitter on every pitch, managed to get into six games, winning one and losing one, before drawing his release. Even in 1935, when the record book said he was fifty, he tried to work for Johnstown of the Middle Atlantic League, but he had thrown too many pitches by then and was released before getting into enough innings to qualify for inclusion in the official averages.

Jack's early life was a hard one, spent first in the mines and then in the shop of a blacksmith. Such work gave him a strong back and the constitution of a rhinoceros, but it also put creases in his face, making him appear older than his years. Baseball people were calling him an old man years before he finally quit the game, and he never thought it was particularly funny. One winter day in 1929 he applied for a hunting license at Bloomsburg, Pennsylvania. "How old are you?" the clerk asked. "A lot of people would like to know that," Jack replied. "Just put down thirty-five. That's as good as any other age."

On another occasion he was warming up to pitch an exhibition game for the Athletics in Louisville. An old man leaning on a cane hobbled down from the grandstand to the fence beside the playing area and cackled at Quinn, "Heh, point out old Jack Quinn to me, will you?" Jack turned away in disgust.

When Quinn was starting out as a pitcher, he told the game's record keepers that he was born at Hazleton, Pennsylvania, on July 5, 1885. Actually he was cheating only by one year. His baptismal certificate has at long last been unearthed, and it reveals that he was born at Janeville, a little mining town near Hazleton, July 5, 1884. This means that he was forty-nine when he came to the end of the line with the Reds in 1933, the oldest man ever signed to a playing contract in the majors.

There have been two cases in which men older than Quinn appeared in big league games, but they represented only stunts, one-time shots by Nick Altrock and Jim O'Rourke. Altrock, once a fine lefthanded pitcher in the American League and later a clown and coach for the Senators, used to make one annual appearance as a pinch hitter, usually on the season's final day. The last time he tried it was on October 1, 1933, shortly after Washington had clinched one of its rare pennants. Swinging for Johnny Kerr, a second baseman, he was retired by Rube Walberg of the Athletics. That time at bat made history of a sort because Nick was then fifty-seven years and sixteen days old.

More extraordinary was the case of O'Rourke, who started playing major league ball in 1872 and who was alert and capable enough to hit .305 for Washington in 1893. After that he continued to play ball in the minors. When the New York Giants were going after their one-hundredth victory of the 1904 season O'Rourke, by this time fifty-two, persuaded John McGraw to let him catch one inning of the game. McGraw agreed, and so well did the veteran do that he remained behind the bat for the entire struggle. In its coverage of this strange affair *The Sporting News* observed:

Jim O'Rourke, the grand old man of baseball, beside whose records those of Pop Anson and other veterans fade into insignificance, yesterday made his first appearance in many years at the Polo Grounds and handled the delivery of Iron Man McGinnity without a flaw. O'Rourke has been playing professionally without intermission for 31 years. He was one of the original Giants who won the pennant in 1888 and 1889 and has never lost his old love for his old team. He had a longing to play once more for his old club and to show his old constituents and their descendents what he can do as a backstop, although he has passed the half century mark in years. Manager McGraw consented to give "Jeems" the opportunity, and O'Rourke not only had the honor of helping the Giants in their one-hundreth victory of the season, but the game that gave them the pennant as well. Those who expected to see a spavined "has been" behind the bat saw a man who has the activity of a youngster combined with the practical experience of a Warner, a McGuire or a Robinson. Not one of the Iron Man's shots got away from "Jeems" nor did he make a wild throw. His one error was the muff of a throw from McGinnity to the plate to force a runner, and this was due to over-anxiety to complete a double play at first base. At the bat O'Rourke made a hit and got to third base on a bad throw by Steinfeldt. He blazed his way around the bases like a minor league colt.

After that triumphant swan song O'Rourke returned to his native Bridgeport, serving as owner and manager of that city's franchise in the Connecticut League and frequently inserting himself in his team's lineup. He caught his last professional game in 1911 at the age of fifty-nine. His son, James Stephen O'Rourke, played shortstop in the same contest.

In comparing O'Rourke with Pop Anson *The Sporting News*, which has recorded the shifting of sands in baseball since 1886, revived the memory of a man who once seemed destined to play the game forever. Anson was on the scene for major league baseball's first season in 1871, and he was still the regular first baseman for Chicago of the National League in 1897 at the age of forty-six. Four times batting champion of the National, one of seven players in all history to make three thousand or more hits, and long a famous playing manager, Anson eventually lost out at Chicago only because of front office politics.

When he began his twenty-seventh season of big league play in 1897, an admiring fan signing himself Hyder Ali penned a long verse that appeared in *The Sporting News*. Two of its stanzas follow:

> How old is Anson? No one knows,
> I saw him playing when a kid,
> When I was wearing still short clothes,
> And so my father's father did;
> The oldest veterans of them all
> As kids, saw Anson play baseball.
>
> How old is Anson? Ask the stars
> That glisten in the hair of night
> When day has drawn her golden bars
> To shut the sunbeams from our sight;
> The stars were present at his birth—
> Were first to welcome him to earth.

But, just as years later Jack Quinn was to resent jibes about his frequent birthdays, Anson became sick and tired of comment on his approaching baseball senility. Chicago newspapers began calling attention to his age when he was still in his prime, and one day during the season of 1891 Anson decided to do something about it. Calling upon a friend who was a theatrical wigmaker, he had made to order a wig with gray locks and a white beard that reached almost to his waist. He entered the clubhouse at the last possible moment before the game and was happy to find that there was only one other player there, his second baseman, Fred Pfeffer. Pfeffer helped him adjust the wig and beard over his uniform, and they then marched out upon the field.

The bewhiskered Anson played the entire game at first base, but the fans, although shrieking in glee, were not quite sure they got the point of his little joke. But when, beard and all, he hit safely to knock across the winning run that afternoon, they realized the beautiful irony of his act, and it was several seasons before the newspapers began to bury him again.

When the Cardinals clinched a National League pennant in 1931, their manager, Gabby Street, though forty-nine, felt playful enough to catch a championship game against Brooklyn. When Babe Herman, third man up that day in the Dodger lineup, heard that Street, out of harness in the majors since 1912 was going to catch, he could hardly hide his elation. "Oh, boy!" he piped. "I hope I can get on base; I can help my stolen base record!" Babe got on base all right and in the first inning, for with two men out and the sacks clear, Gabby had him intentionally passed. He then called for a pitch-out, raised his ancient arm and snapped a throw to the shortstop, Charlie Gelbert, who tagged Herman sliding towards the bag.

In any discussion of the ages of players it is practically impossible to avoid mentioning Leroy (Satchel) Paige, the venerable Negro who was prevented from performing before major league audiences in his prime only because of the customs of the era. But he proved to be tough enough for American League batters in his senescence; what he might have accomplished at his peak is pleasant to ponder. Dizzy Dean, who often faced him in exhibitions along the barnstorming trail, says without qualification that Paige was the greatest pitcher he ever saw.

When Satchel reported to the Cleveland Indians in July, 1948, he said that he was thirty-nine and had been born at Mobile, Alabama, on September 18, 1908. His wife, La Homa Brown Paige, located for an interview in Kansas City, reported that he was forty-one. When Satchel immediately proved that whatever his age he was capable of pitching in the major leagues, the guessing game really began in earnest. Tom Meany, one of the most resourceful of the game's writers, began to collect various estimates of old Satch's age and the hilarious result filled a column in the late New York *Star*. Meany found that Dan Daniel of the New York *World-Telegram* thought Paige was fifty-two; that the New York *Sun* had believed him to be "between thirty-four and forty" in 1941, which was playing it safe, even for the *Sun;* that *Life* magazine, also in 1941, credited him with being thirty-three; and that the defunct New York daily, *PM,* by some bizarre legerdemain of arithmetic, had referred to him as forty-one in 1941 and thirty-four in 1942. Meany also dug up an interview Paige had granted in 1946 in which he said that he had been born on September 25, 1906.

The question was settled once and for all when George J. Flournoy, a correspondent of *The Sporting News,* checked the official birth records at the Board of Health in Mobile. They showed definitely that Paige was born on July 7, 1906. In other words, Mrs. Paige was approximately correct when she said her husband was forty-one at the time Cleveland signed him. Satchel himself had disclosed the correct year, although not the right month, when he stated his age in 1946. But Flournoy's story created scarcely a ripple; to this day newspapermen and radio and television announcers refer to the ancient pitcher as "ageless," whatever that means. Throughout the country fans and players seem to prefer to believe that Satchel is older than he actually is. But he still has not reached the age that Jack Quinn had attained when he was pitching for the Reds in 1933 and will not until after July of 1955.

In a business as perishable as baseball a player certainly cannot be blamed for fibbing about his true age. He knows that his age is one of the factors that determine whether or not he is going to get a job or whether he is going to keep the job he has. For this reason almost every player is a year or two older than he is listed, and a few athletes have been as many as seven years older than they claimed. One example will suffice. In the early twenties the Phillies had a pitcher named Charles (Petie) Behan, listed as born on December 11, 1894. But years later, when President Bob Carpenter organized his former players into an alumni association, Behan indicated on a questionnaire that his birth occurred on December 11, 1887.

When all American men between the ages of twenty-one and thirty-six had to register for military service on October 16, 1940, the Reds were certain they were going to lose a fine pitcher, Jim Turner, to the armed forces. Turner was listed as thirty-five but still had considerable value. A few months later when Warren Giles, the team's general manager, asked Turner about his draft status, Jim smiled and said, "I didn't have to register; I'm too old." But despite his years Turner stayed around and was still an effective relief pitcher for the Yankees in 1945.

It is not always the player who is responsible for the falsification of birth data; sometimes it is the work of a ball club. "I was twenty-four when I joined Memphis of the Southern Association," said a pitcher named Horace Lisenbee. "But when I signed my contract, the president of the team said, 'Let's make you twenty-two. That way I'll have a better chance of selling you to the majors.'" So Horace obligingly became twenty-two and was soon purchased by Washington.

Harvey C. Lehman, the Ohio University professor who has made a survey of players produced by each state, has also studied age differences in baseball proficiency, concluding that batting champions average 29.16 years of age, that pitchers who lead the leagues in percentage do so at an average age of 28.18 and that base-stealing champions reach a peak at 27.96. Unfortunately, however, Mr. Lehman had to base his findings on erroneous dates of birth, using the birthdays supplied by the game's record books. Not until such surveys are based on birth certificates will it be possible to link age with achievement in baseball.

There have been some cases of players who claimed to be older than they actually were, usually because as rookies they considered themselves too young for professional play. Although youth is an asset in baseball, extreme youth is sometimes regarded as a liability.

During the somber but exciting days of the last war when most players were serving in the armed forces, the professional game kept functioning only by the judicious use of mutes, epileptics, players with perforated eardrums and men who were either over or under military age. It was this circumstance that led Cincinnati to express interest in Joe Nuxhall, a boy from Hamilton, Ohio, who showed up at one of the team's tryout camps. A gangling southpaw, promising but wild, Nuxhall was only fifteen. In spite of his lack of years and experience he was signed, and when his manager, Bill McKechnie, threw him into a game that was hopelessly lost to the Cardinals, he was, at the age of fifteen years, ten months and eleven days, the youngest player who ever appeared in a big league box score. Joe retired two of the first three hitters to appear but then found himself facing the great Stan Musial. That sight so unnerved him that he blew sky high, eventually allowing five runs before the inning was completed. After that one brief appearance he went out to the minors to learn the business of pitching, and eight years later he returned to the Reds, ready for the big league at last.

The youngest player in American League history was Carl Scheib, also a pitcher although a righthander. A contemporary of Nuxhall's, Scheib made his bow for the Athletics at the end of the 1943 season, first getting into a score at the age of sixteen years, eight months and five days. Scheib never had to pitch an inning in the minors, and although he spent one year in the armed forces, he was still pitching for the A's and a veteran of ten seasons at the age of twenty-eight.

But Nuxhall and Scheib were veterans compared with Joe Relford, a twelve-year-old Negro bat boy who was used as a pinch-hitter by the Fitzgerald club of the Georgia State League in a game at Statesboro on the night of July 19, 1952. With Statesboro leading, 13 to 0, in the eighth inning, fans close to the Fitzgerald bench yelled derisively at Manager Charlie Ridgeway, "Put in the bat boy!" To their astonishment Ridgeway did exactly that, substituting the lad for Ray Nichting, the team's leading hitter at .330. The boy grounded out, but in the last half of the inning took his position in center field. When a line drive was hit over his head, he dashed back to the fence, gauged the ball's flight carefully, and made a startling catch. But sadly the episode had a bitter denouement. Ed Kubick, the umpire who permitted the horseplay, was fired by the league president. Ridgeway was fined fifty dollars and suspended for five days, and little Joe Relford, hero of the proceedings, was dismissed from his job of hustling bats. The league properly ruled that the bat boy's appearance made a travesty of the game, but Joe's position as baseball's youngest professional player seems secure.

IX
A Letter to Mrs. Gilligan

Although Branch Rickey, the learned chief executive of the Pittsburgh Pirates, has a deserved reputation for manipulating the English language to suit his purposes, it is doubtful that he will ever achieve the heights of rhetoric reached by James (Orator Jim) O'Rourke, the player who caught an entire game for the New York Giants at the age of fifty-two in 1904. O'Rourke was one of the first clubhouse lawyers, and his command of the English tongue was astonishing and bizarre.

When an outfielder named Louis Sockalexis, a Penobscot Indian, signed a contract containing a clause that forbade drinking, O'Rourke read about it; then turned to a friend and said, "I see that Sockalexis must forego frescoing his tonsils with the cardinal brush; it is so nominated in the contract of the aborigine."

On another occasion, when Orator Jim was a manager, one of his players, John Peters, asked for a ten dollar advance. "I am sorry," O'Rourke replied sympathetically, "but the exigencies of the occasion and the condition of our exchequer will not permit anything of the sort at this period of our existence. Subsequent developments in the field of finance may remove the present gloom and we may emerge into a condition where we may see fit to reply in the affirmative to your exceedingly modest request." Understandably, Peters did not try again.

The most remarkable document attesting to O'Rourke's powers appeared in the New York *Sporting Times,* a short-lived journal of the trade, in its issue of November 23, 1890. It seems that a widow named Gilligan who lived in Bridgeport, the Orator's home town, heard a disturbance in the barn where she kept a calf. Not knowing that the intruder was a lion which had just escaped from Barnum's winter headquarters, she rushed into the fray with a pitchfork, routing the beast. The newspapers then made her a sensation. O'Rourke, reading about her feat and overcome with admiration, wrote her as follows:

Dear Mrs. Gilligan:

The unparalleled bravery shown by you, and the unwavering fidelity extended by you to your calf during your precarious environment in the cowshed, when a ferocious, carniverous beast threatened your total destruction, has suddenly exalted your fair name to an altitude much higher than the Egyptian pyramids, where hieroglyphics and other undecipherable mementos of the past are now lying in a state of innocuous desuetude, with no enlightened modern scholar able to exemplify their disentangled pronunciation. The exuberance of my verbosity is as natural as the chrysanthemums exhibited at the late horticultural exhibition, so in reality it cannot be called ostentation, even though the sesquipedalian passages may seem unintelligible to an untutored personality. The lion—or it may have been a lioness—but you, of course, in the impending predicament could only make a cursory and rather unsatisfactory investigation—must have discerned your courageous eye (a trait so characteristic of the Celtic Micks and Biddys), which shows, beyond peradventure, that you are possessed of undeniable hypnotical mesmerization qualities, as well as the diabolical intricacies of legerdemain and therapeutics. We should arise, Phoenix-like, and show our appreciation of your unswerving loyalty. We should extol your bravery to the coming generation in words more lofty than my unprepared efforts can faithfully depict, for your name hereafter will be synonymous with fearlessness in all that the word can unconsciously imply. Standing before a wild, unrestrained pitcher with a mellifluous and unconquerable courageousness is as of nothing compared with the indomitable fortitude exhibited by you when destruction seemed inevitable—when pandemonium rent the oxygenic atmosphere asunder with the tragic vociferation of Barnum's untamed and inhospitable intruder. A thousand blessings to you!

Yours admiringly,
James O'Rourke

Take it away, Mr. Rickey!

Ballplayers differ widely in temperament but are more apt to be laconic than verbose, and there are few O'Rourkes in the profession. Two of the quietest performers of all time were Clyde Barnhart, an outfielder, and Charles (Whitey) Glazner, a pitcher, who roomed together at Pittsburgh from 1920 to 1923. Barnhart never talked at all and Glazner was hard of hearing. One night Johnny Morrison, a pitcher whose name still bobs up in Hot Stove League circles because of his amazing curve ball, visited their room. Only once during his stay was there any attempt at conversation at all. Barnhart opened his mouth to ask the time, but the question was never answered because Whitey failed to hear him.

Charlie Gehringer, the great second baseman of the Tigers, and Elon Hogsett, an Indian pitcher at Detroit, formed another taciturn pair. Like Barnhart and Glazner they roomed together. One morning Hal Walker, a writer for the Toronto *Globe* and *Mail*, had breakfast with them. Hogsett turned to Gehringer and said, "Pass the salt, please." Gehringer obliged, but said in reproach, "You might have pointed."

The stupidity of certain players was acknowledged long before Ring Lardner painted his classic pictures of bushers, alibi artists, boneheads and bores. Pete Browning, a favorite in Louisville and one of the greatest hitters of the 1880's, is supposed to have said, upon hearing of the assassination of James A. Garfield, "Yeah? What league was he in?"

Lardner's creations, by the way, were not at all exaggerated. He is believed to have received the inspiration for one of his more pleasant characters, the busher, after watching Butcher Boy Joe Benz pitch an exhibition game for the White Sox while wearing hip boots. But just as the automobile has helped destroy baseball interest in some sections of the country it has helped destroy provincialism, and the rookie that Lardner knew so well, the kid with his badger haircut and straw suitcase, has disappeared from the scene. The cultural level of players has been raised greatly in the past thirty years. Today's businessman-ballplayer is at ease before the television cameras and in the dining rooms of the snootiest hotels. He buys stocks and bonds and sends his children to private schools. There are still a few who confine their reading to comic books and box scores but their number is decreasing, and it will be a sad day for the game when they disappear entirely because they supply the few splotches of color in the fabric of a game that sometimes approaches the monotony of near perfection.

Almost every anecdote about the illiteracy of players dates back to the period before World War I when Lardner was using his genius to describe the genus. Shoeless Joe Jackson, greatest of natural hitters and one of the unfortunates who became involved in the Black Sox scandal of 1919, had little or no education and the fact that he could not spell was known to the galleries. Once, after Joe had delivered a resounding triple and was perched on third base, a fan shouted from the grandstand, "Heh, Joe. Spell 'cat.' " Jackson glared at him, squirted a stream of tobacco juice out of the side of his mouth and retorted, "Spell 'hit.' "

But long before Jackson certain players were celebrated for their lack of formal learning. William (Blondie) Purcell, a pitcher and outfielder, was a popular member of the first Phillies team in the National League in 1883. One night he was invited to a party at the home of an affluent admirer and arrived late. "Why, hello there, Blondie," his hostess greeted him. "Do come right in; we're having tableaux" . . . "I know," Blondie replied. "I smelt 'em when I come in."

Connie Mack, who has witnessed players of every variety in his unparalleled career, once conducted a clubhouse meeting in which he carefully went over the batting weaknesses of every opposing player. After he finished, a rookie rose to his feet and said, "Mr. Mack, there's one fellow you forgot; this man Totals. I looked at the box score and seen that he got four hits yesterday."

Quite similar is the story, probably apocryphal, about the National League outfielder who could neither read nor write. Each morning he used to sit in the hotel lobby and have other players read the box scores to him. One morning he listened patiently while a mate read the box score of one game in its entirety, even the summary, and concluded by saying, "Time of game, one fifty-three. Umpires, Messrs. Klem and Emslie." Hearing this, the rookie jumped to his feet, shouting, "Don't tell me that Messrs. is in this league! He umpired in the Southern League last year and he was terrible!"

But perhaps the most ridiculous of all these stories is the one involving Heinie Zimmerman, who played second and third for the Cubs and Giants from 1907 through 1919. Zim, so the story goes, was limbering up at third one day in Chicago during batting practice. A boy who worked on the pass gate approached him and said, "Heinie, there's a guy out there from Rockford, Illinois, named Kelly who wants you to leave a pass for him."

"Never heard of him," Heinie grunted. "The hell with him."

But in a few minutes the boy was back. "Heinie, this guy says you will remember him all right. Name's Kelly, from Rockford."

"Look," Heinie insisted. "I don't know any Kelly from Rockford. Now, go away."

When the boy returned the third time, he was almost in tears. "Please, Heinie," he begged. "Help me out. This guy swears he knows you. He said for me to ask you about the hotel episode in Rockford."

"Now I know he's a four-flusher," Zim sneered. "I know Rockford like a book and there ain't no Hotel Episode there."

There is apparently no connection between formal education and success on the diamond, although native intelligence is a great asset. But Moe Berg, the most erudite player the game has ever seen, had a batting average that persisted at the .250 level. Berg is a graduate of Princeton, the Columbia Law School and Sorbonne. He speaks English, Latin, Greek, French, Italian, German, Spanish, some Russian, Japanese, Hebrew and Sanskrit. His thesis on Sanskrit is a valuable work of reference at the Library of Congress.

But when Moe was catching for Washington, the player on the team he most admired was Dave Harris, a hard-hitting outfielder whose schooling had stopped somewhere in the vicinity of the seventh grade. "There's a fellow who really had the pitchers licked," Berg once told Shirley Povich of the Washington *Post*. "He wasn't burdened with too much imagination; he'd just step up there and take a beautiful cut. He used to rib me about my own batting average and say I was too smart to be a good hitter. He may have been right because I liked to try to guess with the pitcher. Once Harris hit a home run and I followed him to the plate. 'Moe, you go on and try your best,' he told me, 'but don't forget, none of them seven languages you know is gonna help you.'"

The best players, educated or otherwise, seem to be those who concentrate completely on the job at hand and who believe absolutely that they can control the outcome of the game. They take baseball seriously and do not exhibit such indifference as was shown by Frank Woodward, a pitcher on the Phillies in 1918. A writer once stopped in the Phillies' clubhouse and asked Woodward, "Who's going to work today?" Frank, who was scheduled to pitch that day, replied, "Who's gonna work? Me and the outfielders."

Woodward may have been an irresponsible kid but he was not lacking in imagination. Two years after leaving the Phillies he found himself a member of the Cardinals in training at Brownsville, Texas. One evening he wanted to go to the movies but did not have the price of admission. After thinking over his problem at some length, he finally strolled down to the theatre, sought out the manager and said, "I was sent here by Branch Rickey. Mr. Rickey has called a meeting of the players and he wants all those who are here at the movies to go back to the hotel right away."

This information was immediately flashed on the screen, and the players filed out. Watching the proceedings from under a tree across the street, Woodward waited until a decent interval had passed, then walked back to the theatre and said to the ticket-taker, "Meeting's over. Now to watch the rest of the picture."

There is no way you can safely generalize about the personalities of players. They can be as verbose as Jim O'Rourke, as quiet as Charlie Gehringer, as ignorant as the Lardner prototype or as erudite as Moe Berg. There are players from the mountains of Tennessee and West Virginia who are as suspicious as moonshiners. There are the college boys with the crew haircuts who collect swing records. There are the Oklahomans, bronzed by the sun, who look older than their years. Club owners have long claimed that baseball, absorbing all these men, is a great social leveler, that it is democracy in action. The claim is not without merit. Charlie Devens was a pitcher who joined the Yankees in 1932. He had attended Groton and Harvard, where he had been a member of the Hasty Pudding Club. His mother was a Vanderbilt. But when he reported to the big stadium across the Harlem, he found that his new team's greatest star, Babe Ruth, was an alumnus of a different institution, a graduate of the St. Mary's Industrial School, a semireform school at Baltimore, Class of '14.

Rookies are supposed to be brash and confident. When Billy Gleason, a young second baseman on the 1921 Browns, was asked the distance between home plate and second base, he quipped, "I don't know. I never ran that way." Such answers are given to cover up any insecurity the player might feel.

Ernie Sulik certainly did not indicate that he felt insecure when he reported to the Phillies as a young outfielder in 1936. In his first game he was called upon to face Dizzy Dean, who was then at the height of his pitching fame with the Cardinals. In his first time at bat Sulik looked at three blistering strikes, tossed his bat away and muttered, "That guy ain't shown me much." When his fellows on the bench looked at him in amazement, he confided, "Just watch me when I go to bat again; I'll hit that ball between the outfielders." Strange to say, that is exactly what he did, splashing a triple into right center. "How is it you looked at those three strikes the first time up?" Ernie was asked after the game. "I wanted to see what Dean had," he explained. "That's how I knew he didn't have anything."

One of the few players who ever achieved more than average success despite the lack of confidence was Emerson (Pink) Hawley, a pitcher from Beaver Dam, Wisconsin, who won 182 major league games in a decade starting in 1892. Hawley was in constant need of reassurance. One day, when he was pitching for St. Louis, he called time and motioned to his catcher, Heinie Peitz, to join him in a conference. "Heinie," he said. "Do you like to catch me?" Peitz was so astonished he had to grope for words, and when he was finally able to mumble that there was nothing he would rather do than catch Pink Hawley, the pitcher seemed reassured and went back to the job of throwing at the hitters.

Charles (Chief) Zimmer was a National League catcher who owned a cigar store and one day, in the dead of winter, Hawley strolled in, walked up to Zimmer and said, "Chief, will you forgive me?" "Certainly," replied the Chief, not having the slightest notion of what Pink was talking about as the two players, in years of acquaintance, had never had cross words.

Early during the following season Zimmer came up to bat in a game against Hawley, who was leading in the late innings, 12 to 0, and just toying with the opposition. "Chief, what's your batting average?" Hawley asked.

"Oh, about .214 I guess," Zimmer admitted.

"Well, boost it a little," Pink said, and when the next pitch was down the middle Zimmer connected for a home run and his team's only score.

Ballplayers simply do not follow any pattern of personality. It is even possible to find some who are genuinely modest. Eddie Moore, for instance. Eddie was an infielder with the Pirates, and during the season of 1924 a

Pittsburgh paper hired him to write his daily impressions of the games. He refused to use a ghost. One day, after winning a 3 to 2 contest by delivering a late-inning home run, Moore did not refer to the feat or even mention his name in the copy. On the other hand, shortly after the Phillies had released a pitcher named Pete Sivess to Milwaukee, a Philadelphia baseball writer received a wire that read, "Please send Milwaukee papers full sketch of Pete Sivess and send pictures." The message was signed by Pete Sivess.

There are even players with a romantic streak. Ed Kenna was a pitcher with the Athletics in 1902. The son of John E. Kenna, a United States Senator from Virginia, he attended West Virginia University and became a hero of sorts when he kicked three field goals in a football game against Grove City. He was a fair pitcher, but his heart really was not in the game, for his principal interest in life was in poetry. They called him the "Pitching Poet" and he could be found scribbling verses in the clubhouse before and after games. Here is a sample of his wares taken from his published book of verse, *Lyrics of the Hills,* written while he was employed to pitch at Wheeling, West Virginia:

> Fall time in the country, when the
> Sunshine filters down
> The tangled maze of cloudland
> And through the beeches brown;
> In the golden rays it scatters
> On the dear, old dirty sod
> I can trace in wondrous letters
> The mystic word of God
> And the goodness of the master,
> Who willed that it should be—
> Oh, the olden, golden autumn
> Is the best of times for me.

Play ball!

X
The Lady Known as Luck

The first mascot of the Yankees was a penny.

When the ground was blasted to start construction of Hilltop Park, a wooden structure that ran from 165th Street to 168th Street along Broadway and served as the first home for the New York club of the American League, an 1817 copper was thrown to the surface. Joseph W. Gordon, the president of the team and like his fellow magnates a superstitious man, had the penny mounted, framed and hung on the wall of his office. Apparently it served as an omen of good fortune; the Yankees have taken in a few other pennies since.

But it has since been demonstrated that the so-called luck of the Yankees is due more to strong executives, sound planning, able scouts and ample resources than it is to a dependence on the vagaries of fortune. Yet many players on the Yankees, like many players on all teams, believe that their success depends, at least in part, on luck.

When you consider the career of Eddie Bennett, the bat boy of the Yankees during the golden twenties, there appears to be some foundation to the belief. Bennett, a sad-faced boy with a malformed spine, first came to the attention of baseball one afternoon during the summer of 1919 when he was found by Oscar (Happy) Felsch, one of the Chicago players who were soon to be shamefully spoken of as the Black Sox. Felsch discovered Eddie at the Polo Grounds, where the Yankees then played their home games.

"Are you lucky?" Happy asked him.

"You bet I am," Bennett replied. "Just keep me with the White Sox and see."

For the rest of that season Eddie traveled with the Chicago players, tending their bats, running their small errands and making himself generally useful. Sure enough, the team won the pennant. But when the World's Series was lost to the Reds, Bennett was puzzled and wondered where the luck he was supposed to generate had gone. Not until the whole sordid story of the Series became known did Eddie regain confidence in himself as a talisman. He was good luck, all right, just as he had told Felsch, but of course if the team were not trying, there was nothing he could do about it.

Meanwhile, liking the life that baseball provided, Eddie obtained another job as bat boy of the Dodgers in 1920. His astonishing good fortune continued when Brooklyn won the National League flag. Then came the World's Series with the Indians. The big set of games was that year played on a best five out of nine basis, and with Eddie proudly wearing his uniform, the Dodgers promptly won two of the first three contests, all played at Ebbets Field. The teams then moved on to Cleveland, but the Dodgers for some strange reason let Eddie remain in Brooklyn. Cleveland thereupon won four straight games and the world championship.

That winter Bennett was employed at Prospect Hall, a Brooklyn arena that featured games played by a professional basketball team, the Visitations. He gave foul-shooting exhibitions at half time, and one night at the conclusion of his performance he noticed that Waite Hoyt, a pitcher who had just been traded from the Red Sox to the Yankees, was in the audience.

"Do you think you could get me a job as bat boy of the Yankees?" he asked Waite.

"I don't know, Eddie. I'll speak to Ed Barrow about it. After all, he runs the club," Hoyt told him.

Barrow was agreeable and Bennett then changed teams for the third straight season. The Yankees then proceeded to win three consecutive pennants, giving Eddie a record of carrying bats for five flag-winning clubs in succession. By this time, convinced that he was far luckier than he had dreamed when Felsch first approached him, he graduated from lugging bats, delegating that humble chore to inferiors, and concentrated on bringing luck to his team. The Yankee record of six pennants in eight seasons starting in 1921 would seem to be adequate evidence of his success, although a few well-timed home runs by Babe Ruth were probably a contributing factor.

Superstition is defined by the dictionary as a belief founded on irrational feelings, especially of fear, and marked by credulity. By that definition most ballplayers are superstitious, although today most of them would have you believe that they are not. But in a game that depends so much on luck it is human nature to look for signs of favor and to avoid anything that resembles a jinx. In 1937 a baseball writer who interviewed numerous players on the subject found that 80 per cent claimed to have no superstitions at all, but he concluded that 80 per cent of them did. However, what passes for superstition is often just a nervous habit or idiosyncrasy. Players can intentionally employ superstition and pretend it is a sort of joke, a cloak to hide behind, a means of attaching blame for defeat on anything but themselves.

The World's Series of 1929 supplies an example of this. When Chicago won the National League pennant that year, the owner of the team, the late William Wrigley, ordered a brand new set of uniforms designed for use in the World's Series against the Athletics. The players immediately raised a howl, maintaining it would be bad luck to discard the suits they had worn throughout the bitter chase for the flag. Although preferring that his hired hands make an immaculate appearance before the big crowds, Wrigley acquiesced, and the old uniforms were sent out for dry cleaning. The Cubs, happy then in their old attire, lost four of the five games and the title. But had Wrigley insisted that the new uniforms be worn, the Chicago players would certainly have attributed their defeat to that circumstance and not, more properly, to the pitching wizardry of the ancient Howard Ehmke, to George Earnshaw and Lefty Grove.

The most common superstition in baseball is the belief that the finding of a hairpin means a safe hit for the finder. Because of this nonsense fans throughout the years have literally showered players with hairpins, have scattered them on the field and have mailed them to their heroes in envelopes. It has often been printed that the first player to succumb to the hairpin theory was Ambrose McConnell, a second baseman with the Red Sox and White Sox early in this century, but actually Amos S. Booth, an obscure third baseman for Cincinnati, was on the prowl for hairpins as early as 1877. Booth later achieved a fair degree of fame as a mounted policeman in Cincinnati, but resigned from the force after an uncertain ride that ended with his charger drowning in one of the city's canals.

In the game's early days superstition was much more common than it is now. A Cleveland newspaper, in explaining the success of that city's National League team, said on June 23, 1884: "The recent streak of winning is attributed to the homely yellow dog the team has adopted." But dog or no dog a few weeks later three of the club's principal stars, shortstop Jack Glasscock, pitcher Jim McCormick and catcher Charles Briody jumped their contracts and joined the Union Association, a major but outlaw organization. The homely yellow dog apparently could do nothing about that, and attendance in Cleveland declined so sharply that the club's owners abandoned the franchise during the winter, depriving the city of National League ball for four years.

Hugh Daly, a one-armed pitcher and one of two hurlers ever to strike out nineteen men in a major league game, pitched at Cleveland a year before the yellow dog showed up, and he was possessed of a superstition difficult to surpass. On the day that he was scheduled to pitch he would never speak to another human being, not even the waiter at breakfast, until he had taken his first round of batting practice. This did not work much of a hardship on his team, however, for Daly had a quarrelsome personality and his mates thought he was at his best when not speaking.

When Mike (King) Kelly once made four hits in as many trips off the delivery of Thomas (Tacks) Parrott, an eccentric who performed for Cincinnati, he was asked what he had had for breakfast that morning. "Ham and eggs," said the King. That evening on his way home from the park Parrott stopped in at a delicatessen and picked up a dozen eggs and a whole ham.

George Stallings, the manager of the Miracle Braves who went from eighth place on July 19 to win a National League pennant and then sweep the 1914 World's Series from the Athletics in four straight engagements, was probably as remarkable a believer in luck as anyone ever associated with the game. He particularly hated to see sparrows light on the turf in front of the players' bench, and he habitually carried in his pockets a supply of pebbles to throw at the birds. The players, knowing this, often would sprinkle oats on the field to attract the sparrows. When Stallings would run out of pebbles, he would demand that one of his substitute players sit on the dugout steps and pound the ground with a bat in an attempt to drive the birds away. Stallings also hated scraps of paper, believing them an evil omen, and he insisted that the area immediately in front of the dugout be kept clear of them. This meant full janitor duty for many players because fans, aware of George's aversion, constantly threw torn paper onto the field.

Many of the strange little beliefs of baseball are related to bats, gloves and other equipment of the game. John (Chief) Meyers, a catcher for the Giants, had a theory that each bat contained exactly one hundred hits; Benny Kauff, later an outfielder with the same team, thought that his bats grew tired, so he frequently rested them; Jimmy Ring, a pitcher for the Reds, Phillies, Giants and Cardinals, always went to bat with his pitching glove jammed into his hip pocket; Urban Shocker, a spitball pitcher of note for the Yankees and Browns, would never throw his glove on the grass, only on the skinned part of the diamond; and Hughie Critz, a second baseman with the Reds and Giants, always moved the glove of his opposing second baseman when taking his station in the field. Critz also invariably put a pinch of dirt in his pocket after each throw by his team's pitcher.

For years Max Carey was an outfielder of repute for the Pirates and a ghost on the base paths, appearing in almost twenty-five hundred National League games. And in each one of those games, after the completion of each inning, while trotting in from his position in center, he would pause to kick third base. One day at the Polo Grounds the other Pittsburgh players in the game formed a cordon around the bag and refused to let Max touch it. One attempt after another was rebuffed and the game delayed so long that Bill Klem, the umpire behind the plate, shed his mask, strolled down the line and said, "All right, boys. Get away from that base and let Carey touch it so we can get on with the game."

A scene equally as ludicrous once took place during a game at Yankee Stadium. Joe Dugan, the home team's third baseman, would never throw the ball back to the pitcher, always leaving that chore for shortstop Mark Koenig, second baseman Tony Lazzeri, or first baseman Lou Gehrig. But on this particular day those other infielders, inspired to deviltry by Lazzeri, decided they would force Dugan to return the ball to the mound. Every time Joe threw the ball to them they would fire it back at him like a bullet. After one such return to Dugan, they all turned their backs on Joe and resumed their positions. Undaunted, Dugan responded by throwing the ball as hard as possible to Koenig, who caught it square in the back.

The number thirteen has of course played its part in the history of superstitions in baseball, particularly during the World's Series of 1911. In explaining why the Giants lost to the Athletics that year, a writer named G. A. Heller pointed out in the *Baseball Magazine* that there were actually thirteen reasons: the name "New York Giants" contains thirteen letters; the series required thirteen days for completion; in the final game on October 26 (2 × 13) there were thirteen Giants used, and in this same game the Athletics made thirteen runs, thirteen hits and thirteen assists; there were thirteen Athletics used in the games; in the six contests the Giants made thirteen runs and thirty-nine safe and sacrifice hits; Mathewson retired thirteen men on strikes; the Giants batted .175 (1 + 7 + 5 = 13); and the New York club's share of the receipts was $90,108.72, being an even multiple of thirteen.

Certain players have tried to defy superstition only to learn that such conduct is in itself superstitious. Ralph Branca, the Dodger pitcher, found that out when he wore a uniform that was numbered thirteen. In defiance of the hoodoo usually associated with the number, Branca originally asked for it because there were thirteen children in his mother's family. He also wore a shoe of that size. When Bobby Thomson of the Giants tagged Branca for the famed home run that brought the 1951 pennant to the Polo Grounds, Ralph thought some of dropping the number but reconsidered and wore it again in 1952.

Another mythical jinx of the game is the conviction that a pitcher who strikes out the first batter to face him is destined to lose the game. George Bulkley surveyed that theory for the *Baseball Magazine* in 1936 and found that in 152 cases the pitcher who whiffed the first hitter won ninety of the games, lost sixty and twice departed with the score tied. That is a percentage of winning that would ordinarily enable a team to finish second and would occasionally produce a pennant.

Just as bad fortune is associated with the number thirteen, good luck is supposed to surround the number seven. It is for this reason that fans in all parks observe the seventh inning stretch, rising from their seats when the home club comes to bat in that inning, regardless of the score. For a long time it was believed that the custom began at a game in Pittsburgh attended by William Howard Taft, then president of the United States. Taft, so the legend went, by chance arose from his seat between halves of the seventh inning. Courteous fans, thinking he was about to leave the park, stood up out of respect for him. However, Bill Bryson, a sports writer for the Des Moines *Register* and one of the game's top authorities, has found that the phrase "lucky seventh" was used by the New York *Times* in 1890.

A. H. Tarvin, an archeologist of the game in Louisville, has uncovered an even earlier instance. He found a letter written in 1869 by Harry Wright, manager of the undefeated Red Stockings of that year, to Howard Ferris, a resident of Cincinnati, in which the custom of stretching in the seventh was described. "The spectators all arise between halves of the seventh, extend their legs and arms, and sometimes walk about," Wright wrote. "In so doing they enjoy the relief afforded by relaxation from a long posture on the hard benches."

Tarvin also found that Tim Murnane, an early player who became a sports writer for the Boston *Globe,* once overheard John Clarkson, a noted Chicago pitcher, refer to the seventh inning as the "lucky seventh." Murnane, anxious to track down the belief, then examined the scores of every game played by Chicago from 1876 to 1886 and discovered that more runs were scored in that inning than any other.

As a matter of fact, the expression "lucky seventh" was well known to baseball even earlier than that. If, as Harry Wright claimed, fans were stretching in the seventh inning as early as 1869, there must have been a reason why that particular inning was selected. Almost certainly it was because sporting people have long associated good fortune with the number seven. It is easy to see how some prehistoric fan, anxious to have the home team forge ahead, might rise, clap his hands, and spur on fans seated around him, saying, "Come on, get up! This is the inning! This is the time!"

O. P. Caylor, who covered baseball for the Cincinnati *Enquirer* in 1876, frequently referred to the "lucky seventh" and the "wonderful seventh." Caylor even began calling Henry Kessler, a Cincinnati infielder, "Lucky" Kessler, because of his habit of delivering safe hits in the seventh inning.

Unfortunately, in his later life, Kessler was anything but lucky. During the winter that followed the season of 1884 he set fire to a hotel at Franklin,

Pennsylvania and served a term for arson. When he emerged from prison, it was too late in his life to resume the career of a professional, and he eventually died in the Venango County poor farm, near Franklin, in 1900.

But the belief in luck has not been a monopoly by the Kesslers of the game; even so intelligent and austere a personage as Kenesaw Mountain Landis was a prey to superstition. A reporter stopped Judge Landis at St. Paul, Minnesota in 1939, when the game's Commissioner was on his way to a fishing camp in Northern Minnesota.

"Aren't you worried, Judge?" asked the reporter. "Don't you realize this is your thirteenth trip up here?"

"Bah!" Landis barked. "Superstition, plain and simple! It has no place in baseball and no place in fishing!"

"Well, then," smiled the reporter. "I have an umbrella here. Would you mind posing with it raised?"

"I should say not," the Commissioner thundered. "Pose with a raised umbrella? Don't you know that's bad luck?"

But despite all the evidence against such beliefs luck does play a vital role in baseball; at least some players are visited by more good fortune than others. A glance at the career of Arndt Jorgens, a catcher with the Yankees from 1929 through 1940, will prove the point. During those twelve seasons Bill Dickey caught 1,408 games for the Yankees and Jorgens 287, but for World's Series play they received identical checks totaling $29,530.44. Jorgens never once broke into a World's Series game, but from the shadow of the bench he watched Dickey catch twenty-three of them. He also received additional money when the Yankees finished second in 1929, 1931, 1933, 1934 and 1935 and third in 1930.

Originally the Yankees considered Jorgens a prize find. He had a batting average of .335 to show for his work at Oklahoma City when he was purchased on the recommendation of Eddie Herr, who scouted him. "I think I've sent Huggins a real coming catcher," Herr boasted at the time. "He's a little fellow like Ray Schalk or Muddy Ruel, but he's built of iron."

Built of iron he was, but on the bench he rusted. He could never compare with Dickey, of course, and later the Yankees brought along another fine pair of young catchers, Joe Glenn and Buddy Rosar, so Arndt remained on the bench and in the bullpen. He appeared in thirty-one games in 1936, thirteen in 1937, nine in 1938, three in 1939 and none at all in 1940, after which he understandably retired.

The career of Jorgens is particularly poignant because his comparative idleness was spent on such a luxurious bench; other players have made more of a science of inactivity without his luck. Ken Silvestri, for example, appeared in only 102 games in ten years on the active list, and was a catcher in only sixty-two of them. Silvestri spent five seasons in the American League with the White Sox and Yankees, then transferred to the Phillies in 1949. In five full years with that club he went behind the bat in only thirteen games, the last one in 1951, although he was listed as an active player in 1953.

Both Jorgens and Silvestri appear to be spiritual descendants of John Churry, who wore the uniform of the Cubs for four seasons. Churry managed to appear in six games in 1924, three in 1925, two in 1926 and one in 1927. Having then exhausted the possibilities of the law of diminishing returns, he called it a career.

XI

Big Night at Strawberry Hill

Many men who played baseball long ago like to believe that the modern game is deteriorating. They maintain that the player of today is coddled, and they are particularly scornful of present day conditioning methods. But if the trainers, diathermy machines and whirlpool baths of today's clubhouse have accomplished nothing else, they have at least brought to a state of decline that painful, muscular affliction peculiar to baseball and known as the Charley horse. The ailment was once so widespread that players were hobbling out of the lineup almost daily, and the number of man hours lost because of it would constitute a challenge beyond the computing powers of the most devoted statistician.

The origin of the term, Charley horse, has long been debated. John McGraw used to tell people there was a story that the name first came into prominence at Sioux City, Iowa somewhere around 1890, when an old horse named Charley, his legs bent after a life of toil, used to require a half-hour to drag the infield.

It seems likely that the source of McGraw's information was Judge Walter McCredie, long head of the Portland team of the Pacific Coast League. McCredie was a member of that Sioux City club, and he has been quoted by Bill Bryson, the Des Moines authority, as saying:

"It was either in 1889 or 1890 that we had a broken-down horse named Charley working on the grounds. He was so old that he was barely able to creep along. So, whenever a player came up with a limp, we used to say, 'Here comes old Charley.' The injury itself then came to be known as a Charley horse, and the Sioux City players carried the term all over the country."

But the probability is that the expression goes back at least as far as 1879, the year in which an infielder named Joe Quest joined Chicago of the National League. Here is what the Cincinnati *Enquirer* had to say on the subject in its issue of June 30, 1889:

> When Joe Quest was employed as an apprentice in the machine shop of Quest & Shaw at New Castle, Pennsylvania, his father, one of the proprietors of the firm, had an old white horse named Charley. Doing usage in pulling heavy loads had stiffened the animal's legs so that he walked as if troubled with strained tendons. Afterward, when Quest became a member of Chicago, he was troubled, along with other players, with a peculiar stiffness of the legs, which brought to his mind the ailment of the old white horse, Charley. All players hobbled like the old horse, and since no one knew what the trouble was, Quest dubbed it "Charley-horse."

The Charley horse is by no means the only baseball expression with an origin shrouded in mystery and doubt. Another is "bullpen," the word now used to describe the area in which relief pitchers warm up for action. Bullpen, of course, is also used in prison slang to designate the fenced-in area where prisoners are permitted to exercise.

In 1909 there were more than 150 Bull Durham tobacco signs painted on the fences of ball parks throughout the country. The bull was twenty-five feet high and thirty-six feet long, and the Bull Durham people paid fifty dollars to any player hitting the bull, an offer which would be costly to the company today but which was a good risk in the era of the dead ball.

Because relief pitchers often got in their preliminary tosses directly in front of the bull, many fans have assumed that the area is referred to as the bullpen for that reason. But the application of the word to baseball antedates the appearance of the Bull Durham signs by a good many years.

When the National League was organized in 1876, the price of admission to the grandstand was pegged at fifty cents. However, some clubs had a policy of admitting spectators for ten cents, after the game had started, herding them within a roped-in area in foul territory, adjoining the outfield. The crowds which patronized these sections were unruly, consisting largely of children, drunks and other undesirables without the price of a grandstand ticket. Because these tattered members of the rabble were penned in like bulls, writers early referred to their abode as the bullpen. On May 9, 1877 a writer for the Cincinnati *Enquirer* observed: "The bullpen at the Cincinnati grounds with its 'three-for-a-quarter' crowd has lost its usefulness. The bleaching boards just north of the north pavilion now holds the cheap crowd which comes in at the end of the first inning at a discount."

Another puzzling baseball expression is "at bat, on deck and in the hole," the terminology used to indicate the first three hitters of an inning. This phrase is commonly used by children in sandlot games. The origin is nautical, and, correctly, the phrase is "at bat, on deck, and in the hold," not "in the hole." The cry was first heard at Belfast, Maine, where many vessels were built, and the date was August 7, 1872, when the Boston Red Stockings, soon to win four consecutive pennants in the old National Association, visited there and played a game with the Pastimes of Belfast, winning, 35 to 1.

There were no scorecards at that game, and as each inning began, the scorer would announce the batters. For example, when Boston came to bat, he would cry, "George Wright at bat; Leonard and Barnes next!" But when Belfast had its inning, he would shout, "Moody at bat; Boardman on deck; Dinsmore in the hold." The salty phrase made such a hit with the visiting scorer that he carried it back to Boston, and it soon became part of the language.

Historians have also been baffled by the date and place of the first game to be played at night. Assuming that no teams were ever foolish enough to attempt a contest by candlelight, this event had to await the first practical demonstration of the incandescent bulb by Thomas A. Edison in 1879. But how soon after Edison's invention was the first night game run off?

The Sporting Life ran a front-page story on March 30, 1887, calling attention to night games being played at the St. George grounds on Staten Island, but it was known that earlier than that, on June 2, 1883, at Fort Wayne, Indiana, a team of professionals from Quincy, Illinois defeated a club calling itself the M. E. College Nine, 19 to 11, in seven innings. But just as Fort Wayne was preparing to celebrate its citation as the scene of the first night game, it was discovered that a still earlier fray had taken place. In it, George Pensinger's Paint Shop trounced Clay Henninger's Nine by an unknown score in a joust at Chambersburg, Pennsylvania.

There matters rested for some time, but it now develops that neither Fort Wayne nor Chambersburg is entitled to the accolade. For a night game was played, beyond doubt, at Nantasket Beach, near Boston, during the summer of 1880, although the exact date is not known. But the Cincinnati *Enquirer,* on September 24, 1880, carried this item as a reprint from the Boston *Advertiser:*

> A novel exhibition of electric light was made at Strawberry Hill, Nantasket Beach, last evening. What especially attracted the 300 spectators to the balconies of the Sea Foam House was the promise of the exceedingly novel sight of a game of baseball in the evening, long after the sun's rays should be dispelled by natural darkness. The real significance of the occasion, however, was the first public experiment in illustration of a new system of illuminating towns by electricity. It contemplates an innovation of startling magnitude. The plan is to illuminate the streets of a city—in fact, the whole atmosphere around and above the buildings. The apparatus in use consisted of 36 carbon lamps in communication with a dynamo-electric generator that is operated by an engine of 30 horsepower. To support the lamps were erected three wooden towers 100 feet high and 500 feet apart, so as to overlook a triangular spot just beneath the northern piazza of the Sea Foam Hotel. The lamps were disposed 12 in a group and possessed a total illuminating power of 90,000 candles, or 30,000 for each tower. An idea of the effect produced by the illumination may be best conceived by stating the fact that a flood of mellow light thrown upon the field enabled the ballplayers, between eight and half-past nine o'clock to complete a game of nine innings. The nines were picked from the employees of Jordan, Marsh & Co. and R. H. White & Co., and tied the game with a score of 16 to 16. It cannot be said that the practice of such sports is likely at present to be carried out extensively by night rather than by day, for the players had to bat and throw with some caution, and the number of errors due to imperfect light was innumerable.

Still another phase of the game that has not been thoroughly investigated is the custom of numbering players. It may come as a surprise to the new generation of fans to learn that when the idea of numbers was first proposed, the cautious club owners recoiled in horror, fearful that the practice might lead to ridicule.

Cleveland was the first team to try it in the majors, in a regularly scheduled American League game against Chicago on Monday, June 2, 1916. The numbers were sewed not on the players' backs but on their sleeves, matching numbers posted on the scoreboard. The Indian lead-off man that day was Jack Graney, later a well-known Cleveland baseball announcer, so to him goes the honor of being the first major league player to step to the plate wearing a numbered uniform.

But the Cleveland experiment was short-lived, principally because the fans had difficulty making out the numbers. Later it was suggested that players might wear numerals on their broad backs. Branch Rickey and Sam Breadon, who jointly ran the affairs of the Cardinals, were early proponents of the scheme, and another of the radicals was Charlie Ebbets, chieftain of the Dodgers. But the other magnates, horrified by the thought of properly identifying their players for the public, voted down all proposals that numbering be mandatory.

One writer, L. C. Davis, outraged not only because the owners banned numbers but because they also refused to indicate hits and errors on the scoreboard, scowled at the absurd situation in the following verse:

Tell me not in mournful numbers
On the baseball player's back
Who that bimbo is that lumbers
To the plate the pill to crack.

While the pastime is progressing
And improving every day,
We must keep the rooters guessing
While they pay and pay and pay.

Likewise, showing hits and errors
On the board, the magnate fears
Would abet the silk shirt wearers
Also known as gamboliers.

Let us then be up and doing
On the old established plan,
Still achieving, still pursuing
The elusive iron man.

Davis penned that tribute to the imagination of the game's operators early in 1923, but six seasons were to pass before the athletes were properly numbered. It was a personal campaign waged by Tommy Rice of the Brooklyn *Eagle* that finally produced results, and surprisingly enough, the first team to adopt the numerals permanently was the often reactionary New York American League club. That was in 1929, and before the season was very old the No. 3 of George Herman Ruth and the No. 4 of Henry Louis Gehrig were well known. Cleveland and Washington followed suit in 1930, and before the passing of another year all big league teams had fallen into line.

The humble rain check also has its place in the lore of the game. In the earliest days spectators turned in oblong tickets, which the takers deposited in boxes and used again and again for subsequent contests. But when it rained before a legal game had been completed, the tickets were returned to the customers. At such times the demand for tickets was always greater than the supply because the numerous deadheads who had gained admission in other ways, including politicians and clergymen who had used the pass gate, lined up for tickets or refunds with the legitimate purchasers. The result was that rain always meant a financial loss to the home club. The idea for a detachable rain check was hatched by Abner Powell, an early pitcher who became a club owner in the minors. Powell invented the rain check in 1888 while operating at New Orleans, and he ordered the first ones from a printing firm in Fort Smith, Arkansas. He failed to apply for a patent, never realizing a dime from his brainchild, which was widely copied.

The squeeze play is an intricate weapon of baseball attack that calls for a runner on third to break with the pitch and requires the batter to bunt neatly, avoiding or delaying a play at the plate. During the days when one run was at a premium the play was greatly respected and widely used, though it was never certain who originated the idea. When a former pitcher named Joe Yeager died in 1937, his obituary named him as the inventor of the squeeze, but that seems unlikely because Joe did not reach the majors until he joined Brooklyn in 1898, and two Yale collegians, George Case and Dutch Carter, are known to have employed the squeeze play in a game against Princeton in 1894.

The first big league use of the play is said to have occurred during the season of 1904 when Clark Griffith was managing the old Highlanders, now the Yankees. With Addie Joss pitching for Cleveland, Jack Chesbro, a New York pitcher, was on third with Willie Keeler batting. Chesbro, thinking he had been given the sign to steal home, broke for the plate but sensed he would be out. Desperate, he yelled to Keeler to do something, and Willie obliged by bunting the ball in fair territory beyond the reach of the catcher. Chesbro was safe, and after the game the other Highlanders asked what had happened. Realizing that his players had hit on a new offensive weapon, Griffith ordered the team to practice the manoeuvre during Spring training in 1905. Before long other teams were copying it. Although John McGraw was a great strategist, his Giant team was the last to adopt the play, although he twice used it successfully during the season of 1907. The double squeeze, a much more difficult play which enables two runners to score on a bunt, was worked out by Hal Chase and Kid Elberfeld when they were with the Highlanders in 1907.

Roger Bresnahan, noted catcher for the Giants, is generally credited with having invented shinguards, first appearing publicly with the protection in 1908. But Charles (Red) Dooin, who caught for the Phillies in the same era, wore shinguards under his stockings as early as 1906.

"Bresnahan always got the credit," Dooin used to say, "but I used them a couple of years before he dreamed of them. I had a special type made, substituting papier mâché for rattan to make them lighter. One day Bresnahan crashed into me at the plate and somehow came in contact with my legs. 'What have you got on under your stockings?' he asked. I told him they were shinguards, and later he appeared wearing big, white cricket shinguards. He took them off when he went to bat, but of course mine had to stay on."

There seems little doubt, though, that Bresnahan did invent the protective cap for batters. He first designed one after being seriously beaned in 1905. He had the device patented and marketed, but it never became popular.

Here are a few other examples of the first-known instances of various obscure practices, phrases and paraphernalia of the game:

1. AUTOMATIC PITCHER—The first pitching machine was demonstrated by Charles E. Hinton, a professor at Princeton, at that institution's gymnasium on December 15, 1896.
2. BANJO HIT—This term, used more by players than writers, indicates a ball that plunks off the bat and falls safe between the infield and outfield, but which is not high enough to be called a "Texas Lea-

guer." It was coined in 1924 by Raymond (Snooks) Dowd, a second baseman then with Jersey City.

3. BONEHEAD—Supposedly first uttered by George Stallings, after his release as manager of the Phillies in 1898, and applied to the owner of that team, Colonel John I. Rogers.

4. BOX SEATS—William H. Cammeyer, president of the Mutuals, introduced them at the Union Grounds in Brooklyn in 1871, according to the New York *Clipper* of June 3, 1871, which said: "Mr. Cammeyer has erected a platform in front of and above the dressing rooms of the Mutual Club to which persons who wish to be exclusive can obtain admission by the payment of an extra quarter."

5. BROKEN LEG—The first such accident to a National League player crippled Archibald (Al) Hall, Cleveland left fielder, in the first inning of a game at Cincinnati, May 13, 1880. Hall collided with his team's center fielder, Pete Hotaling, and was taken to the hospital. J. Ford Evans, president of the Cleveland team, attended the game and released Hall to avoid unnecessary expense. Cincinnati fans passed the hat and raised a fund of five hundred dollars for the injured player.

6. CHEST PROTECTOR—The first known use of this device in the majors was by John T. Clements, a lefthanded catcher with the Philadelphia Keystones of the Union Association in 1884. It was first called a "sheepskin" and was generally ridiculed.

7. DELAYED STEAL—Apparently first employed by Miller Huggins, later manager of the Yankees, in 1903.

8. HIDDEN BALL TRICK—Worked by Louis Say, a shortstop, playing for Albany against Worcester on September 26, 1879.

9. HOLDOUT—The first professional to bargain for a bigger salary was Charlie Sweasy, second baseman of the Cincinnati Red Stockings. Paid eight hundred dollars in 1869, he asked for one thousand dollars in 1870 and got it.

10. HOOK SLIDE—First thought of by William S. Gummere, while playing for Princeton in a game against the Philadelphia Athletics in the 1860's. He slid and buried his face in his right arm, the style later adopted by Ty Cobb. Gummere later became Chief Justice of the Supreme Court of New Jersey.

11. HUNTING ACCIDENT—The first professional player known to be shot while hunting was John Harkins, pitcher for Cleveland in the National League, who accidentally discharged his gun and injured his left hand while hunting in the wilds of New Jersey in February, 1884. The accident did not interfere with his career.

12. "IT ONLY TAKES ONE TO HIT IT!"—The Kansas City *Star* in 1900 attributed this familiar cry to Herman Long, famous as a National League shortstop, making the claim that he first uttered it while playing for Kansas City of the American Association in 1889.

13. OPTIONAL AGREEMENTS—First suggested by the Emporia, Kansas team in January, 1887. The club agreed that if the Cincinnati Reds would supply them with a pitcher and catcher, Emporia would pay their Cincinnati salaries and return them at the end of the season.

14. RUBBER STAMP FOR AUTOGRAPHS—Introduced by Johnny (Pepper) Martin of the Cardinals in 1937. Martin also inspired the phrase "Gas House Gang." In a conversation with Frank Graham, the New York baseball writer, and other players early in 1934, a comparison of the National and American leagues came up. "Why, they wouldn't allow Gas House players like us in the American," Martin snapped.

15. SACRIFICE FLY—The fly that scores a runner from third base first exempted a player from a time at bat in 1908. William J. Murray, manager of the Phillies, led the fight for the legislation because his star outfielder, Sherry Magee, hit them so far and often with a man on third. Club owners have never been able to decide whether they want the rule on the books or not.

16. SEASON TICKETS—First sold in the National League by the Hartford club in 1876.

17. SLIDING PADS—First used by Harry Stovey, a fine outfielder and base-runner for the Athletics in the eighties. He wore them to protect a bruised place in his leg.

18. YANNIGANS—A word without any other known meaning coined by Jerry Denny, third baseman for Providence, in 1884, as a synonym for "rookie."

XII
A Few Myths

When Charles (Gabby) Street, a kindly and witty man, passed away at his home town of Joplin, Missouri in early 1951, many of the notices of his death recalled that he was the first man to catch a baseball dropped from the Washington Monument. This is one of those legends of the game that has been kicked around for years, but like so many other myths that surround baseball, it is without basis in fact. Gabby *did* catch a baseball dropped from the famed obelisk, but he was not the first to do so. That honor properly belongs to William (Pop) Schriver, a catcher with Chicago in the previous century.

The Washington Monument was dedicated in February, 1885. Almost immediately afterwards a man named H. P. Burney, a clerk at the Arlington Hotel in Washington, began to wonder whether or not a skilled professional player could manage to hold onto a ball released at the Monument's peak, five hundred feet of sheer space away. Washington at that time was a member of the National League, and many of the teams stopped at the Arlington while in the city. Burney repeatedly talked to players about his dream, but always claimed vehemently that such a catch could not be made. Finally he found a few players who were willing to try it. But those who made the attempt—Paul Hines, Charlie Snyder, Hardie Richardson and Buck Ewing—all failed.

One man who believed that a ball could be caught under such circumstances was Adrian (Cap) Anson, manager of the Chicago team. Anson was the Rogers Hornsby of his day, gruff, tactless, outspoken and completely honest; and when he believed something, he never hesitated to make clear his view. Once, asked by a Baltimore newspaper to wire his estimate of the Orioles' pennant chances in fifty words, he replied with a telegram that contained only one word—"None."

With the coming of every season, Burney and Anson would renew their annual argument. The Chicago manager always insisted that such a catch could be made; Burney was equally insistent that it could not.

Finally, on the morning of August 25, 1894, Schriver, then the first-string Chicago catcher, agreed to make the attempt. A party which included Frank Bennett, manager of the Arlington, Burney, Anson, and such Chicago players as Clark Griffith, Walter (Jiggs) Parrott, Scott Stratton, George Decker and Bill Hutchinson went out to watch the fun. Their first job was to proceed without the knowledge of the Monument officials, watchful guardians of the shaft who took a dim view of such stunts.

Schriver was immediately impressed with the magnitude of his task, and most of the players in his company were skeptical of any success. Griffith was chosen to drop the ball from the north window, about five feet below the peak. He let the first one go, and Schriver stood aside, watching to see if it would bore a hole about ten feet in the pavement. Instead, it merely bounced high enough to be a high strike. Schriver then took heart, and when the signal was given for the second ball, he was ready. He staggered around, but managed to trap the ball neatly in his big glove, and was jubilant over his success. But by this time the Monument cop was onto the game and flew into a monumental rage, talking menacingly of arrests. But the players cajoled him into a more amiable mood, and the group departed safely. Burney, convinced at last, expressed satisfaction, and the incident became a neglected part of history.

Almost fourteen years later, on August 21, 1908, Street duplicated the performance, catching the thirteenth ball dropped to him. Francis Stann of the Washington *Star* has learned that Street was persuaded to make the attempt because Preston Gibson, a writer and member of Washington's Gridiron Club, had made a substantial wager that it could be done. Bob Ganley, an outfielder, and George McBride, shortstop of the Senators, were witnesses to the affair, and the balls were dropped by Gibson.

The A. J. Reach Company, manufacturers of sporting goods, noting that Street had caught a Reach ball in a Reach glove, ran a full-page advertisement in the *Reach Baseball Guide* for 1909, making the claim that no previous player had been able to do what Street had finally accomplished. The Reach people also proudly announced that the twelve balls that had eluded Gabby's grasp were not damaged in any way and could have been used in a championship game.

Billy Sullivan, a catcher for the White Sox, was the next to try his luck, and one day during the season of 1911 he succeeded in holding on to not one ball but three. "The first one I held was on the third or fourth try," Sullivan later recalled for L. H. Gregory of the Portland *Oregonian,* "then I caught the next one too." Billy said he was anxious to see whether it was easier to snare a ball that was thrown than one that was merely dropped, so on the next attempt he backed away about one hundred feet from the Monument and had the ball tossed down. He nabbed it cleanly, and thought it was a lot more pleasant than receiving the dead weight of a dropped ball.

As hard to down as the myth about Street is the story that in the World's Series of 1932 Babe Ruth "called his shot," slamming a home run out of the park and into the street beyond center at Wrigley Field, in the fifth inning of the third game between the Yankees and Cubs. The curious thing is that not one newspaperman who covered the Series made such a claim at the time. The legend started several years later, supplying a dramatic and sentimental story to Hot Stove League speakers stuck for material and not particular about their facts. The Cubs and Yankees had been riding each other hard during that game, as they had throughout the entire Series, and when Ruth stepped up to the plate with the score tied, 4 to 4, he was the second batter of the inning. Immediately he turned and shouted something at the Cub bench. After the first strike, he held up one finger to indicate that two remained; after the second, he shook two fingers at the bench. Ruth then hit Charlie Root's next pitch on a line, and it carried over the wire fence in center. Here is how the play was described by *The Sporting News,* which covered the game minutely: "Ruth quickly broke the tie and with one of the longest homers ever made at the park. After Sewell grounded to Jurges, the Babe sent a line drive over the bleacher screen in center field, and as he circled the bases he taunted the Cubs, who had been wisecracking about his inability to bend."

Ruth hit two home runs in that game, as did Lou Gehrig, and afterwards Root told reporters exactly how he had pitched to each man. "I put the ball right where I wanted to," Charlie said. "My control was perfect, and I had enough stuff to fool an ordinary batter. Boy, those guys can certainly hit the ball! Ruth made his first home run on a fast ball, low and outside, and his second on a change of pace, high and inside."

It stands to reason that if Ruth had "called his shot," he would not have been thrown a change of pace. Any pitcher as experienced and as capable as Root would have knocked him down after such a haughty challenge, particularly in view of the count of no balls and two strikes.

In later years Root used to do a slow burn whenever the "called shot" home run came up. "I don't mind the fact that Ruth hit such a long home run off my delivery," Charlie always said, "but I certainly resent the legend that he pointed to the place where he intended to hit it. What he did was point to our bench and indicate the count."

As for Ruth himself, in 1937 he confided in Joe Williams, the New York writer, that the episode was a fluke, that on the pitch he had been trying to hook the ball into the Cub dugout to quiet his hecklers.

The fame of Babe Ruth in baseball is secure enough without surrounding his name with spurious achievement.

But one player who actually did predict a home run for himself and then make good on the promise was Paul Hines, an outfielder during the game's infancy, and his prediction was made in writing. While playing for Providence one day in Boston, Hines went over to the scorer's table before the game and facetiously marked a home run opposite his name in the frame that indicated the fifth inning. When he actually hit a home run in the fifth that day, the strange event was widely publicized. It marked one of the few times in early baseball that the populace paid any attention to the home run, a department of play in which few fans appeared to be interested.

Hines was also the central figure in one of the most controversial plays of all time, a triple play made on May 8, 1878 in another game between Providence and Boston. When Harry Hagan, an infielder at Rochester, made an unassisted triple play in 1902, the game's historians scoured the record books to determine whether there was any previous instance of such a play. One who said it had been accomplished was Tim Murnane, the Boston writer who had played first base for Providence in the game at issue. Because of Murnane's insistence, Hines got into the record books as the author of the first unassisted triple play. No one doubted that three men had been put out; the only question was whether Hines had required help in retiring them.

Here was the situation: in the eighth inning Boston was trailing, 3 to 1, with Jack Manning on third, Ezra Sutton on second and Jack Burdock batting. Burdock raised a twisting fly beyond the infield that Hines, the center fielder, and Tom Carey, the shortstop, both chased. Hines ran in about forty yards and picked the ball off his shoe tops. By this time Manning and Sutton had both reached home plate, so Hines continued running and tagged third base before either runner could get back, but then, to make doubly sure, he threw to Charlie Sweasy, the Providence second baseman, who stepped on second.

It was Ernest J. Lanigan, one of the game's foremost authorities, who found that Sweasy had been involved in the play, and that seemed to safely dispose of Murnane's claim for Hines. But others thought that three men had been retired before Hines threw to Sweasy. The issue was not settled until 1953 when Hy Turkin of the New York *Daily News* got a ruling from Tommy Connolly, umpire-in-chief of the American League. Connolly pointed out that two runners who have failed to return to their proper bases cannot be put out just because a fielder touches one base; in other words, the side had not been retired until Hines had made the throw to Sweasy and the latter had touched second, making Sutton the third out. But even Connolly's ruling did not satisfy some observers who claimed that the rule Connolly cited was not in effect in 1878.

The unassisted triple play is one of the real rarities of baseball. Only seven have been made in major league history, six during regular season play and the one executed by Bill Wambsganss for Cleveland in the 1920 World's Series against Brooklyn. Neal Ball made the first for Cleveland in 1909; George Burns of the Red Sox and Ernie Padgett of the Braves each pulled one in 1923; Glenn Wright of the Pirates did it in 1925; and, strangest of all, Jimmy Cooney of the Cubs, brother of the more famous John, and Johnny Neun of the Tigers accomplished the trick on successive days in 1927. The odds against an unassisted triple play being executed in a particular game are about fifteen thousand to one, and yet Tris Speaker of Cleveland has witnessed three, having been on the field when Ball, Wambsganss and Burns made theirs.

Still another example of the game's ample mythology is the so-called sophomore jinx, a delusion on the part of some observers that players, in their second big league season, are apt to find the going rough. The belief in such a jinx is caused by focusing attention only on second-year players who had exceptional first seasons. Players in that category sometimes fail, of course, but when the work of all players is studied, it is found that improvement is the more typical experience of sophomores. Ty Cobb, for example, zoomed from .320 to .350 in his second full campaign; had those two seasons been reversed, he would have been considered a victim of the jinx. Rogers Hornsby, Bill Terry, Lou Gehrig, Mickey Mantle and numerous other players all did better work after a year's experience.

One of the strangest and most fascinating of baseball's legends is an anecdote involving nine towns in Kansas that is included in a book called *Bill Stern's Favorite Baseball Stories*. According to Stern, a network sports announcer whose oleaginous tonsils have pleased their wide audience for many years, there was once living in Chicago a young boy who idolized the Chicago White Stockings at a time when that club was managed by Charlie Comiskey. The Chicago lineup of that era, Stern informs us, included these players: Miller, Admire, Allen, Bushong, Comiskey, Rapp, Helmick, Wisley and Delevan. When the boy grew up, he became an important official of the Missouri Pacific Railroad, and since he had never forgotten the magic names of those nine players, Stern goes on, he bestowed them on nine whistle stops passed by the railroad on its way through Kansas.

Unfortunately, no man by the name of Admire, Delevan, Helmick or Wisley ever broke into a major league box score. There was, however, an Earl Rapp, an outfielder with the White Sox in 1949, but it seems unlikely that a town in Kansas would have been named for him. There have been, of course, plenty of Millers and Allens, some of whom even wore Chicago uniforms. The one Bushong in major league history never played for a Chicago team, and the only year that Comiskey managed a club in that city was in 1890, when he piloted the local franchise in the Players' or Brotherhood League.

According to another book, *History of Emporia and Lyon County*, written by Miss Laura M. French and published in 1929, the Missouri Pacific Railroad first crossed this section of Kansas in 1886, when Charlie Comiskey was a young first baseman with the St. Louis Browns. Miss French also explains how some of the towns in question received their names. For instance:

> Three Osage City men, Jacob Admire, W. E. McElfresh and J. D. Hall worked in the interests of the railroad company to secure the bond issue, and afterwards these men were incorporated as a town company, and the town was named for one of the members of the town company.

That seems to take care of Admire.

> Miller was named for the Millers of Miller Ranch, of which Clyde Miller, of Topeka, is owner.
> Allen, 16 miles north of Emporia, is proud of the fact that it is the direct descendent of Lyon County's first post office, also called Allen.

Stern also seems to be due credit for the legend that William Howard Taft, twenty-sixth president of the United States, as a young man was offered a contract by the Cincinnati Red Stockings. This is a remarkable story for two reasons: the Red Stockings did not sign their players to contracts, and the team disbanded in November, 1870, when Taft was thirteen years old. But we have Stern's word that Taft would have accepted the offer had not his father disapproved of such a career for the boy. "But Dad!" Stern has the lad pleading, "Dad, this is *major league* baseball!" The astonishing thing about that quote is the fact that there was no major league at the time and such a term was not in existence.

There are times, however, when a real hero of baseball, a man to whom legends properly can be ascribed, simply cannot convince an audience of his true accomplishments. Such a man was Joseph Emley Borden, whose career in baseball has long provoked controversy.

Borden was born in Jacobstown, New Jersey, and was a descendent of General John Lacey, who served with Washington at Valley Forge. He grew up around West Chester, Pennsylvania, and during his youth was celebrated for his skill at baseball and boxing. He was signed as a pitcher by Philadelphia of the National Association in 1875, but because baseball at that time was looked upon as a rather disreputable pastime, he preferred to pitch under the name of Josephs and, anticipating Serutan by a number of generations, sometimes as Nedrob, which is Borden spelled backwards.

On July 28, 1875 Borden pitched the first no-hit game in professional history, blanking Chicago without anything that even resembled a safety and winning, 4 to 0. In its account of the game the Philadelphia *Times* observed: "Substantially it was a game between pitchers, both being wonderfully effective, particularly Josephs, who has the proud honor of going on record as the pitcher off whom, for the first time in the history of professional ball playing, not a clean hit was made."

Although apparently not knowing that his performance was a new record, the Philadelphia *Press* was similarly enthusiastic: "Josephs and Golden were very effective, the former particularly excelling, not a base hit being made off his delivery. The support which he received in the field was admirable, the Chicago's being retired in one-two-three order seven times and twice after unearned bases had been reached, their total being three."

When the National League was organized the following year, Borden signed a three-year contract with Boston. But his arm went lame early in the season, and to make him work out his salary the management had him finish the year as groundskeeper.

After that he went back to Philadelphia and worked for a time stitching baseballs in a factory. He escaped further public notice until May, 1889, when *The Sporting Life* printed an item that listed him as one of the victims of the Johnstown flood. This he scornfully denied in a letter, then again disappeared from public view. He became, however, a great huntsman, and one of his dogs, Ruby D III, won every competition in which he was entered.

Borden began clerking in Philadelphia's Guarantee Trust & Safe Deposit Co. in 1891 and devoted the remainder of his life to that institution, rising eventually to the rank of an officer. He often mentioned his baseball career to fellow workers, and they smiled impatiently and looked embarrassed whenever he mentioned pitching the first no-hit game, a story they believed unlikely. He died at the age of seventy-five on October 14, 1929, on the very day that the Athletics won the deciding game of the World's Series against the Cubs. Not one Philadelphia newspaper took any notice of his death.

XIII
Beefsteaks and Bourbon

The Dodgers have Del Bissonette,
No meal has he ever missed yet;
The question that rises
Is one that surprises,
Who paid for all Del Bissonette?
　　　　　　L. H. Addington, 1929

Francesco Pezzolo, who played the outfield for the Yankees under the name of Ping Bodie, once sat down to breakfast at his club's hotel.

"How do you like your eggs?" asked the waitress pleasantly.

"Who're you kiddin'?" Ping glowered. "How do I like 'em? How do I know when I ain't got 'em yet?"

It is probable that more jokes about baseball have involved eating than any other activity of the players. It is assumed, and with a certain justice, that meals are the big events of their daily lives. Back in the twenties when automobiles were new and wonderful and Babe Ruth's Stutz Bearcat was the envy of most players, a writer said to Frank Bruggy, a catcher with the Athletics, "Frank, what's *your* favorite car?" Without hesitating a second Bruggy replied, "The diner." Players rush for the diner as soon as they get on a train. In hotels they like to eat as soon as the dining room opens, then spend the remainder of the day sitting in the lobby.

"I have noticed," said Timothy Sharp, a sports writer of Camden, New Jersey, in a column published on June 18, 1904, "that most of the players sit around the lobbies of hotels in a lazy, indolent way, smoking twenty-five-cent cigars and looking like parvenu millionaires. At the stroke of twelve, you see them face toward the dining room and take in the whole bill of fare from soup to nuts. As is well known, a man cannot do athletic work with his system clogged with so much rich food."

Actually, though, there has been a steady improvement since Sharp's day, not only in the table manners of players but in their choice of food. There is no longer an Ossee Schreckengost around to nail a steak to the wall by way of expressing disapproval of its fiber; the gold toothpick has disappeared; players no longer badger waiters or put out their cigarettes in the ketchup. Some even count their calories, and the player of today is in far better physical trim than his brother of yesteryear.

Night baseball has brought about still another revolution in their eating. When games after dark became general, players first tried eating dinner before going to bed but discovered that sleeping was difficult after a full meal. Now on the day that precedes a game at night, most players will eat a substantial breakfast, skip lunch entirely, and have a full course dinner at about four in the afternoon. If they then order anything after the night's game, it will be only a snack.

But in the past players were noted for the eccentricities of their diet. Edward (Cannonball) Crane, the early pitcher who for years held the record for long-distance throwing, particularly enjoyed two dozen soft-boiled eggs served in a soup bowl, topped off with a dozen clams; Jakie May, a southpaw pitcher with the Cardinals, Reds and Cubs from 1917 to 1932, had to have lima beans at every meal, and they had to be baby limas; "Sunset Jimmie" Burke, long a sidekick of Joe McCarthy's and aide to him on the Cubs and Yankees, had a superstition that made it impossible for him to eat dinner until the sun went down; Wes Schulmerich, an outfielder with the Braves, Phillies and Reds from 1931 to 1934, specialized in the eating of clams, both with and without butter, and was the champion of that department. Then there was Louis (Sea Lion) Hall, a Red Sox pitcher of the early days of this century, who drank so much beer at night that he had no appetite for breakfast, which usually consisted of one lemon, sliced and regally served by itself on a platter as if it were a watermelon.

The Yankees of the twenties were prodigious eaters as well as incomparable players, and Waite Hoyt, who pitched for them throughout that entire decade, recalls that originally the management placed no limit on the amount or cost of their food. But when two rookies shared a fifteen-dollar breakfast at the Brunswick Hotel in Boston, a limit of four dollars per player per day was set. This amount, ample for its day, was doled out at the same time every morning by Mark Roth, traveling secretary of the club. Roth always referred to one eager recruit, a kid outfielder named Camp Skinner who was invariably the first in line, as "the boy with the meal-money stare."

Babe Ruth, of course, was the mightiest eater of them all, though his celebrity was so great he rarely risked an appearance in a public dining room. Ruth always ate in his suite, or when traveling, in his compartment. He was a steak man, as almost all players are, but he liked additional frills. "How about putting a few lamb chops around those steaks for trimmings?" he used to say. Hoyt suspects, however, that Ruth on some public occasions actually ate more than he really required because he felt he was expected to put on a show.

"I remember one incident in particular," Hoyt said. "It was back in 1924, and a kid named Shags Horan had just joined us, as an outfielder. He was a sandlotter from St. Louis. On his first trip with us, Shags said he simply didn't believe all the stories he had heard about Ruth's eating. The Babe overheard him and immediately ordered a porter to set up a table in his section. Then he called the steward and ordered and ate three steaks while Horan and Mark Roth sat across the aisle and marveled at him, much as sidewalk superintendents might admire the progress of a steam shovel at work. But I don't think the Babe would normally have eaten that much."

Ruth's reputation for prowess as an eater was also derived from his habit of munching at snacks between meals; the tales of his consumption of eight hot dogs, washed down with soda pop, are not exaggerated.

The hot dog, by the way, has been an integral part of the baseball scene for more than a half century. Harry M. Stevens, the concessionaire, first offered them to the public on a cold day at the Polo Grounds when ice cream would not sell. He dispatched two vendors to round up one thousand frankfurters, which he immediately steamed and served on soft rolls. They made such an immediate hit that they became a ball park staple, and the name "hot dog" was given to them by the noted cartoonist, Tad Dorgan.

One of the game's most repeated stories involves the hot dog. Here is the way it was told by Harold Burr in the *Baseball Magazine* of March, 1935:

> The Tigers were playing the Athletics and Connie Mack's sluggers were making it too hot on the mound for a parade of Detroit pitchers. Kyle Graham, a Tiger rookie, watched the slaughter from the bullpen and to keep up his strength bought himself a light snack of a hot dog from a passing vendor. He bit pensively into the roll when he heard a dread voice calling to him, "Heh, Graham, they want you to get in there and pitch!" "Who's up?" asked the flustered rookie. "Cochrane, Simmons and Foxx are coming up and the bases are full," said his informant cruelly. Graham laid down his afternoon meal on the bullpen bench and started for the distant hill. "Nobody touch that puppy," he called back over his shoulder. "I'll be back in a minute."

A few months later, in the July, 1935 issue of the same magazine, Dan Daniel had this to say: "Talking about eating in the bullpen reminds me of a funny story involving Henry Johnson, when he pitched for the Yankees. One day he was in the bullpen eating a hot dog. The call came to relieve. 'Who is up?' asked Johnson. He was told, 'Al Simmons.' Johnson put down his hot dog. 'Listen, nobody touch this. I'll be right back.' "

Al Schacht, the clown of the diamond who pitched for Washington for three years, for years has made the rounds of the banquet circuit telling the same story on himself, with Ruth, Gehrig and Meusel being substituted for Cochrane, Simmons and Foxx.

But it remained for H. B. Salsinger of the Detroit *News* to trace the story to its true source. When the inimitable Ring Lardner wrote a sketch for Ziegfeld Follies, Salsinger found, he included a scene in which a relief pitcher was munching a sandwich on the bullpen bench when he was suddenly summoned to the mound. "Who's up?" he asked the catcher, simultaneously handing him the sandwich. "Cobb, Crawford and Veach," was the reply. "Well, hold this, then," the pitcher said, "I'll be right back."

While playing the outfield for the Reds in a game in 1940, Morrie Arnovich was all set to catch a fly ball when he was struck in the face by a flying hot dog, roll, mustard and all. It had been thrown from the stands, and Morrie vowed that if he ever laid his hands on the thrower, he would break him in two. Several years later, Arnovich, by this time a weary infantryman in New Guinea, sat in the grass beside a dusty road, enjoying a brief respite from the march. "Heh, aren't you Morrie Arnovich?" the soldier next to him suddenly asked. Morrie acknowledged that he was. "Well, do you remember the time that a guy socked you in the face with a hot dog at Crosley Field? Well, I'm the guy!" Morrie was so astonished that he forgot his vow, and the two shook hands.

A lavish pattern of serving food, drinks and entertainment for the press has been established in major league baseball, and every World's Series and league meeting is the scene of considerable revelry. This custom was established by Garry Herrmann, president of the Reds, at the World's Series of 1919, an ill-starred occasion if there ever was one, although Charlie Comiskey, chief of the White Sox, had earlier set up a press room with free drinks and food for the scribes.

Herrmann was most at home with pigs' feet, sauerkraut and various sausages, but since that day the palates of the magnates have become so refined that they attempt lobster and *pâté de foie gras.* One of the most epic parties of club owners was a dinner given by Horace Stoneham, shortly after he inherited the New York Giants from his father in 1936. There were only thirty guests that night, but a staff of 125 made the preparations at a cost of about ten thousand dollars. It was held at the Rainbow Room of the Waldorf-Astoria, and because the Giants were about to depart for a training trip in Havana, a Cuban motif was employed, including a garden with ducks swimming in a miniature lake. The menus were hand-painted on cedar wood, and behind the diners parrots and cockatoos fluttered in their cages.

Drinking to excess in baseball is not as common as fans are apt to believe. The average player of today usually has a few beers before turning in for the night, but hard drinkers among the players are really scarce. The game occasionally encounters an alcoholic player, but such unfortunates are few, and some of the club owners have learned that they deserve sympathy and help.

This is a remarkable change from the old days, when the conduct of players off the field was generally scandalous and alcoholism actually threatened to destroy the game. It would be impossible to exaggerate the situation; club owners, players and umpires traveled in a fog compounded largely of bourbon, and hardly a day passed without some shocking arrest, thrashing, shooting or instance of delirium tremens.

To select the most dissolute team of this era would be an almost impossible chore. Drinking in baseball reached a peak in the 1880's, and two of the worst behaved clubs were the Pittsburgh team of the American Association, known as the Alleghenies, in 1883, and Columbus, Ohio of the same league in 1889. The Columbus team was so bad that it was nicknamed "Lusher's Rest." As late as 1903 the Cincinnati *Enquirer* offered shaky players this advice:

Whenever a ball looks like this:

O

O

O

Take a chance on the middle one.

As early as 1879 baseball realized the seriousness of the drinking evil, and at the winter meeting that year the National League suspended a handful of players for one year each. But such prohibitive measures failed to work. Almost a decade later the 1889 *Spalding Guide* observed editorially:

The saloon (is) the evil of the baseball world at the present day; and we see it practically exemplified in the failure of noted players to play up to the standard they are capable of were they to avoid these gross evils. One day it is a noted pitcher who fails to serve his club at a critical period of the campaign. Anon, it is the disgraceful escapade of an equally noted umpire. And so it goes from one season to another, at the cost of the loss of thousands of dollars to clubs who blindly shut their eyes to the costly nature of intemperance and dissipation in the ranks. We tell you, gentlemen of the League and Association, the sooner you introduce the prohibition plank in your contracts, the sooner you will get rid of the costly evils of drunkenness and dissipation among your players. Club after club have lost championship honors time and again by this evil, and yet they blindly condone these offences season after season. The prohibition rule from April to October is the only practical rule for removing drunkenness from your teams.

But when reform came, it was not because of prohibition planks in contracts. Baseball grew to be so popular that the supply of players became greater than the demand for them, and competition between clubs eliminated the most objectionable athletes. It was a gradual process that required years. Night baseball, forcing on the player an arduous schedule, requires his services at an hour when temptation might be greatest. When Mike Donlin, the old Giant star, first heard that major league games were to be played at night, he was working as a carpenter in the studios of Hollywood. He shook his head sadly and said, "Just think of it! Taking away a ballplayer's nights!"

But the saloon still serves as a social center for some fans, even though the cuspidors have been removed and the television set has joined the jukebox and the shuffleboard to compete for the attention of the customers. Many former players still operate taprooms, although not so many as in the old days.

August (Gus) Weyhing pitched major league baseball from 1887 to 1901, mostly for the Phillies, and after his retirement he purchased a liquid emporium that was a mecca for players and fans. But during a period of economic depression business dwindled, and eventually the property had to be sold by the sheriff. The proprietor was told that he must vacate the premises by July 1, but he was philosophical about it and put a sign in the window that read: "The first of July will be the last of August." This, however, did not prove to be the case, for Gus was still hale and hearty at his home in Louisville at the age of 88 in 1954.

Training rules in baseball no longer have the importance they once did, and conditioning has come to be pretty much an individual matter. Wise managers have learned that each player has to be handled as a separate case. Rules that were once necessary to keep a minority of players in line only offended the majority. Occasionally today a club owner or manager, irked by a team's losing streak, will suddenly adopt a sweeping new set of training rules, but such a policy is apt to cause grumbling and further losing.

John McGraw was severe in his insistence that players observe stringent discipline, and the system paid off in numerous pennants, although such tactics might very well be ineffective with the more sensitive and intelligent player of today. Frank Chance, on the other hand, was the most lenient of managers, and his Cubs managed to win four flags in five years starting in 1906.

Even McGraw, in his later years, learned to exempt certain players from his laws. When he traded George Kelly to Cincinnati for the highly talented outfielder, Edd Roush, he was astonished when Roush wrote him he was not sure he would report. "I guess it is an honor to be a member of the Giants," Roush wrote, "but I'm not sure that you and I would ever get along. I take good care of myself at all times, and I don't want to be awakened by some trainer or house dick knocking on my door at midnight to find out if I'm in. By that time I'm asleep."

Brooklyn was the first team to enjoy the luxury of a fulltime trainer, hiring Jack McMasters, a former conditioner of pugilists, in 1887.

Cincinnati hired the first actual physician as a trainer in 1898, obtaining the services of Dr. M. A. Frey, a Swedish massage professor. A graduate of the leading medical college in Stockholm, Dr. Frey spoke seven languages and weighed only ninety pounds. He knew absolutely nothing about baseball, but was a tireless worker and gave twenty-two massages on the day he reported. He remained with the team for two seasons but then acquired a devotion to the racing business, and when the Reds last saw him at New Orleans he was attempting to learn to become a jockey.

Few managers have attempted to prohibit smoking on the part of players, although Clark Griffith banned cigarettes when his Highlanders were in training at Atlanta in 1907.

Barney Dreyfuss, for years president of the Pirates, had an aversion for cigarettes, and it was because of that that he passed up one of the greatest players of all time. Dreyfuss scouted Tris Speaker in Texas but refused to buy him after observing that Tris had a habit of leaving the bench each day after the fourth inning to sneak a few puffs. The cigarette was then considered effeminate. "No man who smokes them will ever be a big league player," Dreyfuss predicted. It will also be recalled that Dreyfuss ignored the letter recommending Walter Johnson, a tip offered by a cigar salesman. "What does a cigar salesman know about ballplayers?" Dreyfuss snorted. What, indeed!

XIV
Land of the Potted Palm

Spring training, once a paradise for the sports writer but always a scene of drudgery for the ballplayer, has evolved into a scientific and monotonous assembly line for the mass production of major leaguers. The rustic rookie who once went South to be victimized in badger games and snipe hunts now finds his life governed by mimeographed instruction sheets and the inexorable truth of the stop watch.

The pressure of competition and the curse of efficiency are responsible for the change in the nature of training camp life, but better baseball is probably the result. After inspecting several hundred players that he controlled at the Vero Beach, Florida factory shortly after the last war, Branch Rickey, then boss of the Brooklyn Dodgers, said he had cut the time required to make a big league player out of a hopeful recruit from five to less than four years, and he added that a further speed-up was possible.

Some baseball people think that a player, other than a pitcher, could annually get into shape in about two weeks. But because the training period is so widely publicized and because so many exhibition games are now scheduled (at major league prices in such settings as Miami), teams head for camp at the end of February and work their way back northward in early and frequently chilly April, stopping in uncertain weather for exhibitions at unlikely places, risking their valuable arms and legs on hazardous diamonds, and losing the fine physical edge gained in the semitropics. The typical big league player on Opening Day is a well-tanned man with a cold.

When the Dodgers flew from New York to Ciudad Trujillo in the Dominican Republic for their preseason work in 1948, they reached their destination just seven hours and twenty minutes after boarding a Pan-American Clipper at La Guardia Field. Veteran writers who accompanied them first looked out over the azure Caribbean, then considered the appointments at the swank Hotel Jaragua; and their thoughts went back to earlier Dodger camps at Macon, Georgia and Columbia, South Carolina, where one tired bellhop made innumerable trips on a creaky elevator to deliver ice water, where married players yawned away the evenings playing lotto with their wives, and single ones sneaked down a side staircase to investigate the possibilities of the night.

The custom of heading South before the season is older than major league baseball itself, and it began because Chicago was envious of Cincinnati. When the first professional team, Cincinnati's Red Stockings, went through the season of 1869 without experiencing the humiliation of a single defeat, a group of Chicago civic leaders vowed to form a club that could beat them. In February, 1870, more than a year before the birth of the first major league, the National Association, that new Chicago team, christened the White Stockings, was organized by Tom Foley, a famous billiard player of the day and one of four brothers who had played for an early Chicago amateur baseball team, the Actives. Foley's first move was to import a captain and manager, Jimmy Wood, a second baseman from Brooklyn who had played with the Williamsburgs and Eckfords of that city. Wood immediately rounded up the best available players in the East; and to assure himself that his men would be in the finest possible shape he took them to New Orleans for a period of training. The plan worked so well that Chicago beat the Red Stockings not once but twice. So in the years that immediately followed many of the old National Association teams would winter at New Orleans, playing games whenever the weather permitted, which was often.

Frank Bancroft was something of a nineteenth century Bill Veeck. Trained in the circus business but more inclined towards baseball, he staged the first wedding at home plate, signed the famed one-armed pitcher, Hugh Daly, and took his Cleveland, National League club of 1883 to train in the nation's capital, even arranging an audience for his players with President Chester A. Arthur. Asked why he had chosen Washington for the site of his camp, Bancroft said, "Well, we selected Washington because it is a good place in which to practice. Out West and up North the season is very backward and precludes any possibility of outdoor work."

Billy Sunday, the weak-hitting Chicago outfielder who later became a celebrated pounder of pulpits, is responsible for the legend that the first team to go South to train was Chicago's club of 1886. Late in his life Sunday made that assertion in correcting a newspaper story that awarded the honor to Ned Hanlon's Baltimore Orioles of 1896. Anson's White Stockings did go to Hot Springs in an effort to boil out after a winter spent largely in grogshops, but Sunday was not aware that an earlier Chicago team had preceded them by sixteen years. Anson's training camp paid off when Chicago won the National League pennant in 1886, but the following year, after another visit to the Spa, the White Stockings were dethroned by Detroit, a team that did its conditioning at home.

The Boston team of the National League visited New Orleans in 1884; Harry Wright took his Phillies to Charleston, South Carolina in 1886; and apparently the first team to find Florida was Washington in 1888, a team assembled in Jacksonville. Connie Mack was on that squad and has often recalled how the manager, Ted Sullivan, used to obtain extra service in restaurants through a ruse. Sullivan would customarily start a meal by extracting a silver dollar from his vest pocket, slipping it onto the tablecloth as the waiter's eyes popped. Then, after a meal that consisted largely of double portions, he would put the coin back in his pocket and take his leave.

The conduct of the players in those early camps was often quite offensive to the people of the town. The Chicago team of 1898 insulted so many women on the streets of Waycross, Georgia that the players were actually forced to leave. Afraid of being mobbed, they abandoned the Waycross base and finished the conditioning process at Savannah.

As late as 1914 a big league team made itself unwelcome at its training site. The Phillies of that year held their sessions at Wilmington, North Carolina and considered themselves lucky to get out alive. The team ran into a blizzard, and for a week the players sat in idleness at their hotel. The sports writers, necessarily short of copy, filed stories about Wilmington life in general, commenting on the weather, the food and the habits of the natives. An enterprising Wilmington newspaperman bought as many Philadelphia papers as he could find, then reprinted the stories on the front page of the local gazette, under this screaming headline:

WHAT THEY THINK OF US!

But despite these incidents, other communities stumbled all over each other in an effort to attract teams. A civic booster in San Antonio, Texas, anxious to have the Reds train there in 1898, wrote to John T. Brush, the team's president, proclaiming, "The water here has cured scores of cancers, rheumatism cases, paralysis, and blood diseases. We can offer you a free park, free street-car rides and free mineral baths." The Reds snapped up that offer but remained only one Spring, moving to Columbus, Georgia the following year, their cancers presumably uncured. San Antonio, however, has been referred to often as the finest possible training site, particularly by John McGraw.

At the Columbus camp the Cincinnati players were startled to find awaiting them engraved invitations to a triple hanging at Troy, Alabama. A grandstand had been constructed for spectators at the execution of three unfortunates named Tom Johnson, Richard Hale and Sam Rivers. Alabama law decreed that the hangings be conducted in private, Sheriff S. M. Reeves explained in an accompanying note, hence the invitations. Not one player attended.

Before World War I most teams had their bases in Georgia and Texas. An early booster for Florida was Al Lang, a former Pittsburgh laundryman who to this day sings hymns in praise of St. Petersburg. He managed to induce the Browns to train there in 1914, and since that time the Tampa Bay area has deservedly become the real capital of the Grapefruit League. The land boom of the twenties lured teams away from other states, and for the past thirty-five years more than half the major league teams have trained in Florida. The Miami area was first invaded by the Braves, who were stationed there in 1915.

When the Giants experienced a rainy spring at Sarasota in 1924, writers of course sent home word of the wetness, and the local paper ran an outraged editorial that said, among other things, "If it rains any more, keep your darned mouths shut."

The Yankees are the only team to train on British soil, having pitched camp on Bermuda in 1912. But they found the food bad and discovered that the soil was of a coral composition that seemed to cause pulled leg muscles.

No team has trained in Mississippi since the Phillies visited Biloxi in 1938; Texas has not provided a camp since the Braves and Browns were at San Antonio in 1941; Alabama has not supplied a base since 1924, when the Athletics were at Montgomery and the Browns at Mobile; and the Red Sox and Pirates, encamped at Hot Springs in 1923, were the last to visit Arkansas.

Although Bucky Harris took his first Detroit club to Phoenix in 1929, it has only been in the past decade that Arizona has been a popular site. The Giants and Indians popularized working out in that desert air, with the Cubs later joining them.

California was first investigated by John McGraw and his Giants in 1907. The first manager to lead his charges out of third-class boarding houses and into swank resort hotels, McGraw disconsolately watched it rain for thirteen straight days at Los Angeles and became so disgusted that he did not return until 1932, his last year in harness. When Bill Terry succeeded him in 1933, he visited Los Angeles again and experienced the nightmare of an earthquake. But the Cubs long were advocates of California training and were at Avalon on Catalina Island for twenty-one consecutive years, starting in 1922 and at Pasadena before that. Their string of visits to Catalina constitutes a record, although the Yankees prepped at St. Petersburg for eighteen straight years, and the Braves stopped at the same place sixteen seasons in a row.

The Giants trained at Marlin Springs, Texas for eleven consecutive years beginning in 1908 and came to look upon the place as a second home. There it was that Rube Marquard, the star southpaw, used to chase boredom by firing his revolver out the window, and Larry Doyle, the second-base marvel, amused himself by tossing lighted firecrackers under the chairs of startled assistant managers and bookkeepers.

The Cardinals of 1919 were the last team to train at home. Branch Rickey returned from World War I as a major in the chemical warfare division of the Army and found that his team was insolvent. He rented from Washington University a field and gymnasium that had been built for the 1904 World's Fair and put the team to work.

There has been only one hiatus in this annual trek to the South and West, a three-year interruption brought about by the last war. Joseph B. Eastman, the nation's director of defense transportation, warned all clubs that in 1943 they must shave mileage from their itineraries by training north of the Ohio and Potomac rivers and east of the Mississippi, an exception being made for the two St. Louis clubs, which were permitted to work out in Missouri. As a result of this order, teams had to condition themselves in such exotic and chilly locales as Wallingford, Connecticut, Bear Mountain, New York and Medford, Massachusetts. And although, in such settings, the players were able to work their way into shape, as soon as the ban was lifted in 1946, the clubs understandably returned to Florida and California.

Although spring training has become increasingly more efficient, a process culminating in the almost frightening atmosphere of such factories as Vero Beach, human nature remains much the same, and from a psychological standpoint the training camp is the same today as it was a half century or more ago.

March, for the ballplayer, is the time of promises and resolves. The pitcher who won five games the year before visualizes for himself a modest victory total of twenty; the outfielder who hit .253 knows it was because he spent too many evenings as a baby sitter or was the victim of ptomaine caused by the poisoned filet mignon in Philadelphia; and this time he will hit .320 sure; the fat catcher is going to lose at least thirty pounds; the veteran never felt better; the rookie is certain he can make it.

And the manager? "Well," the manager will say at a public banquet the day before the season opens, "Now I can't tell you where we're going to finish. But I'll tell you one thing. I never had a club that worked harder than my boys did in Florida this year. Now, I can't tell you how they're going to make out in the pennant race, but you can bet on one thing. We're going to be hustling out there every minute. We started hustling the minute spring training opened up, and we're going to be hustling right down to the World's Series." The audience, thrilled by such originality, will applaud vigorously.

Here is how the various big league teams have moved around their training headquarters in the past thirty-five years:

DODGERS: 1920, Jacksonville, Fla.; 1923, Clearwater, Fla.; 1933, Miami, Fla.; 1934, Orlando, Fla.; 1936, Clearwater, Fla.; 1941, Havana, Cuba; 1942, Havana and Daytona Beach, Fla.; 1943, Bear Mountain, N. Y.; 1946, Daytona Beach, Fla.; 1947, Havana; 1948, Ciudad Trujillo, Dominican Republic; 1949, Vero Beach, Fla.; 1951, Vero Beach and Miami, Fla.

CUBS: 1920, Pasadena, Calif.; 1922, Catalina Island, Calif.; 1943, French Lick, Ind.; 1946, Catalina, Calif.; 1948, Los Angeles, Calif.; 1950, Catalina, Calif.; 1952, Mesa, Ariz.

REDS: 1920, Miami, Fla.; 1921, Cisco, Texas; 1922, Mineral Wells, Texas; 1923, Orlando, Fla.; 1931, Tampa, Fla.; 1943, Bloomington, Ind.; 1946, Tampa, Fla. (Also at San Juan, Puerto Rico in 1936).

BRAVES: 1920, Columbus, Ga.; 1921, Galveston, Texas; 1922, St. Petersburg, Fla.; 1938, Bradenton, Fla.; 1941, San Antonio, Texas; 1942, Sanford, Fla.; 1943, Wallingford, Conn.; 1945, Washington, D.C.; 1946, Fort Lauderdale, Fla.; 1948, Bradenton, Fla.

GIANTS: 1920, San Antonio, Texas; 1924, Sarasota, Fla.; 1928, Augusta, Ga.; 1929, San Antonio, Texas; 1932, Los Angeles, Calif.; 1934, Miami Beach, Fla.; 1936, Pensacola, Fla.; 1937, Havana, Cuba; 1938, Baton Rouge, La.; 1940, Winter Haven, Fla.; 1941, Miami, Fla.; 1943, Lakewood, N.J.; 1946, Miami, Fla.; 1947, Phoenix, Ariz.; 1951, Sanford and St. Petersburg, Fla.; 1952, Phoenix, Ariz.

PHILLIES: 1920, Birmingham, Ala.; 1921, Gainesville, Fla.; 1922, Leesburg, Fla.; 1925, Bradenton, Fla.; 1928, Winter Haven, Fla.; 1938, Biloxi, Miss.; 1939, New Braunfels, Texas; 1940, Miami Beach, Fla.; 1943, Hershey, Pa.; 1944, Wilmington, Del.; 1946, Miami Beach, Fla.; 1947, Clearwater, Fla.

PIRATES: 1920, Hot Springs, Ark.; 1924, Paso Robles, Calif.; 1935, San Bernardino, Calif.; 1942, El Centro and San Bernardino, Calif.; 1943, Muncie, Ind.; 1946, San Bernardino, Calif.; 1947, Miami Beach, Fla.; 1948, Hollywood, Calif.; 1949, San Bernardino, Calif.; 1953, Havana, Cuba; 1954, Fort Pierce, Fla.

CARDINALS: 1920, Brownsville, Texas; 1921, Orange, Texas; 1923, Bradenton, Fla.; 1925, Stockton, Calif.; 1926, San Antonio, Texas; 1927, Avon Park, Fla.; 1930, Bradenton, Fla.; 1937, Daytona Beach, Fla.; 1938, St. Petersburg, Fla.; 1943, Cairo, Ill.; 1946, St. Petersburg, Fla.

RED SOX: 1920, Hot Springs, Ark.; 1924, San Antonio, Texas; 1925, New Orleans, La.; 1928, Bradenton, Fla.; 1930, Pensacola, Fla.; 1932, Savannah, Ga.; 1933, Sarasota, Fla.; 1943, Medford, Mass.; 1945, Atlantic City, N.J.; 1946, Sarasota, Fla.

WHITE SOX: 1920, Waco, Texas; 1921, Waxahachie, Texas; 1922, Seguin, Texas; 1924, Winter Haven, Fla.; 1925, Shreveport, La.; 1929, Dallas, Texas; 1930, San Antonio, Texas; 1933, Pasadena, Calif.; 1943, French Lick, Ind.; 1946, Pasadena, Calif.; 1951, Palm Springs and

Pasadena, Calif.; 1952, El Centro and Pasadena, Calif.; 1953, El Centro, Calif.; 1954, Tampa, Fla.

INDIANS: 1920, New Orleans, La.; 1921, Dallas, Texas; 1923, Lakeland, Fla.; 1928, New Orleans, La.; 1940, Fort Myers, Fla.; 1942, Clearwater, Fla.; 1943, Lafayette, Ind.; 1946, Clearwater, Fla.; 1947, Tucson, Ariz.

TIGERS: 1920, Macon, Ga.; 1921, San Antonio, Texas; 1922, Augusta, Ga.; 1927, San Antonio, Texas; 1929, Phoenix, Ariz.; 1930, Tampa, Fla.; 1931, Sacramento, Calif.; 1932, Richardson Springs and Palo Alto, Calif.; 1933, San Antonio, Texas; 1934, Lakeland, Fla.; 1943, Evansville, Ind.; 1946, Lakeland, Fla.

YANKEES: 1920, Jacksonville, Fla.; 1921, Shreveport, La.; 1922, New Orleans, La.; 1925, St. Petersburg, Fla.; 1943, Asbury Park, N.J.; 1944, Atlantic City, N.J.; 1946, Panama and St. Petersburg, Fla.; 1947, Puerto Rico and St. Petersburg, Fla.; 1948, St. Petersburg, Fla.; 1951, Phoenix, Ariz.; 1952, St. Petersburg, Fla.

ATHLETICS: 1920, Lake Charles, La.; 1922, Eagle Pass, Texas; 1923, Montgomery, Ala.; 1925, Fort Myers, Fla.; 1937, Mexico City, Mexico; 1938, Lake Charles, La.; 1940, Anaheim, Calif.; 1943, Wilmington, Del.; 1944, Frederick, Md.; 1946, West Palm Beach, Fla.

ORIOLES: 1920, San Antonio, Texas; 1921, Bogalusa, La.; 1922, Mobile, Ala.; 1925, Tarpon Springs, Fla.; 1928, West Palm Beach, Fla.; 1937, San Antonio, Texas; 1942, DeLand, Fla.; 1943, Cape Girardeau, Mo.; 1946, Anaheim, Calif.; 1947, Miami, Fla.; 1948, San Bernardino, Calif.; 1949, Burbank, Calif.; 1953, San Bernardino, Calif.

SENATORS: 1920, Tampa, Fla.; 1930, Biloxi, Miss.; 1936, Orlando, Fla.; 1943, College Park, Md.; 1946, Orlando, Fla.

Fans who watch Spring training games in St. Petersburg are most likely to see future champions in action because the Yankees and Cardinals, who have long trained there, have the best records for winning pennants in their respective leagues. In the past thirty-two years in which teams were allowed to go where they wanted to train, forty-one out of a possible sixty-four flag winners have conditioned in Florida, eighteen of them in St. Petersburg. California has trained seven pennant winners over this period, Texas six, Louisiana four, Cuba three, Arizona two, and Mississippi one.

California has not trained a World's Series winner since the 1933 Giants began practice at Los Angeles; Arizona had one only because the Giants and Yankees swapped bases in 1951 until both the Giants and Indians won in 1954; and Texas saw its last one when the Cardinals were assembled by Rogers Hornsby at San Antonio in 1926.

Although Cuba was long the favorite winter quarters of John McGraw, he never considered taking his team there because of the presence of too many frozen daiquiris and unfrozen señoritas. "It would be an ideal place to train," he said, "were the temptations not so great." However, the Giants made their base there after his death in 1937 and went on to win the National League title.

XV
Don't Kill the Umpire

Though sticks and stones his bones may crack
And bottles inundate his back,
The harshest names
From men and dames
Won't jar his self-possession.
Though folks all call him "Jesse James"
And "crook" and "yegg" and such like names,
And say he's blind,
He doesn't mind.
Now, what is his profession?
Baseball Magazine, January, 1926

The forlorn, abused umpire, buffeted through the ages, a target for the oaths and sometimes the fists of players, the censure of club and league officials, and the senseless venom of partisan fans, has at long last secured the stature and protection that his position warrants. Although a few of today's officials, perhaps befuddled by the heady wine of their new authority, are a little hasty in banishing offending players and a trifle too aware that their every gesture is recorded on the television screen, umpiring is better now than at any time in history.

Some, of course, are better than others, although the leagues have never asked the managers and players to grade their work. But in 1935 *The Sporting News* polled more than two hundred major leaguers and found that the most popular and respected of all was the National League's Albert (Dolly) Stark. Strangely, in spite of the acclaim for his work, Stark quit his job three times. A pleasant, conscientious man, slight of build but agile as a panther, he simply could not put up with the stupid tirades of players and the ignorant mockery of many spectators. Stark actually revolutionized umpiring, but it was a quiet revolution, and fans were not aware that it was taking place. Long after his third and final retirement, Dolly, in a conversation with Frank Graham of the New York *Journal-American,* explained how he had changed the nature of an umpire's work. "I just followed the ball," he said. "When I was working on the bases, I called plays from inside the diamond because I found I could see them better that way. And when I was working back of the plate and had only one umpire working with me, I ran down to first base or third on close plays when the other umpire, as he often had to do, was looking for a play at second." Conditions have improved since Dolly retired, and now there are at least three, and often four umpires for every game in the majors.

It would not have been possible for anyone as intelligent and sensitive as Stark to have worked in the early days. The hand-to-mouth existence of those first officials constitutes a sad chapter in baseball's history. Originally they were paid five dollars a game, and for that pittance they had to dodge beer mugs hurled from the stands by irate loudmouths, engage in postgame fistfights with players, and absorb the daily abuse of partisan sports writers. Some of them were former players down on their luck, many were unable to function properly because they had deadened their senses with whiskey, but they were impartially tormented. Billy McLean was the best umpire in the National League's first decade, but this is what the Boston *Herald* had to say about him on June 28, 1884:

"In Providence they have no use for McLean. He acts like a crank and, in my opinion, he is not right in his upper story. His eyesight is poor; he cannot read without spectacles; and he does not take a position which enables him to fairly judge balls and strikes. I have never seen worse decisions than McLean has made since we have been in Chicago."

John Gaffney was called "King of the Umpires" all through the eighties and early nineties, and up to that time he was considered the best of all, but his profession paid him so poorly that he ended his days as a ticket seller on the Brooklyn El. Gaffney umpired his first big league game at Boston on August 9, 1884, with Old Hoss Radbourne of Providence beating the home team, 1 to 0, and although not much remained of the season, he early discovered the sort of life he had entered. A writer covering a game between New York and Buffalo on September 26 explained the umpire's absence: "Gaffney did not umpire because he was slugged yesterday at the hotel by Ward. They got into an altercation about Wednesday's game, when Ward struck the umpire twice in the face, one blow laying open the flesh to the bone, over the left eye. Humphries and the bystanders separated them."

The Ward in question was John Montgomery Ward, a Giant manager who married an actress, Helen Dauvray, a half century before Leo Durocher met Laraine Day; author of a perfect game as a pitcher, manufacturer of more than two thousand hits, a star shortstop, organizer of the Brotherhood, and later an attorney for the National League. Throughout his career Ward conducted himself as a thorough gentleman, and although it may seem absurd to take sides in his battle with Gaffney seventy years after the event, the only logical conclusion is that he had some provocation.

Misfortune dogged the steps of the early arbiters even into old age. Charlie Daniels was on the National League staff in 1876, the first year of operation, and he held his job for thirteen years. But Daniels was in the news as recently as 1932. In his old age he shared a farm home with a brother two years his junior near Colchester, Connecticut. Both were unmarried and very poor in their last years. First, the brother died; then one night the house burned down, and Daniels moved in with understanding friends. One March day shortly afterward he tried to walk to town but slipped and fell, cutting his head badly, and a passing truck driver found him in a ditch. Rushed to Norwich Hospital twelve miles away, he died the next day. There were no near relatives, and only a handful attended the funeral. Allen Willey, an old newspaperman, conducted a public subscription through the Hartford *Times* to assure him a decent burial.

One umpire who thrived in an environment of tumult and mayhem was Tim Hurst, a red-headed bantam from Ashland, Pennsylvania, who spent his boyhood picking slate in the collieries and learning to fight during his lunch hour—a period at which the miners always beat each other up for the sheer pleasure involved. Hurst's career in the National and American leagues was featured by a constant uproar. The way he spent the afternoon of August 4, 1897 at Cincinnati was typical of his career. When a beer stein thrown from the stands hit him in the back, he casually picked it up and returned it, but had the misfortune to see it land on the nose of a city fireman. Fans then emptied onto the field, but alert police escorted him to the safety of the station house. Ashley Lloyd, the treasurer of the Reds, went his bail, and when the fireman had his face patched up and was on the way to recovery, Hurst was let off in court with a fine of one hundred dollars. That winter the National League released him, but Chris Von der Ahe, the droll, Rabelaisian character who ran the St. Louis Browns, made him manager of that club the following year. Although only a few months removed from the ranks, Tim immediately developed into the most virulent umpire baiter of all time. But when the Browns finished twelfth in a twelve-club field, Von der Ahe saw unlimited possibilities of progress and let him out.

Ban Johnson, the great builder of the American League, was the first baseball executive to back up his umpires and curtail ceaseless wrangling by giving them full authority on the field. He also increased their pay in an effort to lend some dignity to the profession. When Hurst, in retirement, saw what an easy time umpires were enjoying under the new code, he applied for a position on the American League staff and was accepted in 1905. He managed to control his temper for several seasons, but on August 4, 1909, twelve years to the day after the melee at Cincinnati, he punctuated an argument over a disputed play by spitting into the eye of Eddie Collins, the great second baseman of the Athletics, precipitating another riot, and then refused to turn in a report on the incident. Johnson then regretfully suspended and released him.

There have been greater umpires than Hurst, but probably none so fearless, and of all the men in baseball elected or appointed to the Hall of Fame at Cooperstown, he is certainly the only one who got there on the sole basis of pugnacity. Tim is believed to have inspired the common observation about umpiring, "You can't beat the hours." It is said that once, after a hectic game, he was taking a stroll with a fellow in blue, Silk O'Laughlin.

"It's a dog's life we have, Tim," Silk moaned. "Worse than that, for some people are kind to dogs. But every afternoon between three and five, standing out there, taking the insults."

"I know," Tim agreed, "but Silk, me boy, you can't beat thim hours."

The best known umpire in history was undoubtedly Bill Klem, who worked in the National League from 1905 to 1940. Klem began officiating in industrial leagues around Berwick, Pennsylvania at the turn of the century, and he advanced steadily in his profession, refusing to remain in a league longer than one year. Next to Ban Johnson, Bill probably did more to improve the working conditions of his craft than any other man. It was at his insistence that umpires were first given dressing rooms. The first one was at Baker Bowl in Philadelphia, and proved to be as dank as a dungeon. When Klem complained to the league president, Harry Pulliam, he was asked why he did not dress at his hotel.

"For two reasons," Klem said. "In the first place, I refuse to risk pneumonia by going back to the hotel in wet clothes. In the second place, it's embarrassing to be on a street car in uniform, particularly after the home club has lost a game."

Klem was a great umpire because he concentrated completely on the job at hand, always following the ball. When Jim Tobin pitched a no-hit game for the Braves in 1944, Bill Stewart was the umpire behind the plate. "That Stewart is a lucky fellow," Klem observed. "That's the third no-hitter he's umpired, and I never worked in one." Actually, Bill watched five no-hitters from his perch behind the catcher, but he was so intent on calling balls and strikes that he was not aware of what was taking place.

Bill Byron, who worked with Klem for several years, was justly celebrated as "the Singing Umpire." He carried a chip on his shoulder and was asked to leave the National League for that reason, but he was one of the best of his day (1913–1919). Byron often rendered his decisions in verse. He was a masochist and a true artist, as sensitive to the crowd as a violin string is to rain. When his ear would detect faint stirrings in the multitude, he would begin to chant, "Fandom must be very sore; listen to the awful roar."

At about the same time that Byron was delighting his audience, the Pacific Coast League boasted an umpire named Quigg, a dignified, dried-up man with sparse hair who resembled the popular conception of a clergyman. Quigg liked to bawl the batteries as sanctimoniously as possible and then say in almost a whisper of reverence, "And now, let us play."

Although it is commonly believed that umpires never change their decisions, they have on occasion, and with unexpected results. George Moriarty, later a well-known umpire himself, found that out one day when he was a player for the old Highlanders. When Tim Hurst called a strike, George said over his shoulder, "Why, Tim, that pitch was worse than the one you called a ball." "In that case," Hurst snapped, "we'll call them both strikes."

But when players argue with the officials, their logic is not always clear to the spectators. One day at Sportsman's Park in St. Louis fans were startled to see Jim Walkup, a pitcher for the Browns, protest because the man behind the plate called one of his pitches a strike, and a third strike at that. What they did not know was that Walkup's manager, Rogers Hornsby, fined his pitchers fifty dollars whenever, with a count of no balls and two strikes, they threw the ball over the plate. Walkup protested bitterly that the pitch was a ball, but the decision stood, and so did the fine.

There is a legend that in the low minors one day an umpire punched one dollar out of a player's cafeteria meal ticket in order to fine him. Mickey Heath, for years a top first baseman in the minors, had an experience almost as strange. An umpire named Casey in the Pacific Coast League was so angered when Heath kicked dirt over his shiny, blue suit that he made him bring two hot dogs and a bottle of pop to his dressing room after the game and also charged him $1.25 to have his suit dry-cleaned.

Umpires may appear to be dictatorial, but their aura of dignity is usually assumed only to assure a well-run game. Actually, many of them are sentimentalists who like the life because it keeps them around the game. Bill Klem was not joking when he said, "Baseball is more than a game; it's a religion." Billy Evans, the great American League umpire who covered the 1924 World's Series as a reporter, cried unashamedly when Walter Johnson finally won the seventh and deciding game, the crowning triumph of his incomparable career. "This is the greatest thrill I have ever received from baseball," Evans informed the press gallery.

Charlie Rigler, a National League umpire, is usually credited with being the first to raise his right arm to indicate a strike. But long before Rigler entered the league in 1905, Cincinnati coaches used to signal strikes in the same manner for the benefit of William (Dummy) Hoy, their star outfielder, who was a mute. In the eighties mutes in baseball were plentiful, most of them graduating from an institution near Columbus, Ohio, where baseball was encouraged. When they were batting, some way had to be found to let them know what the count was. Arlie Latham, the clownish third baseman, would kick his right leg or try to stick his tongue into his right ear to signal a strike, but more conservative coaches would merely raise their right arms. By the time Rigler came on the scene the practice was general.

When Columbus of the American Association played at St. Louis one afternoon in 1883, the umpire, Bob McNichol, showed up with such a severe case of laryngitis that he was unable to speak at all. Only one umpire was scheduled for each game in those days, so McNichol's disability created a real dilemma. Horace Phillips, the Columbus manager, solved the problem by standing next to McNichol all through the game, shouting out that each pitch was a ball or strike after watching the umpire indicate his decision with his arms.

Fans have often been amused by the names of umpires, and they chuckled when the National League hired a man named Robb to officiate in 1947, but he proved to be a good one. And although the date and place cannot be pinned down more exactly, about thirty years ago there was an umpire in the minors named Raspberry.

Harry Colliflower was a pitcher for the most inept major league team of all time, the hopeless Cleveland club of 1899 that won twenty and lost 134 National League games. Later he tried his hand at umpiring in the American League, and Billy Evans advised him to change his name. "Colliflower is made to order for wise guys in the stands," Evans told him. "You'd be smart to pick something else." So the arbiter changed his name to James, but that only made things worse. "Where's your horse, Jesse?" the hecklers would shout.

Umpires have never received proper recognition. Until Hy Turkin and S. C. Thompson published their *Official Encyclopedia of Baseball* there was not even a complete list of them in existence. There still is no roster showing the number of games they umpired in each major league city, although that formidable chore is now being undertaken.

The first umpires admitted to the Hall of Fame at Cooperstown, a group of eleven, included Tommy Connolly, Bill Dinneen, Bob Emslie, Billy Evans, John Gaffney, Tim Hurst, Bill Klem, Honest John Kelly, Tom Lynch, Silk

O'Laughlin, and Jack Sheridan. The omission of Hank O'Day from his galaxy is a mystery, for he was one of the greatest.

League presidents like to say that the best umpires go completely unnoticed. By that definition O'Day was the perfect official. Umpiring was his whole life. It was he who had to make the crucial call when Fred Merkle failed to touch second base in the game that precipitated a replay to decide the issue between the Giants and Cubs in 1908, and he was the center of hundreds of dramatic incidents in his thirty-three years of service to the National League; but off the field he seldom spoke, and in hotel lobbies you could find him sitting, wearing a cap and staring out into space as if he harbored some strange secret. Hank seldom engaged in the luxury of conversation, and he seemed to consider pleasantness on the part of others as an intrusion. But he was a great umpire.

Hank also served brief stretches as manager of the Reds and Cubs. It was during his year at Chicago that one of his rare spoken sentences became the title of a book. Ring Lardner was sitting in the lobby of the Aldine Hotel in Philadelphia one day, and standing near him were O'Day and the owner of the Cubs, Charlie Murphy. Just then the genial manager of the hotel stepped up and greeted Murphy profusely.

"Oh, by the way," Murphy said. "Have you met our manager, Mr. O'Day? Hank, this is the manager of the hotel."

"What of it?" O'Day asked.

Lardner was so amused by Hank's rejection of social amenities that the phrase stayed with him, and his next book, a delightful collection of miscellaneous pieces, was called, "What of it?"

Another who probably will reach a pedestal at Cooperstown some day is George Magerkurth, the most controversial umpire of recent times. Solid as marble and usually angry, he looked exactly the way fans thought an umpire should look. When he retired from the wars after nineteen years with the National League in 1947, the game lost one of its most colorful advertisements.

Magerkurth once put Burleigh Grimes, then the Brooklyn manager, out of a game for calling him a "nanagoadgie," and later both were summoned to the league office by President Ford Frick.

"I fined you for calling Mage a bad name," Frick said.

"What did I call you, George?" Burleigh asked.

"I don't know what it was," Magerkurth admitted. "I couldn't even spell it. But it was terrible."

"What does 'nanagoadgie' mean?" Frick asked.

"It's a new word," Burleigh explained. "It stands for anything."

XVI
Spitters and Sliders

The pitching record of Walter Esau Beall is so devoid of brilliance that followers of the game can certainly be pardoned for not remembering his name. Anyone sufficiently curious can easily verify this estimate of him as a pitcher; a leafing through the records will show that in five seasons with the Yankees and Senators from 1924 to 1929 Walter won exactly five games. And yet he is remembered to this day by baseball men who glow in fond recollection whenever pitching is discussed, for Beall had the most stunning curve ball that anyone has ever seen. He could not control it, and for that reason he never won a regular job on a big league staff; but it was a curve that simply exploded, and when he got it over, the batters would grunt, swing, miss, and walk away, shaking their heads in wonder.

Beall had short arms, and the curve seemed to snap when it left his fingers. It was next to impossible for a batter to tell whether the curve or fast one was coming, because he threw them with the same straight, overhanded motion. Sam Rice and Goose Goslin, the fine Washington outfielders, were talking about him one day. "The greatest curve I ever saw," Goslin said. "Better even than Johnny Morrison's," Rice added. This was a real tribute, for Jughandle Johnny Morrison, a Pittsburgh employee, received his nickname as a result of his dazzling curve. There have been other great hooks: Mordecai Brown had one, Joe Wood, Alexander the Great, George Dauss, Win Ballou—but Beall surpassed them all.

The game's partisans have long been fascinated by trick pitching equipment. They dote on the fadeaway or screwball, the spitter, the knuckle ball, the sinker, and, in recent years, the much maligned but useful slider. Any pitcher who employs a strange delivery or uses a weird type of pitch instantly stands out and attracts a following.

The spit ball was declared illegal in the major leagues starting with the season of 1920 because the club owners, realizing the financial possibilities of more home runs, were anxious to restrict pitching. It was ruled, however, that any hurler then on a big league roster who included the spitter in his repertoire could continue to use it. Burleigh Grimes, who hung around until 1934, was the last of the breed. Now that home runs have completely changed the game, agitators have asked that the spit ball be brought back, but it seems unlikely that they will succeed in this campaign in the near future.

Although it has been claimed that Bobby Mathews employed a damp delivery while pitching for the Lord Baltimores in 1868, what we know as the spit ball was discovered at the turn of the century. It was developed, strangely enough, not by a pitcher but by an outfielder, George Hildebrand, who later became an American League umpire. One day in Providence Hildebrand noticed a pitcher named Frank Corridon dampening the tips of his fingers to produce a slow ball. The effect was good, and Hildebrand thought he could improve on it. Applying more saliva to the ball than Corridon had used, he threw it with a straight, overhanded motion, and saw that it broke sharply down. At Hildebrand's suggestion Corridon then tried it in a game, and struck out nine men in five innings.

Hildebrand found himself on the Pacific Coast, employed by an outlaw club at Sacramento, in July, 1902. When he heard that a pitcher named Elmer Stricklett was about to be released because of ineffectiveness, he taught him the new pitch. Stricklett, spitting happily, promptly won eleven games in a row and was purchased by the White Sox. Before an exhibition game at New Orleans in the spring of 1903, Elmer showed the pitch to Jack Chesbro, a big righthander of the Highlanders. Chesbro added it to his bag of tricks and became such a master of it that in 1904 he won forty-one games.

But the greatest spit-ball pitcher of all was Ed Walsh. He too picked it up from Stricklett. Drafted from Newark by the White Sox, Walsh was lightly regarded, but the spitter soon made him the ace of the staff. He won forty games in 1908, and remained with the team for thirteen years. Stricklett, meanwhile, became the victim of a sore arm, and was shunted off to Brooklyn, where he never enjoyed a winning season.

One of the first knuckle balls to bewilder major league batters was exhibited by Oren Summers, a righthander who joined the Tigers in 1908. Summers won twenty-four games that season, but in each succeeding year the batters took more liberties with his offerings, and he was around for only five campaigns. The knuckler was later brought to a higher stage of development by Eddie Rommel of the Athletics.

Working as a steam fitter's helper on a ship in World War I, Rommel scalded his hand severely. While recovering, he began experimenting with the knuckle ball, a pitch he learned from Cutter Drury, a veteran minor league first baseman. Rommel knew he was not too fast and needed something extra; by this time the spit ball was on the way out and his curve was not sharp enough. He perfected the knuckler while working for Baltimore, and when the Athletics bought him, he was ready to win. Ed won twenty-two for the A's in 1922 when the entire team earned only sixty-five triumphs and finished seventh. But he used the pitch sparingly. One day, when he beat George Uhle, of Cleveland, 2 to 1, in a game that required only fifty-six minutes to complete, he did not call on it once, but the batters were always expecting it and were caught off stride. Rommel, unlike most knuckle-ball pitchers, never gripped the ball with his fingernails, but threw it off the butt of his hand.

Jim Tobin, a young pitcher who started out in the Yankee chain, first reached the majors with the Pirates in 1937. He had good stuff, but in sliding into second one day, he tore the muscles of his pitching arm. That was the end of his fast ball, but Tobin, a resourceful fellow, picked up the knuckler and kept his job. One day in 1943 while pitching for the Braves, he noticed that he could get more of a break on his knuckler and control it better if he threw it sidearm. This was unorthodox, for although the slider is now often thrown with a sidearm motion, the knuckle ball is almost always an overhanded delivery. But Tobin kept throwing it the way he found easier, and as the ball fluttered and danced up to the plate, he began to win. From the stands it looked like the easiest sort of a pitch to hit, but it annoyed batters to a frenzy.

Trick pitching reached its heights in the days before World War I. Home runs were not popular and seldom hit, the games were reeled off in an hour and one half or less, and the pitcher was king. The same ball often remained in play for an entire game, and the pitchers would spit on it and cut its seams; the catchers would dirty it up. Every pitcher had his pet trick in those days, and the sports pages were full of wondrous explanations of shine balls, mud balls and every conceivable variation.

Russell Ford and his emery ball were typical of the era. Ford, a young righthander, was pitching one day for Atlanta when a ball was fouled off his delivery into the stands. When it was returned to him, he noticed a wingy surface on the cover from bouncing against the boards. Whenever he pitched a fast ball after that, it would sail, so he learned that a rough spot on the surface of the ball caused wind resistance. Ford then began wearing a ring on the third finger of his left hand, covering it with a piece of emery cloth. He then cut a small hole, no larger than a quarter, in the corresponding finger of his glove. By twisting the ball against the ring, he produced a rough spot big enough to make his pitches weave crazily. The Yankees bought him, and also his catcher, Ed Sweeney, the only man who could hold his strange shoots. Ford and Sweeney kept their secret, and the pitcher won ninety-eight games in six seasons.

The slider is the most controversial pitch of modern times. Such old-timers as Frankie Frisch dismiss it as a "nickel curve." But it is a legitimate pitch that in proper hands can be extremely deceptive. It has been printed that batters who faced George Blaeholder of the Browns in 1936 first called the delivery a slide. It was supposed to have been a slider thrown by Irving (Bump) Hadley, then of the Yankees, that fractured the skull of Mickey Cochrane, the great playing manager of the Tigers, that same year. But Waite Hoyt thinks the slider is older.

"George Uhle taught it to me when we were together at Detroit in 1930," Hoyt has often said. "It was a wonderful pitch. Uhle threw overhanded with his fast-ball motion. It didn't curve, but actually skidded, almost at right angles, like an auto on ice. He practiced it hour after hour. Sometimes the umpire would be about to call it a ball when it would hop over into the strike zone at the last fraction of a second."

"You know," Hoyt will say. "Uhle had much better luck with Ruth than most pitchers did, and I think it must have been the slider he was throwing.

Batters can't always tell. Of course, George was a righthander, and the ball would veer in towards the Babe; but it would come in right at his fists, and Ruth never could hit it solidly."

The slider today is probably not usually the same pitch that Uhle threw. It has a bigger sweep, and it is likely that pitchers do not control it so well. After a home run, they will come to the bench and say, "That was a slider that big lug hit." Maybe. Lefty Gomez of the Yankees was once induced to try throwing it by Clint Brown of the White Sox. The first time he used it in a game, the batter tripled. "That must have been my slider, all right," Gomez quipped. "I pitched, looked up, and the batter was sliding into third."

The sinker pitch has also come into favor in recent years. It is the same delivery that schoolboys refer to as a "drop," and is most effective when kept low. Wilcy Moore brought the pitch to a high state of development. An Oklahoma dirt farmer who reported to the Yankees at a comparatively advanced age, Wilcy worked mostly in relief for the Yankees in 1927 and posted a nineteen and seven record. His pitching was so gratifying that Miller Huggins let him start the fourth and final game of the World's Series, and he responded with a 4 to 3 victory over the Pirates.

There are two legends about Moore. First of all, it was said that Ed Barrow bought him for the Yankees after noticing that he won thirty and lost four for Greenville, South Carolina in the Sally League in 1926, not actually scouting him but merely seeing his record in the league averages. It was also popularly believed that Moore developed his sidearm sinker after cutting his hand severely.

"Both stories are strictly the bunk," Wilcy has often said. "The Yankees first scouted me in July of 1926 and purchased me in August. They paid $4,500 for me before the season was over. If Ed Barrow saw my record in the averages, he was reading about a man he already owned. As for the injury, I did drop a five-gallon water bottle one day in 1924, and cut the second and third fingers of my pitching hand. The story was that there was a change in the formation of the flesh in those fingers, and that I was able to pitch a good sinker as a result. That wasn't so. What happened was this: at Greenville I got hit by a line drive and fractured my right wrist. I had won ten and lost ten at the time and was strictly an overhanded pitcher. When I started pitching again, my wrist was rather sensitive, so to favor it I started going sidearm. To my surprise, the new delivery gave a new snap to my sinker. The pitch would approach the plate in the strike zone, then zip down so fast that the batter would always top it and hit the ball on the ground. Naturally, most ground balls are fielded, and the pitcher who can keep the batters hitting the ball on the ground is going to be a big winner."

When Moore returned to Greenville in 1926, he concentrated on the sinker, and after losing the opening game, he won seventeen in a row. It was that streak that brought him to the attention of the Yankees. After a scout recommended him highly, Ed Barrow merely picked up the phone, talked to the Greenville business manager, Frank Walker, and arranged terms. Wilcy would have reported immediately, but Greenville found itself in an important post-season series with Richmond, champion of the Piedmont League, and he remained there to pitch.

Moore was a big favorite on the Yankees, and the players enjoyed kidding him about his age (he swore he was only thirty), his baldness and his freckles. He was constantly amazed at the change in fortune that sent him from the Sally League to the staff of the world champions, and he remained on the big league scene for six seasons, continuing to perplex the opposition with his pet pitch.

Although he did not employ freak stuff, Carl Mays was one of the most frightening pitchers that players have ever been called upon to face. Mays was a submariner, twisting his body into a pretzel and shooting it at the batter from a starting point only inches off the ground. He also kept his pitches low, as a rule, and batters hated to face him.

Mays will probably be remembered longer than most pitchers because of his misfortune in throwing the ball that killed Ray Chapman, the plucky little shortstop of the Indians, late in the season of 1920. Chapman was the only player ever killed on the field in a major league game, although Johnny Dodge, a former National League infielder, died after being struck by a pitch while playing for Mobile in 1916. Because he had a surly disposition and had often been accused of throwing at batters, Mays was the target for anonymous threats after Chapman's death, and there was even a movement to have him barred from baseball. But the pitch that struck Chapman was in the strike zone. Ray was a notorious plate crowder, and Muddy Ruel, who was catching Mays that afternoon, has often recalled that the pitch was over, that Chapman simply seemed paralyzed and unable to get out of the way.

But after that tragedy, batters were even more wary of Mays and hated the days he worked.

"Batting against Carl Mays was an unforgettable experience at any time," Luke Sewell, an American League catcher for twenty years, recalls, "but I had the tough luck to face him in my very first trip to the plate in the American League. I was just a kid with the Indians in 1921, the year after Chapman had been killed. Tris Speaker had brought me up from Columbus only a few days before, and in this game he threw me in as a pinch hitter. Mays was tough to face at any time—I was to learn that later—but on this particular day he had had a tooth pulled and was feeling meaner than usual. I also remember that he hadn't shaved for several days. Believe me, my knees were knocking when I walked up there. He went into that puzzling, submarine windup, and the first pitch was a strike that I just blinked at. I kept hoping the Cleveland bench would keep quiet, but they started yelling at Mays, reminding him about Chapman and cursing him in general. You can imagine how I felt. When the next ball was over, I hit it down to Everett Scott at short on a couple of hops, and I was never so happy in my life to be called out at first, for I knew that I was out of there."

The submarine style was not natural to Mays, but he went underground as a young man so as not to aggravate injured muscles. He then found the style comfortable and continued it. But Ad Liska was a born submariner, having thrown that way even as a boy on the sandlots of Nebraska. He never achieved the prominence that Mays did, but he was with Washington for four seasons and the Phillies for two, and his strange delivery made him memorable. Liska even threw to the bases underhanded, which Mays did not.

When his major league days were over, Liska signed with Portland of the Pacific Coast League, a broken-down pitcher with a sore arm, hoping that by some magic he might be able to hang around for a season or two. During his first winter in Oregon he worked in an iron foundry. His fellow employees, delighted to have a professional player in their midst, presented him with a token of an iron baseball, complete with seams, that weighed five pounds. Liska began to swing it daily in anticipation of a comeback, and succeeded beyond his wildest dreams, so strengthening the arm that he won twenty-four games for the Beavers in 1937. He then remained in the Pacific Coast League for more than ten years, and crowned his career with a no-hit game in 1946, a decade after he thought he was washed up.

Eldon Auker, who pitched for the Tigers, Red Sox and Browns for ten years starting in 1933, was the last submarine pitcher to make the major league grade, but he was actually more of a sidearmer, not nearly so radical in his style as Mays or Liska. When Auker was a young, blocking halfback for Kansas State, playing for the late A. N. (Bo) McMillin, he broke his shoulder on the first play from scrimmage in his first collegiate game against Purdue. After that he wore a brace, but broke the shoulder again. When he went out for baseball the following spring, he found he could not pitch over-handed at all, and adopted the semisubmarine stuff to favor his shoulder.

It has been said that the late Walter Briggs, owner of the Tigers, found Auker's style so annoying that he got up from his box and left the park almost every time he worked, but if that is true, he missed some good ball games. Eldon won eighteen and lost seven in 1935 and was seventeen and nine two years after that.

Fans who get disgusted with the occasional futility of their favorite bat-ters should remember that pitchers have had more than a century to develop their craft and share their secrets; and that a pitched ball travels more than ninety miles an hour. That is no rough estimate, for Dr. I. M. Levitt of the Fels Planetarium in Philadelphia measures the speed of thrown balls with a pitchometer, a device with electric eyes. The ball breaks through two beams of light a foot apart, setting off an electronic timer, and the exact speed is computed without any possible error. Bobby Feller was timed at 98.6 miles per hour in 1946, when he was slightly past his pitching peak, and Atley Donald of the Yankees was clocked at 94.7. It is considered probable that if such an instrument had been available in the pitching days of Walter John-son, it would have been found that he threw the ball more than one hundred miles an hour.

But a ball travels just as fast when it leaves a bat as it does when thrown, and so marked is the emphasis on long-distance hitting in the modern game that pitchers, whatever tricks they employ, are strictly at a disadvantage. The rise of that most recent of baseball specialists, the reliever, is proof that pitching is more of a burden today than ever before. The three biggest assets in a reliever's book are courage, control, and a rubber arm. There are various reasons why pitchers take up this specialty. Johnny Murphy of the Yankees, one of the greatest of the breed, had such heavy muscles in his back that he found he got tired after six or seven innings. For this reason his manager at Newark, Al Mamaux, often worked him in the seven-inning second games of double-headers that were not only legal but frequent in the International League. By the time Murphy reached the Yankees he was conditioned to that distance.

Baseball has had fewer changes in its rules than any other major sport, one of the reasons for its constant appeal. But almost every change that has come has worked some sort of a hardship on the poor pitcher. In the early days of the game Will White, of the Reds, was not only the first big league player to appear on the field wearing glasses, but one of the best pitchers of his time. White liked to drive batters away from the plate by hitting them; that brought about the rule adopted by the American Association in 1884 that a player struck by a pitch is given his base. White was never effective after that, but the rule was a good one, and the National League put it on its books three years later.

The pitching distance has twice been lengthened, first from 45 to 50 feet and then, in 1893, to its present distance of 60 feet, 6 inches. One of baseball's greatest mysteries is the reason for those six extra inches. The change from 50 feet was at the instigation of an Eastern writer who thought that the pitcher ought to be exactly halfway between home plate and second base. This would be 63 feet, 7 inches. Eastern teams favored the idea; the Western clubs were opposed. A compromise was effected, but why the extra six inches? No one has ever been able to find out. When writers who covered the meeting at which the change was made asked John B. Foster, an authority on the rules, he said, "Ask Mr. Soden," referring to the dignified owner of the Boston Braves. Soden, in turn, referred them to Colonel John I. Rogers of the Phillies. But the Colonel was not talking, which for him was rare.

XVII
Fanatics

During the years he ran the Athletics from the bench, Connie Mack was always a mild citizen who spurred on his players with soft words rather than pyrotechnics; but he was good and mad on the afternoon of September 15, 1927. In the middle of that day's game with the visiting White Sox, Connie summoned a policeman and pointed an outraged finger at a fan later identified as Harry Donnelly, aged twenty-six. The police removed Donnelly from the park, and after the game Connie visited the station house and swore out a warrant, charging the spectator with disturbing the peace.

"This man's rooting has damaged the morale of my team," Mack said. "He has been razzing us all year, and because of him I have had to dispose of Bill Lamar, a competent outfielder. He has assailed other players until they are of little use to the club at home. Sammy Hale, for instance, is a nervous wreck. I want Donnelly under a bond that will restrain him from any more of this abuse."

In view of Donnelly's loud dissatisfaction with the Athletics of that year, a peek at their lineup in the game that brought about his arrest seems to be in order. Here it is: Max Bishop, 2b; Sammy Hale, 3b; Chick Galloway, 3b; Walter French, rf; Ty Cobb, cf; Mickey Cochrane, c; Jimmy Foxx, 1b; Al Simmons, lf; Joe Boley, ss; Jack Quinn, p; Lefty Grove, p.

Fans are presumed to be hard to please, but just what sort of a team could have been constructed by the Athletics to placate Donnelly is uncertain.

Five of the eleven men that Connie called on that afternoon—Cobb, Cochrane, Foxx, Simmons and Grove—are now in the Hall of Fame at Cooperstown, and four of them followed each other at the plate in the contest with the White Sox. There have been, roughly, one hundred thousand games of major league baseball played, but not often has a manager been fortunate enough to be able to use five immortals in the same one. Connie Mack, however, could have employed a sixth, as Eddie Collins was resting on his bench. The Athletics won the game in question, 5 to 4, and finished second in the American League race; yet a home fan had to be restrained from abusing them.

On the other hand, there are rooters as fanatical in their adulation as Donnelly was in his scorn. Bob French of the Toledo *Blade* has reported that one afternoon in Detroit the Tigers, having trailed all through the early stages of the game, filled the bases in a late inning. Gerald (Gee) Walker, a tremendous home favorite, walked up to the plate and struck out. But Hank Greenberg then belted the ball between the outfielders, and the Tigers went ahead to stay. When the teams changed sides at the inning's end and Walker assumed his position in the field, the bleacher gods rose to a man and greeted him with a mighty roar of approval.

A fan from another city turned to a Detroiter and said, "Why on earth are they applauding Walker? He struck out, didn't he?"

"Of course," was the reply. "But they're cheering him for Greenberg's hit. They always do that here."

Somewhere between the abusive scoffing of Donnelly and the Detroit idea that Gerald Walker could commit no wrong lies the attitude of the average fan. His emotions are on the surface and he is mercurial; he forgets the defeat of yesterday in the excitement of today's triumph; he may boo, but usually he comes to cheer. The word "fan" was coined by Ted Sullivan, the legendary manager and scout of the early days, as an abbreviation of fanatic. Sullivan employed the word in the early eighties to describe spectators in St. Louis, where enthusiasm knew no bounds and attendance, particularly on Sunday, was extraordinary. Before that fans were known as "cranks."

It was early recognized that avid followers of baseball are a breed apart. The Boston *Globe* observed in 1884:

There is a man in the Government Hospital for the Insane who is perfectly sane on every subject except baseball. He knows more about baseball than any other man in America. The authorities have humored him so that he has been able to cover the walls of his large room with the intricate schedules of games played since baseball began its career. He has the record of every important club and the individual record of every important player. He takes an astrological view of the game. He explains every defeat and every success on astrological principles. He has it all figured out. His sense has gone with it. He is the typical baseball crank.

It did not take long after the start of professional baseball for fans to lionize players. When the first professional team, the Cincinnati Red Stockings, returned from an undefeated Eastern tour early in the summer of 1869, a swarm of four thousand rooters buzzed around the Little Miami depot and, led by a Zouave band, escorted the players to a banquet at the Gibson House. A fan named Carter Gazley presented the team with a bat that was 27½ feet long, 19 inches in diameter at the butt and 9½ inches at the wrist and weighed 1,600 pounds. It had been turned by a Mr. Heisel in ten hours on a lathe built expressly for the purpose, and the names of the nine Red Stocking regulars and the two substitutes were hand-painted on it.

"The Eastern papers frequently remarked that you were heavy batters," Gazley said in making the presentation. "If you have any more batting to do, you now have a heavy bat to do it with. The papers also said you were good fielders, and we regret that we are unable to present you with a field proportionate in size to the bat."

It was at that banquet, by the way, that players first demonstrated that there is no connection between skilful play and oratory. Here are some of the responses they made when asked to say a few words, as quoted by the Cincinnati *Commercial Gazette*.

Doug Allison, catcher: "I thank you, gentlemen, but you will have to excuse me, for I can't talk."

Fred Waterman, third baseman: "You'll have to excuse me for this is something I never did. (Cry of 'Out on first.')"

George Wright, shortstop: "Gentlemen, you must excuse me, as nobody else is making speeches. My forte is baseball and not speaking; therefore, I'll stop short."

"Leonard got up and sat down without saying anything," the *Commercial Gazette* reported. "McVey asked to be excused. Sweasy was called on but declined, and then loud calls were made for Harry Wright, the manager. He arose and rather bashfully asked to be excused from making a speech."

But program chairmen have never given up, and in the eighty-five years that have elapsed since the Red Stockings refused to talk, organizations have ceaselessly continued to seek out players as speakers, operating under the delusion that the ability to bat a baseball is an adequate qualification for batting the conversational breeze.

But just as those Red Stockings were the first players to be made aware of fan adulation, they were the first to feel the sting of public neglect. When they lost a few games in 1870, interest in the team slackened to such a degree that the franchise had to be abandoned and the lumber used to construct the fence at the park had to be sold so that the management could pay its bills.

The custom of booing players was originated by loafers who were merely demonstrating the churlish nature of their personalities. Early teams were maintained by saloons, and a boy had to be an idler to become skilful. The better classes did not patronize games on saloon grounds, and the typical fan of the time was a roughneck. Liquor was sold in the stands, and there were from six to eight fights at each game.

With the passing of each succeeding generation, the conduct of spectators has become more refined, and there probably will come a day when booing will be considered a quaint but somewhat embarrassing relic of the past. Even so, it has prevented countless players from doing their best work, even in recent times. As late as 1929 a veteran St. Louis writer, John B. Sheridan, who had followed the game from the gutter days, said sadly: "Booing at athletic events exists in no other country. In Australia it's known as "larriking" and the person who indulges in it is called a "larrikin," a synonym for boor."

Jake Fournier was a first baseman of more than ordinary talents who was so singled out for abuse by fans at his home park, Ebbets Field, that he almost quit the game. Fournier batted .350 for the Dodgers in 1925, a mark that rated him fifth in his league, but he was subjected daily to such a torrent of obscenity from the mongrel element in the crowds, that he issued a public statement announcing his retirement and blaming it on the fans. He was finally induced to reconsider, and was back in the Brooklyn lineup as usual in 1926, and the public reaction to his retirement threat was one of the finest things that ever happened in baseball. Tommy Rice painted a vivid picture of it in the Brooklyn *Eagle* when he wrote:

> The reception of his protest was amazing. Club owners have suddenly awakened to the fact that they have permitted in baseball parks language and conduct that would have been tolerated in no other sort of gathering of supposed civilized people. Some of the largest newspapers in the United States have treated Fournier's protest editorially and in every instance, so far as I can ascertain, they treated it seriously. . . . Fournier, himself, has received scores of letters from Brooklyn fans. I have examined them and they are wonderfully alike. Those letters express sincere regret that Fournier thinks of jumping the team, and condemn in severest terms the low-brows who have been allowed to misconduct themselves at will in ball parks, to the shame of the cities and the citizens.

Conduct in major league parks has generally been slightly better than in the minors; some of the worst riots have been in the towns of the smaller circuits. In speaking of certain bleacher fans at Wilmington, North Carolina, a few years ago, Eddie Rommel, then serving as manager of the Richmond, Virginia, club of the Piedmont League, said, "I'll bet if you'd throw a quarter of raw beef into those bleachers, those fellows would eat it up before it hit the seats."

A subspecies of spectator is the professional fan, who is either an eccentric or one who attends games for business reasons. In the former group were such well-known rooters as Hilda Chester, the bell-ringing die-hard from Brooklyn; Harry Thobe, of Oxford, Ohio, a bricklayer who liked to wear a red, straw hat, carry a parasol and dance a jig around the bases at Cincinnati; and Mary Ott, of St. Louis, a familiar figure at Sportsman's Park who used to whinny at the players like a horse. In the latter category were such fans as Jack White, operator of Club 18 on New York's West 52nd Street, who always put out a sign that read, "No Game Today," whenever the Giants lost; and Brooklyn's balloon-bursting Jack Pierce, who appeared on the Ebbets Field scene in 1940 and singled out the Dodger third baseman, Harry (Cookie) Lavagetto, for shrill screams of affection.

Pierce always sat in a box behind the dugout of the visiting team, and his daily visit to the park cost him about forty dollars, which took care of seats for his friends, two fifths of Scotch and taxi fare for his balloons, which he filled with helium from a hand bellows and released at appropriate moments. As each balloon burst, he would scream C-O-O-K-I-E at the top of his lungs. Other fans took up the cry and Lavagetto, slightly puzzled, became one of the most popular of the Dodgers.

No fool, Pierce was the owner of a downtown Brooklyn restaurant and a heavy investor in several other corporations. The Dodgers were a rising team at the time, so his public exhibitions served as a satisfactory means of entertaining his customers. Born in Manhattan and a Giant fan in his youth, Pierce was normal until he moved to Brooklyn.

Fans frequently reveal what is on their minds in letters to ball clubs, and not all their mail is as ridiculous as the post card sent to the Pittsburgh management by a Pirate fan who asked for an autographed picture of Forbes Field. Many letters offer advice, some make predictions about the team's chances of success in future seasons, a few ask for jobs, others have medical hints for players who are injured or ill, and still others send in presents for players. They are all read, and most clubs now answer those that are signed.

Probably the strangest complaint ever received by a ball club was contained in the letter of a man who wrote to the Reds in 1902 and asked, "Will you kindly tell the night watchman at the ball park to please discontinue whistling? We stood it all last summer, and this winter he has been worse than ever. We have a sick person at our house, extremely nervous, and the whistling is awfully annoying." That is the only known instance of ballpark noise creating a nuisance in winter. The same team also received in the mail the first known autograph request, a letter written on May 10, 1890, by a lady who said she was working on a quilt and thought it would be nice to embroider the signatures of the players.

The autograph nuisance began in earnest with Babe Ruth, but now even the lowliest substitutes know that when they leave the clubhouse, they will have to fight their way through mobs of admirers, most of them teenaged girls. If an autograph is all that is wanted, the players are usually glad to oblige, although the nearly fatal shooting of Eddie Waitkus, first baseman of the Phillies, by a crazed girl fan in Chicago in 1949 is still fresh in their minds.

Some of the nation's greatest celebrities have been proud to consider themselves fans. The love affair between Tallulah Bankhead and the New York Giants is of long standing and is not the work of a press agent. Ethel Barrymore is another star of the stage who finds her happiest hours in the ball parks. In the early days Eugene Field, the poet, was always on hand for games at Chicago, as was Clarence Darrow, the famed attorney. Field became so outraged when the White Stockings sold their star, King Kelly, to Boston for ten thousand dollars in 1887 that he began bombarding Chicago newspapers with indignant letters. Robert Ingersoll, the great infidel, was a warm friend of the players, and during the Brotherhood uprising in 1890 he told them that the reserve clause in their contracts would not hold up in court. James T. Farrell, the novelist and critic, is the despair of his intellectual friends because of his passion for baseball; and it is said that when Thomas Wolfe died, a ticket to the Baseball Writers' dinner in New York was found in the suit he was wearing. One of Wolfe's greatest characters, Nebraska Crane, was a big league player, although a completely fictional one. It is thought that he represented Wolfe's childish ambition to become a player.

Presidents of the United States have found the game enjoyable since the day that Frank Bancroft took his 1883 Cleveland team to shake hands with Chester A. Arthur. It is believed, however, that the only chief executive who could actually score a game was Warren G. Harding. In his days as editor of the Marion, Ohio *Star,* Harding also served as an official of the local team in the Ohio State League, and in that capacity he tipped off the Indians to a young first baseman named Jake Daubert and a rookie pitcher, Wilbur Cooper. Cleveland ignored the tip, but Daubert played first base for the Dodgers and Reds for fifteen years, and Cooper was a prominent southpaw for the same length of time, working mostly for the Pirates.

Occasionally a fan will have enough money to buy the ball club of his choice, and when that happens, everyone benefits. Such an event took place when Walter O. Briggs acquired the Tigers. Briggs became the sole owner of the team in 1936, but in the years just before that he had supplied the money to buy Mickey Cochrane as a playing manager, a move that brought about successive pennants in 1934 and 1935. As a young man, Briggs had been such a noisy Tiger rooter that Tommy Connolly, the umpire, once threatened to have him evicted from the park; and after he was able to buy into the club, baseball in Detroit, which had long been a business, became a sport again. He paid his players, scouts and office staff so handsomely that other owners began to mutter about his foolishness. He violated all known rules of operation to realize his dream of a winning team.

Only one team in a league can win each season's pennant, of course, so fans, perennially hopeful, have to endure all sorts of heartbreak. When the Reds won the National League pennant in 1919, a Negro rooter in Cynthiana, Kentucky, then walked sixteen miles every day merely to learn the inning-by-inning results of the World's Series against the White Sox. His disillusion must have been complete when he learned more than a year later that the games had been fixed.

But fans have been known to exert a mass influence, and by their attendance they can determine what sort of a game baseball is to be. On occasion they have even forced a team to use a certain player.

When Brooklyn bought Fred (Dixie) Walker, an outfielder, from Detroit for the bargain basement price of ten thousand dollars in 1939, Larry MacPhail, the general manager of the Dodgers, thought he was merely adding a part-time performer who would fill in for a while and then pass on. Repeatedly banged up in collisions, Walker, a veteran of seven big league seasons, had only twice been able to participate in one hundred or more games. Because of his ability to hit, particularly against the hated Giants, Dixie immediately became a Flatbush favorite. Whenever the Dodgers benched him or threatened to trade him, the public response was so spontaneous and raucous that the management always reconsidered. Dixie remained in the Brooklyn lineup for nine years because of the fans' insistence, to the benefit of the ball club and its stockholders.

XVIII
The Wansley Affair

Baseball is all right, and it will be for ages to come. There is nothing that can shake it. It is the only sport that lives on its own merits. It has no betting privilege to keep it going.

Adrian C. Anson

The belief that big league baseball is completely honest is not a myth; it is a fact. Anyone who has ever associated with professional players knows that they not only do not bet on games, they even avoid the company of persons who do. Although throughout the United States there is an enormous amount of money daily wagered on games, the players are disinterested. Their complete divorce from the gambling element cannot be traced to any superiority of character on their part, but is a tradition of the game, a heritage from the stern administration of Kenesaw Mountain Landis, who even barred for life an owner of the Phillies, Bill Cox, for betting on his own team.

Organized baseball has a phobia about gambling. The parks are policed to prevent it, the clubhouse bulletin boards have placards that shout in bold print the penalties meted out to players and club employees caught at it, and the most witless jockeys of the dugout know better than to joke about fixing games. Even when a player faced with a day off spends a harmless afternoon at the race track, he does it as quietly as possible and with the same sense of doing something naughty that a small child experiences when he raids the cookie jar.

Because of this fine record, the scandals that beset the game in its infancy become more piquant, racy reminders of an era when baseball belonged to the pool seller and the crook. It was the formation of the National League in 1876 and its subsequent firm dealing with dishonesty that made possible the reform, although there have been a few picturesque scandals since that time.

When the National League in 1877 expelled four Louisville players—George Hall, Al Nichols, Jim Devlin and Bill Craver—for selling games, newspapers hinted at an even earlier scandal, an episode mysteriously referred to as the *"Wansley affair."*

William Wansley was a catcher for the Mutuals, an early team in New York City, and the day of his downfall was Thursday, September 28, 1865. Baseball at that time was still an amateur endeavor in theory, although some players were accepting money for their services and had been for about five years, and there was considerable gambling at the Elysian Fields in Hoboken, New Jersey, where the Mutuals played their games against such opponents as the Atlantics, the Eckfords and the Excelsiors.

On the day in question the Mutuals were to meet the Eckfords, and on the night before Wansley had been given one hundred dollars by a gambler named Kane McLoughlin to make sure that the Eckfords won. According to the terms of the plot, which was hatched at the residence of one S. O'Donnell, Wansley was to bribe at least two other members of his team so that there could be no possible doubt about the result. He first asked the third baseman, Ed Duffy, to go along with him, and Duffy said he would only if the shortstop, Tom Devyr, would join them. Several hours before the players were to take the field, McLoughlin picked up Wansley, Duffy and Devyr in a wagon and drove them to the Hoboken ferry. Wansley gave Duffy and Devyr thirty dollars each, keeping forty for his share. All these details were later freely confessed by Devyr.

The Mutuals took an early lead in the game, but then collapsed, errors by Wansley being largely responsible. Here is the line score:

Mutuals	3	0	1	1	3	0	0	1	2	= 11
Eckfords	0	2	1	1	11	1	0	5	2	= 23

Wansley's histrionic abilities were apparently not subtle; in that horrible fifth inning his work as a catcher was so glaringly bad that he was forced to change positions with McMahon, the right fielder. But by that time the damage had been done. In five appearances at bat Wansley failed to reach first base, and his defensive contribution to the Mutual cause included six passed balls.

There was a crowd of 3,500 at the game, and the fans, many of whom had a financial stake in the proceedings, quickly spread rumors of crooked work. In taking notice of the reports, Henry Chadwick, writing in the New York *Clipper*, said of Wansley: "The comments on his errors made him mad, and that is all there is to this talk of selling the game. Baseball has never yet been disgraced by any such thing, and never will, we hope."

But John Wildey, the president of the Mutuals, was highly suspicious, and bluntly accused Wansley of selling out. William H. Dongan, the club's secretary, then handed the player a note in which he was ordered to report to a committee of players at 8 P.M. on October 20 at the club's offices at 397 Hudson Street. Wansley appeared, made a full confession that implicated Devyr and Duffy, and the trio was expelled. But the episode was soon forgotten as the sport continued its rise to popularity.

Several years later Wildey was about to attend a game between the Atlantics and the Haymakers of Troy, New York. Seated in the park with James McKean, president of the Haymakers, he was astonished to hear that august official say that the result of the game was a foregone conclusion and that if he wanted to make a barrel of money to bet on the team from Troy.

It was this same McKean who, in 1869 removed his Haymakers from the field after they had forged from behind to tie the score, 17 to 17, in a battle with the undefeated Red Stockings at Cincinnati. That action almost precipitated a riot among the twelve thousand customers, and at the Gibson House that night McKean had to have police protection for his players. The pretext on which McKean made his players leave the field was a silly controversy about a caught foul tip. The umpire, John R. Brockway, awarded the victory to the Red Stockings by forfeit, but the Haymakers claimed a tie. Later it was revealed that McKean and his friends had wagered sixty thousand dollars on Troy but, fearing defeat, he had avoided a payoff by stopping the game as soon as the score had been tied. The owner of the Haymakers was that fragrant politician, John Morrissey.

All through the five-year history of the National Association, the first professional league that began operations in 1871, contests were casually sold to the highest bidder, and frequently different players on the same team were betting on opposite sides. The result was almost complete chaos.

Even after the founding of the National League, which was formed to put an end to pool selling, fixed games and contract breaking, gamblers tried their best to influence the outcome of games. A New York pool seller, F. H. Seibert, apparently thought that the Mutuals, although by now a National League member, would be doing business at the same old stand, for in 1876 he offered that team's star pitcher, Bobby Mathews, two hundred dollars a game for every one he would sell.

Seibert gave Mathews in writing a code, as follows:

> Mutuals—Anderson
> St. Louis—Bertram
> Cincinnati—Charlestown

If Mathews wanted Seibert to bet on St. Louis, he was to send a wire saying, "Buy Bertram," and so on, addressing all messages to George Howard at the New York Turf Exchange and signing them "Robert."

Mathews nodded that he understood the arrangement, pocketed the code, and at the first opportunity turned Seibert in to the organizer of the league, William A. Hulbert. That display of honesty by Mathews must have discouraged the betting gentry, but not greatly enough to prevent them from reaching the four Louisville players in the following year.

The credit for exposing the mess at Louisville should go to the team's vice president, Charles E. Chase, who first became suspicious when so many telegrams were being sent to Al Nichols, who was only a substitute third baseman. But recent research also reveals that John A. Haldeman of the Louisville *Courier-Journal*, a baseball writer who accompanied the team, played a large part in getting at the truth. Haldeman, suspecting the actions of the four, boldly confronted them and accused them of crooked work even before Chase was aware of what was going on, just as years later another courageous newspaperman, Hughie Fullerton, was to print the details of the Black Sox scandal despite threats from the gambler, Arnold Rothstein. Hall, Nichols and Devlin all admitted their guilt, but the case against Craver was never actually proved. But the league's firm action in making their ineligibility permanent bolstered public confidence in the game.

The baseball world breathed more easily after the expulsion of the Louisville four. In an editorial, the 1881 *Spalding Guide* said,

> It is quite a mystery to us how any professional player possessed of common sense can ever be induced to enter any crooked-play conspiracy. Experience so plainly points out the policy of pursuing an honest course in his occupation, that it becomes a matter of surprise to see him adopt any other. Integrity of play is part of a professional's capital, as much so as his record for special skill at his home position. And yet, until within the past two or three years, occasional instances were known of men being led to risk reputation and character by the temptation of acquiring a few hundred dollars extra money. Here is an occupation which is healthy and recreative in its nature, involving nothing out of the way in the form of fatiguing labor, and for which the remuneration is five-, and in some cases tenfold, what the same individual would obtain in any ordinary business he is competent to engage in.

This was good advice, but it was not the whole story. It is true that the early players were in theory earning five or ten times what they might have made in some other occupation, but they were seldom paid on time and in some cases not at all. When Craver was asked by the Louisville directors if they could read his wires, he replied, "You can if you will pay me the two months' salary you owe me." The wires were not opened: Devlin, Nichols and Hall had not set such a condition on the reading of theirs.

The next episode of dishonesty to confront the game involved an umpire, Richard Higham. The year was 1882, the scene was Detroit, and the nature of his offense was to announce in advance the probable winners of games that he was to umpire.

It was William G. Thompson, president of the Detroit team, who first thought Higham's work was peculiar. In fact, he was sick and tired of watching his Wolverines lose games at which Higham officiated. For reasons of economy an umpire in those days stayed with a team for several weeks at a time. Of the first twenty-nine National League games played by Detroit, Higham called the decisions in twenty-six, and Thompson thought that was too much of a bad thing. Suspicious of the umpire's work, he hired detectives who succeeded in intercepting two letters that Higham had written and posted. One was completely innocent; the other is here printed verbatim:

Friend Todd:
    I just got word we leave for the East on the 3 p.m. train, so I will not have a chance to see you. If you don't hear from me, play the Providence Tuesday, and if I want you to play the Detroits Wednesday I will telegraph you in this way, "Buy all the lumber you can." If you do not hear from me, don't play the Detroits but buy Providence sure, that is in the first game. I think this will do for the Eastern series. I will write you from Boston. You can write me at any time in care of the Detroit BB Club. When you send me any money, you can send a check to me in care of the Detroit BB Club, and it will be all right. You will see by the book I gave you the other day what city I will be in.
Yours truly,
Dick

Armed with the two letters, Thompson summoned the other club owners to a special meeting of the league at the Russell House in Detroit on June 24. Higham readily admitted authorship of the innocent letter, but claimed he had never seen the other one. However, Thompson had the foresight to have in attendance a handwriting expert who gave his professional opinion that the letters had been written by the same person. Higham was then immediately blacklisted.

For a long time after his expulsion there were only occasional charges of dishonesty or suspicions that it existed. In 1886 a newspaper accused Tony Mullane, a prominent American Association pitcher, of throwing a game, but Mullane asked for an investigation and easily cleared himself. When the first World's Series of this century was played between the Pirates and Red Sox in 1903, gamblers tried to reach Cy Young, the great Boston pitcher, through his catcher, Lou Criger. When Criger reported the bribe attempt to his league president, Ban Johnson, the plot was exposed. Because of his honest action, Criger for years was given a pension out of American League funds, long before the philosophy that all faithful employees should be pensioned became general. Ill of tuberculosis in Arizona, he put the money to good use.

Finally the Black Sox scandal came along to give the game its greatest challenge. The atmosphere of baseball at the time was murky. Prominent players had been mysteriously released; rumors were rife that a few players, operating on their own, had been selling games for years. Public confidence was shaken, and stern measures were called for. The dirty laundry that had accumulated in baseball's basement was finally brought out for airing and washing.

Although the eight Chicago players were acquitted in court of throwing the 1919 Worlds Series to the Reds, they were permanently barred from the game, along with others who had knowledge of their scheming. The public exposure of their plot was, in the long run, a happy thing for baseball, because it helped bring about a revolution in operation and led to the establishment of a Commissioner, Judge Landis.

In the first years of the Landis reign there were numerous rumors of scandal, but most of them involved games played before 1919. Although all such reports were carefully investigated, it finally became necessary to impose a statute of limitations, setting five years as the period after which charges against ballplayers would be void. Only in this way could an end be brought to the charges and counter-charges that filled the air.

Since that time there has not been the slightest suspicion about a single major league game and only a few instances of crookedness in the minors. In an editorial in the *Spalding Guide* for 1927 the veteran writer, John B. Foster, summed up the new spirit:

> The moral strength of this country is bound up in its sports. A nation that plays honestly deals honestly. The baseball player of today, instead of permitting himself to be warped by the whine and sophistry of the mercenary, should glorify himself by feeling that he is honored to be an exemplar to the best game in the world and one that holds a superlative brief for its existence in the splendid fact that it is honest to the core, and played by men who are as honest as their game, for *men* make the game, and crooks try to unmake it!

XIX
Little Women

It is probable that the world outside Chattanooga, Tennessee, would never have heard of Virne Beatrice (Jackie) Mitchell had she not accomplished the noteworthy but strangely unfeminine feat of striking out Babe Ruth and Lou Gehrig in succession on the afternoon of April 2, 1931. The occasion was an exhibition game between the Yankees and their hosts, the Chattanooga Lookouts of the Southern Association. With all due credit to Miss Mitchell, her accomplishment is more of a tribute to the gallantry of Messrs. Ruth and Gehrig than it is to her pitching.

The owner of that Chattanooga team was Joe Engel, an experienced promoter of the bizarre. A few months before signing Miss Mitchell, an attractive girl of seventeen, he succeeded in trading his shortstop, Johnny Jones, for a twenty-five pound turkey. Engel made that deal with Felix Hayman, the president of the Charlotte Hornets. Hayman had been after Jones for some time. When Engel visited Charlotte he said to Felix, "Okay, you can have him, and since you run a butcher shop on the side, you can send me a nice, fat gobbler." The turkey was then eaten by members of the Southern Baseball Writers' Association.

The Jones deal was probably not the strangest transaction in the game's annals. Earlier, Joe Cantillon had swapped Booth Hopper for a bird dog; Barney Burch of Omaha had traded two players for an airplane; Fred McJunkin, owner of the Dallas club, gave pitcher Joe Martina his release for two barrels of oysters; and Homer Hammond of San Antonio traded infielder Mike Dondero for a dozen doughnuts.

But if Engel did not establish a record in the Jones trade, he certainly did when he signed Jackie Mitchell. The depression had severely sliced baseball attendance, and he figured that she might lure a few extra admissions from customers he otherwise might miss. Miss Mitchell's motivation was plain enough: she wanted to buy an automobile, and Engel gave her enough money for that one pitching appearance to get one.

The attendance was a disappointing turnout of 3,500. Clyde Barfoot, who had earlier seen service with the Cardinals and Tigers, was the starting Chattanooga pitcher, but after he yielded a double to Earle Combs and a single to Lyn Lary, Jackie was brought in. Ruth and Gehrig then obligingly fanned on three pitches each, but Tony Lazzeri went to the full count and then walked. That ended her performance, the first experiment in signing a girl to a contract in organized baseball.

It was not, however, the last. In June, 1952 the Harrisburg club of the Inter-State League signed a shapely shortstop named Eleanor Engle (no kin, of course, to the Chattanooga executive, who spells his name with the "e" before the "l"). The wife of a carpenter, Mrs. Engle at the time was a twenty-four-year-old stenographer. Dr. Jay Smith, the president of the team, added the girl to his squad without the knowledge of his manager, Clarence (Buck) Etchison, a former first baseman for the Braves who looked on the project in disgust.

Eleanor worked out during infield practice before a game with Lancaster, but the following day George Trautman, president of the National Association, the governing body of the minor leagues, squarely put down his thumb. Trautman, who had already consulted with Commissioner Ford Frick, ruled that women could not be signed to contracts in organized baseball, and warned that any repetition of the Harrisburg nonsense would bring a fine and perhaps a graver penalty against the offender. Just as there had been no rule barring a midget when Bill Veeck had signed Eddie Gaedel, there was no law prohibiting girls from playing, but Trautman and Frick reached the proper conclusion that the presence of a woman on a team tended to make a travesty of the game.

Mrs. Engle did not agree and expressed shock. "I think baseball is making a big mistake," she told Johnny Travers, a Harrisburg sports writer. "I love the game. More women should be playing."

Although Jackie Mitchell and Eleanor Engle are the only two women known to have actually signed contracts, the interest of women in baseball, even as players, is not so recent as is popularly believed. As early as the eighties teams of girls traveled around the country, and like the theatrical companies of the era, were frequently stranded by their promoters. One of the best players of that time was Lizzie Stride of Mahanoy City, Pennsylvania. The daughter of Hugh Stride, a sportsman interested principally in foot races, she pitched under the name of Lizzie Arlington. Ed Barrow, the conservative executive of the Yankees, as a young man often hired Lizzie to pitch exhibitions when he was running the old Atlantic Association.

When Cincinnati organized its first professional team, its famous red stockings were sewed by a girl whose name, believe it or not, was Margaret Truman, and who married the team's star pitcher, Asa Brainard. A little later Mrs. Sallie Van Pelt was named baseball editor of the Dubuque *Times,* and she was considered one of the foremost authorities of the game in Iowa. Still later, the wife of Adrian (Cap) Anson acted for a season as official scorer of the Chicago White Stockings.

One girl, Amanda Clement, of Hudson, South Dakota, had ambitions as an umpire. At the age of seventeen in 1905 she was captain of the basketball team at Yankton College and the leading tennis player in South Dakota. Dressed nattily in a blue suit with her hair tucked neatly under her cap, she made an impressive sight on the diamond. Although she started umpiring more or less as a joke, officiating in games between teams representing lodges, she did so well and the players had so much respect for her decisions that she worked for several years throughout the Dakotas, Minnesota and Iowa. She wanted to get into organized baseball, but there were no offers.

The first woman to own a major league team was Mrs. Helene Hathaway Robison Britton, who inherited the Cardinals from her uncle, M. Stanley Robison, just before the season of 1911. A handsome woman of thirty-two and a militant suffragist, she actually ran the club for eight years, hiring and firing managers, making deals, and attending all the league meetings. Her greatest accomplishment was to make it possible for Miller Huggins to become a big league manager, naming him to succeed Roger Bresnahan in 1913. Bresnahan, a rough and tough product of McGraw baseball, argued with her continually, and although he could hold his own in any dispute with a member of his own sex, wrangling about baseball with a woman was a new experience for him, and he was utterly defeated. When Mrs. Britton sold out to a group that included Sam Breadon, she got $350,000 for the franchise.

During the winter that followed the 1930 season, the Tulsa team of the Western League was sold to Mrs. Lucille Thomas. The wife of an oil operator, she had previously managed a string of theatres. Sports writers were alarmed by this threat of petticoat ownership and had bad dreams about the possibility that she might install cretonne curtains in the dugouts, but their anxiety was relieved when Mrs. Thomas found herself unable to raise the money for a new park and had to forfeit the franchise to the league.

One of the most remarkable women in baseball history was Florence Knebelkamp, who for years served as traveling secretary of the Louisville Colonels of the American Association. A sister of William F. Knebelkamp, the club's owner, she assumed every duty that the male secretary knows, making the railroad and hotel reservations, checking the turnstiles and comforting the players.

Johnny Marcum, a pitcher who started his major league career with two shutouts, was on the Louisville team when Florence served it, and he recalls one embarrassing circumstance in which she found herself. The team visited a hotel for the first time, and the secretary had wired ahead for reservations, signing herself "F. Knebelkamp, Secretary."

When she went up to the desk, the clerk said, "Who are you?"

"Why, I'm Florence Knebelkamp, the traveling secretary."

"Now, let me see," the clerk stammered. "Oh, yes, I see I have you in with Johnny Marcum. I'd better give you a room to yourself."

Another unusual woman is Bessie Largent, who, with her husband, Roy, for years scouted Texas players for the White Sox. At first she went along on scouting trips just for the ride, but she became an astute judge of players, and Roy considered her opinions expert. Among the players sent to the majors by the Largents were Carl Reynolds, Smead Jolley, Art Shires, Bruce Campbell, Luke Appling and Zeke Bonura.

But most women involved in baseball serve as the wives of players. Ballplayers as a rule marry early in life, and do not necessarily choose a girl who knows anything about the game. Often they marry some beauty they knew in school or in the lower minor leagues. Very few remain bachelors, and for some reason unexplained, the divorce rate among players is extremely low. Being married to a player has its compensations, but it is not always an ideal existence. Players are apt to be affected emotionally by the results of the games or by the progress of their careers. Wives have to live with them through their slumps and losing streaks when the evenings are apt to be a burden. A good wife is by far the best influence that an athlete can have; a bad one is ruinous. It is doubtful if any player's wife has been more helpful than Edna McIntosh, who married Clem Dreisewerd, a pitcher for the Red Sox, Browns and Giants during the last war. The Dreisewerds carried a catcher's glove in their automobile, and whenever Clem felt like limbering up, he would stop the car and "play catch," his wife serving as his receiver.

When professional baseball began, the players were often ostracized and were seldom able to meet decent girls. When the Chicago White Stockings visited New Orleans in 1882, they stopped at the Lee House, a hotel more elegant than those in which players were usually housed. Mrs. Frank Flint, wife of the team's catcher, found herself rebuffed whenever she tried to strike up an acquaintance until she met a beautiful girl from Virginia named Nettie Tucker, who had a rare warmth. They went to the game together the following day, wearing big bouquets of violets. As they were being seated, George Gore smashed out a home run, and Nettie told Mrs. Flint that if he did it again, she would throw the violets at his feet. Gore did not repeat, but Ned Williamson later hit one, so Nettie pelted him with her bouquet. After the game they were introduced, and before the team left New Orleans, they were married. There has been a story of that kind behind almost every baseball romance that has since taken place.

A much sadder fate was in store for another White Stocking fan of the same era. Nellie Dolan was the girl's name, and she worked at Marshall Field's. Although she was engaged to a wealthy contractor, Nellie became enamored of Ed (Cannonball) Crane, who pitched for the Giants. Much against the wishes of her parents, she eloped with the Cannonball and married him at St. Bridget's Church in Jersey City, September 11, 1892. For a brief time they were happy, but Crane became a heavy drinker, and the marriage was dissolved. The strange part is that Crane had been a teetotaler until he made a world tour with two teams of major league players under Al Spalding following the season of 1888. Nightly, in such unlikely places as Egypt and Ceylon, the teams were entertained at lengthy banquets, and Cannonball, perhaps out of sheer boredom, began sipping wine. After Nellie left him, the trail led to the minor leagues: Springfield, and then, in 1896, Providence. When he drew his last release from the latter club, he drifted to Rochester and holed up in a hotel, desperately trying to stay on the wagon. The cunning had vanished from his arm; he had no job, no wife, no friends except the saloon loafers who reminded him of how great he used to be and then, as always happens, laughed at him behind his back because they were envious of his talent. The crowning indignity came when the hotel clerk reminded him that his unpaid bill amounted to sixty-five dollars. Ed Crane knew what to do then. They found his body in the room the next day, a picture of Nellie Dolan clutched in his hand. The coroner said he had swallowed chloral. He was thirty-four years old.

Most girls who go to the ball parks have better luck than Nellie Dolan, and they have been watching games from the very start. A. H. Tarvin, the Louisville historian, has traced the custom of ladies' day back to the eighties, saying that the originator of the practice was Aaron S. Stern, a clothing manufacturer who owned the Reds. Pitching for Stern's team was Tony Mullane, a handsome fellow born in County Cork, Ireland, and known as "the Apollo of the box." Stern noticed that although a few ladies were always on hand, they were out in abundance whenever Mullane was scheduled to pitch. Seeing an opportunity to increase attendance, the owner then decided that Mullane would always pitch on Monday and that all ladies with escorts would be admitted free.

Stern did sponsor such ladies' days, but he was not the first to do so. Bill Bryson, the Des Moines writer, has found the phrase "ladies' day" in a story published by the Chicago *Inter-Ocean* in 1883, and in that same year women were admitted free on specified days for National League games at Cleveland and New York.

Weddings at home plate have become a rather common ball park occurrence, particularly in the minor leagues. Young players often believe that there is sentimental value attached to a marriage performed in front of the team, and many a couple has marched to the blessed state under an arch of crossed bats. The front office, recognizing that such an extra-curricular attraction might produce a few more paid admissions, is usually glad to co-operate in such a venture.

It is believed that Frank Bancroft, the same man who introduced his Cleveland players to Chester A. Arthur, arranged the first home-plate wedding at the Cincinnati ball park on September 18, 1893, just before a game between the Reds and the rowdy Baltimore Orioles.

Louis Rapp was a former bat boy and an assistant groundskeeper at the park, and Bancroft, who then served as business manager of the club, was his boss.

"I'd like the afternoon off next Monday," Rapp told Bancroft.

"Why?"

"I'm getting married."

"Why not do it at the game?" the business manager proposed. "Get married at home plate, and I'll give you some furniture."

The bride was Rosie Smith, who lived conveniently near the park, and the bridal party made the trip to the scene by carriage from her home. Amidst the booming of cannon and to the stirring strains of the wedding march rendered by Cook's band, the group assembled at the outfield gate. Groundskeeper Dutch Oehler notified the crowd that the party was ready by firing an old mountain howitzer that had been used at Bull Run, and the procession to the plate began. The management of the Reds presented the couple with a parlor set and two tickets to the World's Fair at Chicago. Fans chipped in with an ice box, and a local character named "Cheese" Glozier, an ancient waiter of the vicinity, contributed a huge limburger cheese.

A big factor in teaching baseball to women has been the broadcasting and televising of games. When ladies began going to the park in droves, their knowledge of rules and strategy was understandably vague. They often squealed at obviously foul balls and chatted about the cuteness of uniforms. They are now more discerning, thanks to a daily diet of baseball in their own living rooms, and if they feel so inclined, they can throw the ironing board through the television screen whenever the umpire, in their studied judgment, misses a call. It is noticed, though, that few of them at the park yet keep score, and it is probable that they could double their enjoyment if they would chart the progress of play as assiduously as they add up grocery bills.

Of all the women whose lives have touched the game, the undisputed queen is now Laraine Day, the movie star who became Mrs. Leo Durocher. Before meeting Leo, she had never been to a ball game and had never even read the sports page of a newspaper. At the Stork Club, where she first got a glimpse of her future husband, she had to ask who he was and what he did. Remarkably, she had never even heard of the Dodgers, the team he was then riotously managing.

But Miss Day, to use her professional name, in a very few years became a fanatic and a student of the game. She and Mrs. John McGraw, widow of a similarly noted manager of the Giants, are the only two women who have given their names to books about baseball. In the pre-game television interviews that, from time to time, she has conducted, she has displayed a remarkable memory and a rare insight. So now, after a Giant defeat, as she waits for her famous husband in a creamy convertible, she can say with real authority, "You lug! You should have lifted the bum in the sixth!"

XX
No Joy in Mudville

There must have been times in the life of Ernest Lawrence Thayer when he wished he had never written "Casey at the Bat." Surely, when he composed baseball's most famous verse as a harmless filler for the San Francisco *Examiner*, he had no idea that he was to become the center of a storm of controversy that would rage for more than half a century. A shy, cultured gentleman of unusual sensitivity and intelligence, he was destined to spend his life warding off the spurious claims of frauds who maintained either that they had written the poem themselves or that they had inspired the character of Casey. For a while the authors of the verse outnumbered the descendants of passengers on the *Mayflower*, and by the time that Thayer died at Santa Barbara, California, at the age of seventy-seven in 1940, the hassle was still raging.

Thayer was born to wealth at Lawrence, Massachusetts, on August 14, 1863. He attended Harvard, where he edited the *Lampoon*, served as ivy orator on Class Day, 1885, and earned with honors his degree in English composition and philosophy. After his graduation, he drifted to the Pacific Coast, anxious to secure employment without the aid of his family, and settled in San Francisco, where he took a position with the *Examiner*. After a year or so, he returned to Massachusetts, but continued to mail contributions to the paper. He wrote "Casey" at Worcester, and the *Examiner* published it on June 3, 1888, an important bit of evidence to consider in the swarm of claims that were to arise.

Almost a year later, the McCaull Light Opera troupe was about to open a new show, *Prince Methuselah,* at Wallack's theatre, Thirtieth Street and Broadway, New York City, the performance featuring the famed actor and raconteur, DeWolf Hopper. Archibald Clavering Gunter, a novelist, dramatist and friend of Hopper's, learned that the two most famous ball clubs in America, Adrian Anson's Chicago White Stockings and Jim Mutrie's New York Giants, were to be in the audience on opening night. Gunter, a baseball fan, remembered Thayer's verse, which he had clipped from the *Examiner,* and thought it might be an appropriate bit of business for Hopper to use it as an encore. Hopper, in complete agreement, was seized by the charm of the poem and immediately memorized it. When he recited it, the Chicago and New York players set up such a pleasant din that the actor made the recitation a permanent feature of his performance. When he long afterward penned his autobiography, "Once a Clown, Always a Clown," Hopper said the date of his first recital was May 13, 1889.

For the rest of his life DeWolf Hopper and "Casey" were inseparable, and to think of one was to think of the other. The verse in the *Examiner* had not been signed, and for three years Hopper tried desperately to learn the identity of the author. One day when he was billed to appear in Worcester, an old family friend who was living there addressed a note to the theatre, asking Hopper if he would not like to meet Ernest L. Thayer, the man who wrote "Casey at the Bat." The actor was delighted, and when Thayer appeared at his dressing room, they spent a pleasant couple of hours. Hopper was very much amused to discover that Thayer could hardly recite the poem, delivering it in clipped, effete accents that did not do justice to the lines.

The impact of the verse on the country was tremendous. Fans loved every syllable of it, possibly because it echoed the frustrations that they knew so well, because so many different Caseys in so many different Mudvilles had swung and missed throughout the years. Certainly if Casey had won the game for his team with a hit, the verse would soon have been forgotten. Although Grantland Rice did an extremely able job in writing "Casey's Revenge," a verse in which the mighty slugger atoned for his earlier strikeout, it will never have the impact of the original.

With Hopper responding to cries from the gallery and reciting it in every state in the union, newspapers everywhere began to print the poem, not always in its correct form. The New York *Sun* ran a version that omitted the first five of the thirteen stanzas. Then a man who had heard Hopper recite the original version tried to rewrite the first five stanzas from memory and attach it to the truncated verse published by the *Sun*. The result was horribly garbled, but even in that form was circulated widely. In the resulting confusion various people stepped forward with the claim of having written it, but most of them stepped right back whenever Thayer put them straight. Thayer repeatedly asserted that Casey was not an actual person, that he had had no particular player in mind when he wrote the verse. But the parade of claimants continued steadily, and the last of them has probably not yet appeared.

The first person who tried to discredit Thayer was F. T. Wilstach, business manager of the Viola Allen company of players. Wilstach said the poem was written in his presence by Will Valentine, a young Irish poet who came to the United States in 1876 and who died in New York in 1897 while a staff member of the old *World*. According to Wilstach, Valentine first published the verse in the Sioux City *Tribune* in 1882. Valentine had been city editor of the Kansas City *Star* until he moved to Sioux City and the *Tribune* in 1882. He contributed parodies to his paper, signing himself "February 14th," which, of course, was a play on his surname.

Wilstach and Valentine shared rooms in Sioux City, and the former said that one drowsy afternoon they had been reading aloud from Macaulay's *Lays of Ancient Rome*, and that he suggested to Valentine that the style could easily be parodied. Wilstach added that Valentine read "Horatius at the Bridge," then sat down and wrote "Casey at the Bat." Thayer was informed of the claim for Valentine, and replied that if he had indeed written it in 1882 and published it in the Sioux City *Tribune*, it would be a simple matter to prove it. Later, when Albert G. Spalding was gathering material for the history of baseball that he published in 1911, he wrote to Thayer about the Valentine matter and received this reply:

"While a certain Will Valentine may have written a baseball poem in a Sioux City paper before 1888, it could not have been 'Casey at the Bat,' and if anyone is anxious enough to search the files of that paper this fact will become patent." Apparently no one was anxious enough, least of all, Mr. Wilstach.

O. Robinson Casey was a resident of Syracuse, New York, and the honored president of the local chapter of the Society for the Prevention of Cruelty to Animals until his death in 1936. During his last years he decided that he had inspired the poem by striking out with the bases full while playing for Detroit of the National League against Minneapolis in 1885. But the only Casey on the Detroit team that year was Dan Casey, a pitcher who also claimed to have inspired the verse; Minneapolis was not in the National League or any other league that year; and the bases were not full when Casey struck out, Blake was on second and Flynn on third. (Fortunately, Casey represented the winning run; otherwise he might have been given an intentional pass and posterity would have had no poem at all.)

The Syracuse *Post-Standard* wrote to Thayer about the claim of O. Robinson Casey, and received a reply that should have settled the issue for all time. Thayer wrote:

The verses owe their existence to my enthusiasm for college baseball, not as a player, but as a fan, and to my association while in college with Will Hearst, who engaged me to come to the *Examiner* in San Francisco after I graduated.

I wrote voluminously for the *Examiner* during a period of a year and a half, beginning in the summer of 1886, and had most success with a series of so-called ballads. Some of these were written after I had resigned from the *Examiner* staff. "Casey" was the last and very much the best of the lot. It was written in Worcester, Mass., in the late Spring of 1888. I called it "A Ballad of the Republic" as a subheading.

The poem has no basis in fact. The only Casey actually involved, I am sure about him, was not a ballplayer. He was a big, dour Irish lad of my high school days. While in high school, I composed and printed myself a very tiny sheet, less than two inches by three. In one issue, I ventured to gag, as we say, this Casey boy. He didn't like it and he told me so, and, as he discoursed, his big, clenched, red hands were white at the knuckles. This Casey's name never again appeared in the *Monohippic Gazette*. But I suspect the incident, many years after, suggested the title for the poem. It was a taunt thrown to the winds. God grant he never catches me.

Daniel M. Casey, the man who actually played for Detroit in 1885, was also with the Phillies from 1886 through 1889 and was a notable southpaw pitcher of his time. After his retirement from baseball, he became a street car conductor at Binghamton, New York, but moved to Washington, D.C., in 1929. Although he had never been anything but a pitcher and had never posted a batting average higher than .183, he decided that he must have been the slugger that Thayer had in mind. He remembered that the neighborhood around Broad and Huntington streets, where the Phillies moved in 1887 to occupy the park later known as Baker Bowl, was often referred to as Mudville, a fact that was true enough. The property was a real mudhole owned by Franklin Gowen of the Philadelphia & Reading Railroad before Alfred Reach and Colonel John I. Rogers bought it for the Phillies.

The Phillies' Casey thought that the Flynn and Blake referred to in the poem must have been Charlie Bastian and Joe Mulvey, weak-hitting infielders who preceded him in the batting order. He also remembered that he once struck out in a game against the Giants, stranding two runners in the ninth, with the Phillies losing, 4 to 3. He said the date of this game was August 21, 1887. No such game was played on that date, although on August 20 the Phillies and Giants battled to a 5 to 5 tie.

On the strength of his story Casey made an appearance on the network radio program, "We, the People," then conducted by Gabriel Heatter. Thayer was still alive when this performance was presented on March 3, 1938, but whether or not he had the strength left to protest is not known.

At about the same time there died in Rowe, Massachusetts, one George D'Vys, who had long told the world that he wrote "Casey at the Bat" while lying in the grass of Franklin Park in Boston. A former sandlot player, Mr. D'Vys said that he had been a member of a team known as the Mudville nine at Somerville, and that his boyhood idol had been Mike (King) Kelly of the White Stockings. D'Vys saw Kelly strike out with the bases loaded one day in August, 1886, and it was this spectacle, he said, that inspired him to write the verse. D'Vys maintained that he changed the name of Kelly to Casey and sent the verse to O. P. Caylor, editor of *The Sporting Times*.

It remained for Fred Hoey, the baseball writer and radio announcer, to dismiss the D'Vys claim. He discovered that *The Sporting Times* was not in existence in 1886 and that Caylor did not become its editor until 1890. Hoey did find that a badly mutilated version of the ballad appeared in *The Sporting Times* of July 29, 1888, but that the name Kelly had been substituted for Casey, only eight stanzas were printed, and it was frankly stated that the verse was adapted from the one that had appeared in the *Examiner*.

Whenever D'Vys had been asked why his poem appeared anonymously, he always replied that he sent it in that way to avoid censure by his father, a sea captain who did not like poetry in any form.

Thayer's letter to the Syracuse paper and Hoey's fine work in blasting the D'Vys claim should have ended the matter, but, after a decent interval had elapsed, the Chamber of Commerce of Stockton, California, entered the Casey sweepstakes with the claim that Thayer had written the poem after witnessing a game in Stockton. That busy group went so far as to re-enact the famous strike-out at the local ball park in 1952, with the assistance of Max Baer, the former heavyweight champion, who took the part of Casey.

The only players mentioned in the poem, aside from Casey, are Cooney, Barrows, Flynn and Blake. All four of those names were also the names of players in the California State League of the eighties, although they were all on different teams. That is apparently the sole basis of the contention that Thayer had the community of Stockton in mind when he wrote the verse.

Here is "Casey at the Bat," exactly as it was written by Ernest L. Thayer and first published in the San Francisco *Examiner* on June 3, 1888:

Casey at the Bat
(A ballad of the Republic. Sung in the year 1888.)

The outlook wasn't brilliant for the Mudville nine that day;
The score stood four to two with but one inning more to play;
And then, when Cooney died at first, and Barrows did the same,
A sickly silence fell upon the patrons of the game.

A struggling few got up to go, in deep despair. The rest
Clung to that hope which "springs eternal in the human breast";
They thought, If only Casey could but get a whack at that,
We'd put up even money now, with Casey at the bat.

But Flynn preceded Casey, as did also Jimmy Blake,
And the former was a lulu and the latter was a cake;
So, upon that stricken multitude grim melancholy sat,
For there seemed but little chance of Casey's getting to the bat.

But Flynn let drive a single, to the wonderment of all,
And Blake, the much despised, tore the cover off the ball,
And when the dust had lifted and men saw what had occurred,
There was Jimmy safe at second, and Flynn a-huggin' third.

Then from five thousand throats and more there rose a lusty yell,
It rumbled through the valley; it rattled in the dell;
It knocked upon the mountain and recoiled upon the flat,
For Casey, mighty Casey, was advancing to the bat.

There was ease in Casey's manner as he stepped into his place;
There was pride in Casey's bearing and a smile on Casey's face,
And when, responding to the cheers, he lightly doffed his hat,
No stranger in the crowd could doubt 'twas Casey at the bat.

Ten thousand eyes were on him as he rubbed his hands with dirt;
Five thousand tongues applauded when he wiped them on his shirt.
Then, while the writhing pitcher ground the ball into his hip,
Defiance gleamed in Casey's eye, a sneer curled Casey's lip.

And now the leather-covered sphere came hurtling through the air,
And Casey stood a-watching it in haughty grandeur there,
Close by the sturdy batsman the ball unheeded sped—
"That ain't my style," said Casey. "Strike one," the umpire said.

From the benches, black with people, there went up a muffled roar,
Like the beating of the storm-waves on a stern and distant shore.
"Kill him; kill the umpire!" shouted someone from the stand;—
And it's likely they'd have killed him had not Casey raised his hand.

With a smile of Christian charity great Casey's visage shone;
He stilled the rising tumult; he bade the game go on;
He signalled to the pitcher, and once more the spheroid flew;
But Casey still ignored it, and the umpire said, "Strike two."

"Fraud," cried the maddened thousands, and echo answered "Fraud,"
But one scornful look from Casey, and the multitude was awed.
They saw his face grow stern and cold; they saw his muscles strain,
And they knew that Casey wouldn't let that ball go by again.

The sneer is gone from Casey's lip; his teeth are clenched in hate;
He pounds with cruel violence his bat upon the plate.
And now the pitcher holds the ball, and now he lets it go,
And now the air is shattered by the force of Casey's blow.

Oh! somewhere in this favored land the sun is shining bright;
The band is playing somewhere, and somewhere hearts are light.
And somewhere men are laughing, and somewhere children shout;
But there is no joy in Mudville—mighty Casey has Struck Out.

XXI
A Word About Home Runs

Until he recently became president of the South Atlantic League, Bill Terry, who managed the Giants for almost ten years, had been out of baseball, but the game was in his blood, and very often he showed up in the grandstand to watch the proceedings at some training camp.

When he put in an appearance at a game in Florida not long ago, a reporter friend said to him, "Bill, you hit .401 in 1930, and there hasn't been a National League average that high since, but if you were playing today, you wouldn't do it."

"What do you mean?" Terry glowered. "Don't you think I was as good as these kids who are around now?"

"I think you were probably better than most of them," the reporter admitted. "But that's not the point. Bill, you like money, and the money today is out in those seats. You were a lefthanded hitter, but you often poked the ball into left field. You wouldn't do that today; you'd be pulling everything to right because that's where the money is. It might cost you fifty points in batting percentage, but you might hit fifty homers too."

"I guess you're right," Terry agreed.

Terry has not been an active player since 1936, but in the brief interval since then the game that he played so well has undergone an almost complete metamorphosis. Today the home run almost completely dominates the action. The National League reaped a harvest of 936 homers in 1950, upped the record to 1,100 in 1952 and 1,197 in 1953. The American League has lagged behind but not far.

Never has there been such a steady cannonade of balls hit over the fences. The home run, once as exotic and mysterious as the orchid, has become as commonplace and monotonous as the dandelion. The continual bombardment has resulted in the lengthening of games, the establishment of numerous records and the ruination of some pitchers. The spectator who once thrilled to the homer is now in much the same state of mind and body as the man who tried to eat quail every day for a month.

Naturally, in view of this revolution of baseball style, magnates, managers, players, umpires and fans have been attempting to determine the cause. Many have been satisfied to blame the ball itself. But the manufacturers deny that the ball has been tampered with and say that, although they have frequently been accused of adding jackrabbit serum to the ingredients that make up the ball, no player yet has come down with a case of tularemia. Others are content to blame the pitcher, claiming that it is not the ball but the decay in the art of pitching that had led to the current unbalance in the game. Even so important a figure as Commissioner Ford Frick has suggested that the pitcher be aided by the restoration of the unhygienic spitball. It is his belief that the easily mastered but mystifying spitter would so confuse batsmen that not only home runs but hits of all proportions would begin to decline. Still others, unable to determine whether home runs have caused bad pitching or vice versa, a problem somewhat akin to the ancient query about the chicken and the egg, are inclined to blame the managers. They suggest that managers have ruined pitchers by removing them too soon from game after game, establishing a conditioned reflex that renders pitchers psychologically unable to finish their starts.

But apart from the ball, the pitching and systems of managing is another reason why baseball developed into a form of carnage, and that reason is George Herman (Babe) Ruth. It was the Babe who, along with Judge Landis, saved baseball after the Black Sox scandal of 1919. Landis restored public confidence in the game by his intolerance of dishonesty; Ruth filled the parks by developing the home run into a hit of exciting elegance. For almost two decades he battered fences with such regularity that baseball's basic structure was eventually pounded into a different shape.

When Ruth finally retired in 1935, the operators of the pastime, unable to find his like, solved the problem by enabling lesser players to duplicate his feats. This may have been accomplished by making the ball more lively and by enforcing new restrictions on the poor pitcher, but a bigger factor was the systematic reduction in the dimensions of playing fields.

Most of the parks in which major league clubs now play were constructed in the years between 1910 and 1915. They were built without regard for the home run, and it was expected that few balls would be hit beyond their confines. An interesting example is Crosley Field in Cincinnati, called Redland Field until the name was changed to honor the current owner of the club, Powel Crosley, Jr. Redland Field was thrown open to the public for the opening game of the 1912 season. Not a single fair ball was hit out of that park for more than nine years, or until Louis (Pat) Duncan, an outfielder of the Reds, smashed one over the left field fence on June 2, 1921. The feat rated headlines in the local newspapers, but today home runs are hit at Cincinnati, as elsewhere, with a regularity that some fans consider tiresome. The terrain has also been shortened at Ebbets Field in Brooklyn, Comiskey Park at Chicago, Municipal Stadium in Cleveland and Forbes Field in Pittsburgh.

Ruth hit his first major league home run at the Polo Grounds, May 6, 1915, when he was a rookie pitcher for the Boston Red Sox. He accounted for three more that year, three in 1916 and two in 1917. Those hits attracted scant attention outside of Boston, but in 1918 when Ed Barrow, Ruth's Boston manager and later his front office boss at New York, began to use him in the outfield, the Bambino's home run total began to swell. He hit eleven that year, tying for league leadership with Clarence (Tillie) Walker of the Athletics.

Ruth's influence began to be felt in 1919. He ended that season with twenty-nine homers, a major league record. But the writers were at a loss to explain just whose mark he had beaten. Someone dug up the information that John (Buck) Freeman had blasted twenty-five for Washington of the National League in 1899, and when Ruth passed that total, he was believed to have set a record. But Ernest J. Lanigan, then as now the foremost statistician in the game, unearthed Ed Williamson's record of twenty-seven with the 1884 White Stockings, giving the Babe a new goal that he surpassed without difficulty.

The home-run carnival began in earnest in 1920, when Ruth, sold to the Yankees for $100,000 and a loan of $385,000, belted fifty-four home runs, wiping off the books all previous marks, including those registered in the minor leagues. For instance, Perry Werden had hit forty-five home runs for Minneapolis of the Western League in 1895, a figure so grandiose as to have been considered safe for all time. But by 1920 Ruth was definitely in the business of eliminating all his predecessors. Then the Babe upped his annual total to fifty-nine in 1921.

An interesting by-product of the home-run craze was the insertion of the "runs-batted-in" column in the official averages. Writers noted how many runs Ruth accounted for with his long drives and began keeping track of the runs driven across by all players. Although the previously mentioned Ernest J. Lanigan had kept such figures since 1907, the "runs-batted-in" column did not become an official phase of the averages until 1920. This interest in slugging emphasized the shift in the game from defense to offense. An even more drastic example of the trend occurred in 1950 when statisticians added a new column to pitching records that showed the number of home runs hit off each pitcher.

Ruth's record of sixty home runs hit during the season of 1927 has withstood the assaults of twenty-six seasons. Such sluggers as Hack Wilson, Jimmy Foxx, Johnny Mize, Hank Greenberg, Ralph Kiner, Ted Williams and Ed Mathews have tried in vain to exceed the magic total. But even if a modern player should connect for a new record, that would not make him another Ruth by any means. When Ruth hit sixty, the entire American League produced only 439. Ruth, in other words, accounted for more than 12 per cent of the home runs hit by his entire league. A National League player in 1953, when the circuit manufactured 1,197 homers, would have had to smash 145 in order to dominate his league as Ruth did. Unless the club owners do away with outfields entirely, putting the fences on the grass behind the infield, it is not likely that any player will ever account for as high a percentage of home runs hit as the Babe did in his golden year.

Ruth's lifetime total of 714 home runs also appears to be beyond the capabilities of any performer now active, although Mathews must be given at least a mathematical chance.

But the excitement generated by Ruth was not merely the result of his homers. He was a crowd pleaser; he performed his greatest stunts before his greatest audiences. He was a star in nine of the ten World's Series in which he appeared. When the Yankee Stadium was formally dedicated, Babe won the game with a three-run homer. He produced three in a single World's Series game in 1928. A home run from his bat contributed to the American League victory in the All-Star game at Comiskey Park in 1933, the first such game ever played, and by that time he was on his last legs. And even in his final dismal season, with the Boston Braves in 1935, he delighted a huge opening-day throng at the Polo Grounds with a home run off Carl Hubbell. Still later, just before his retirement, he knocked out three terrific home runs in a game at Pittsburgh, his final burst of glory.

So naturally the magnates searched, without success, to find another Ruth. Unable to discover replicas of the Babe, they then attempted to create his duplicate by reducing the square yards of playing surface.

The first such attempt was made by the Boston Braves in 1928. During the previous winter the Braves had acquired the contract of Rogers Hornsby, probably the most fearsome right-handed hitter who ever lived. Judge Emil Fuchs, the Boston president, installed "jury-box" seats in left field, forming an inviting target for Hornsby's bat. Actually, Fuchs had changed the geography of his park before adding Hornsby, making the alteration to please his catcher, Shanty Hogan, who went to New York in the Hornsby deal. But he figured the new arrangement would be to the Rajah's liking. But for some reason Hornsby never did hit into those seats with regularity, while visiting players did. Early in June three Cincinnati pitchers, Pete Donohue, Ray Kolp and Eppa Rixey hit into the pews in successive games. That was enough for Fuchs. The seats were promptly torn out and the first experiment in field alteration abandoned.

But other parks were permanently changed, and the fans, delighted with homers, gave their approval. Sports writers and broadcasters, warming up to the popular demand, soon were on the prowl for all sorts of new home-run records: the most ever hit by a Dodger, the most by a third baseman, the most on the road during a season, the most in a double-header, the most in a month—all these were added to the bulging record books. When Mickey Mantle began hitting extremely long home runs for the Yankees, his club began the practice of measuring them, and buying back the baseballs from fans so they could be sent to Cooperstown.

In view of the current popularity of home runs, it is difficult to realize that there was a time when they were of little moment. The first National League leader in the department, George Hall, hit only five for the Athletics in 1876. There was so little interest in extra-base hits that they were not included in the averages, and only in recent years have historians combed them from the box scores. The Chicago White Sox of 1877 failed to hit a home run all season long, but there was a good reason for it. So close to the plate was Chicago's right field fence that any ball hit over it became a grounds rule double. When the two-base rule was finally rescinded in 1884, the way was paved for Williamson to hit his twenty-seven.

Despite the frequency with which Williamson delivered long hits that year, the home run continued to be unattractive to the game's patrons. Henry Chadwick, generally considered to have been the greatest writer of that early period, despised homers and continually growled about them in print. "Just think of the monotony of a game marked by a series of home runs in each inning," Chadwick wrote in 1891. He should be around today!

During the first decade of this century the four-base hit was still neglected. Low-score contests were the rule, and players tried to excel in such intricate departments of play as the bunt, the hit-and-run and the steal, the squeeze bunt and the double steal. It was not considered good baseball to hit one out of the park. Tommy Leach of the Pirates led the National in homers though hitting only six in 1902, and Sam Crawford of the Tigers tagged only seven while setting the pace for the American in 1907. The White Sox of 1908 hit only three as a team. Many of the home runs that were hit in that era were inside-the-park affairs, involving a contest of speed between the runner and outfielder climaxed by a close play at the plate.

J. Franklin (Home Run) Baker, the fine third baseman for the Athletics, acquired his nickname by hitting two important homers in the World's Series of 1911 and not by leading the league four years running, as he did, with totals of nine, ten, twelve and eight.

Then along came Ruth and the revolution.

Because the Babe spent twenty-one of his twenty-two major league campaigns in the American League and hit 708 of his 714 homers in that circuit, fans have always had the impression that the American was a league for power hitters and the National the one in which pitchers flourished. That was true for a time, but the fact is the National League has witnessed more home runs than the American in the first fifty-three years of their joint existence, the exact number of homers being 26,164 for the National and 24,620 for the American in the period from 1901 through 1953.

Ruth himself, in his later years, said that records were made to be broken, and he promised not to be too disconsolate when his were topped. His personal choice to hit more than sixty in a season was Johnny Mize, a distant cousin. But Mize retired without making it, although he hit a high of fifty-one in 1947. Ruth did say, though, that cheap home runs were ruining the game. "If someone beats my record," he stated, "I want them to do it under the same conditions under which I operated."

It is too late for that, but the game is by no means ruined. Despite the ennui among certain fans, others still shriek with joy whenever a home run, be it ever so phony, is hit. Besides, there is a well-founded suspicion that baseball cannot be ruined by anyone. The game has survived three wars in which the United States has participated, countless economic depressions, and four disturbances in its own ranks brought about by attempts to form outlaw major leagues. It has prospered more than ever after each of these temporary interruptions that might have been ruinous.

Baseball has gone through these cycles before, some of them even more drastic. When the pitching distance was increased in 1893 from 50 feet to 60 feet, 6 inches, it took the pitchers several years to adjust themselves to a different throw. Conditioned to breaking off their curve balls at a distance that was ten feet shorter, they had to learn to pitch all over again, which led to a feast of hitting that threatened to ruin the game even in that early day. In 1894 the National League, then composed of twelve clubs, produced ninety-four players who batted .300 or higher, and the scores of the contests were tremendous. The Philadelphia team batted .343 with outfielder Billy Hamilton scoring 196 runs in 131 games. That was the year that Hugh Duffy batted .438, the highest mark ever recorded if you ignore the .492 figure registered by Tip O'Neill of the Browns in 1887, when a base on balls was counted as a hit. But when the fans, alarmed by the high scores of that year, expressed a preference for a different style of play, the game was given back to the pitcher, and he kept it until 1920.

That is quite likely what will happen again because of the home run. Fans usually get what they want from the game's operators in the long run, and when enough of them express disgust with the homer, the shift to a pitcher's game, or to something else, will be made again.

Branch Rickey usually thinks several years ahead of his competition. And in 1953 Rickey disposed of Ralph Kiner and decided to restore Forbes Field to its original dimensions. He is trying to build a club of young players who can run and throw. If he succeeds and the Pirates win, that style will be imitated and the home run will again go into decline.

XXII
The Good Old Days Are Now

Ty Cobb, exercising his prerogative as a fan but speaking with the authority of one conceded to be the greatest ballplayer of all time, stirred up a violent controversy when he collaborated on an article called "They Don't Play Baseball Any More" that appeared in the March 17, 1952 issue of *Life* magazine. Declaring that Stan Musial of the Cardinals and Phil Rizzuto of the Yankees were the only two modern players who could be compared with those of his era, Cobb deplored the accent on slugging, the decline of bunting and the base-stealing art, the absence of strategy, sign stealing and "inside baseball." He particularly singled out Ted Williams and Joe DiMaggio as players who had not realized their potential ability, and commented acidly on the brittleness of modern players. He was also disturbed about the low estate of batting averages.

The reaction was as violent as Cobb's original article. Players replied emotionally, many of them missing the point and citing gate receipts and attendance figures as proof of the superiority of the modern game.

Thus was revived the old argument that can never be settled. Could Joe Louis beat Jack Dempsey? What about Ben Hogan and Bobby Jones? Was the fighting at Tarawa harder than at Verdun? There is not a barroom or living room in the land that has not provided the setting for this eternal battle of the generations.

Some fans operate under the delusion that baseball began when they began to follow it. For this reason they are not interested in hearing about or reading about men who played when the game was young. But by the same token, old men who played the game in their youth tend to glorify the past.

Jimmy Wilson was a National League catcher for twenty years, and at the time of his death in 1947 he insisted that baseball was better than ever. "I'll tell you about these old-timers," Jimmy used to say. "They forget the average player of their time and remember only the stars. It's human nature. When I broke in with the Phillies in 1923, there were some great ballplayers in the National League; but there were plenty of bums too. Who remembers them? The competition today is greater, the equipment is better, and the men are better men. So how could the game be worse?"

Cobb should not have been mystified by the absence of high batting averages today, for the accent on the home run has naturally reduced them. Baseball today is an entirely different game than Cobb's game, not necessarily superior, but there is no proof that it is inferior. Why should players bunt and steal and play for one run if they are followed to the plate by men who can win the game with one swipe of the bat?

The 1927 World's Series offers an illustration of the point. The Pirates entered that series with players who, by the Cobb definition, were good men: the Waner brothers, Pie Traynor, Glenn Wright. They could hit-and-run, bunt and play "inside baseball." During the regular season they led the National League in batting percentage, hitting .305 as a team. But in the World Series the Yankees beat them four straight, and in three of the four games scored more runs in one inning than the Pirates did in the entire game.

It is charged that modern players lack aggressiveness. Old-timers seem dismayed because the athlete of today does not climb into the grandstand and punch spectators, and because he is able to make a circuit of the bases without spiking three infielders. Just where does aggressiveness cease to be an asset? Where does it conflict with sportsmanship? How aggressive should a player be?

Here is a glimpse of the evening activity of major league players of 1884. In reporting a typical episode of that time the Cincinnati *Commercial-Gazette* printed the following:

> Lynch, one of the pitchers of the Metropolitan Baseball Club, and Rose-
> man, one of the fielders of the same club, gave a free entertainment last

evening on the curb in front of the Grand Hotel. The thing began in a good-natured sparring match, that by some hook or crook, developed considerable spirit, and from fun worked up to earnest.

Roseman altogether worsted Lynch in the sport and the latter grew chagrined, and then angry, and began pummeling Roseman so vigorously that he was compelled to resort to extreme measures for self-protection. He therefore seized Lynch and bodily threw him into the gutter. Lynch was now doubly exasperated, and returned to the contest with increased force. Then the contest developed into a brutal fist fight. The participants knocked each other about without ceremony, and were both battered and blood-stained before they could be separated and cared for. They were walked off to different dressing rooms, and in soap and water repented of their folly.

That nice, aggressive evening by two old-time ballplayers if duplicated today would cause any decent hotel to seek a different class of patronage. We have become civilized enough not to settle differences with our fists. Perhaps that is proof of decadence, and in that case the moderns have to plead guilty.

Not only players but fans have become more intelligent and less aggressive. At least in recent years there has been no repetition of this scene described by the Baltimore *American* in its account of a game between Baltimore and Louisville in the former city on June 12, 1884:

The umpire, John Brennan, declared the man out but many in the audience did not agree with him, and gave vent to their indignation by hissing. . . . Several hundred persons immediately jumped over the fence and made a rush for Brennan, but were prevented from doing any harm by York, Emslie and several other players, who told the excited individuals that Sommer had been fairly put out, and that the decision was perfectly right. Still the mob refused to leave the field, and demanded that the umpire be turned over to them. Brennan in the meanwhile stood near the home plate, surrounded by Louisville players, fearing to move one way or the other. At this time fifty or more men from the western, open stands jumped the fence, and advanced threateningly toward Brennan, but Keeper Foy and several other special officers managed to keep them at a safe distance. During the row one of the men drew a huge revolver and threatened to shoot the umpire if he rendered another such decision. . . . While Brennan was leaving the field, one of the persons who was loudest in his denunciation of the umpire's decision advanced toward that official, and almost without warning dealt him a powerful blow in the face, and then escaped in the crowd.

Brennan was gotten safely into the clubhouse, where he remained until a little after seven o'clock, when he went to Jimmy Clinton's house, on Huntingdon Avenue, until after dark.

It seems likely that a fan who took part in that mob scene would have found the baseball played in the Cobb era that was to follow unnecessarily tame. But baseball's long history has been featured by a gradual but steady improvement in the conduct and sportsmanship exhibited by both players and spectators. With rare exceptions, they are today too mature emotionally to punch umpires. Old-timers may, if they like, seize on this as an example of the lack of desire to win.

George Wright, the shortstop of the Red Stockings in 1869, did not remain long on the scene as a regular after the National League began play because he was not able to hit curve pitching, but he made a fortune manufacturing sporting goods, and he was a frequent patron of games. One day in the nineties he told a reporter as he was leaving the park, "These modern players all wear gloves now. It wasn't like that in my day."

True enough. Putting on gloves became necessary when the game grew faster, and if George Wright had been in his prime when they were worn, he would have found it necessary to adopt one. But he preferred the good old days.

Charles (Spider) Baum was a pitcher who won 262 games in the Pacific Coast League. Known as the "Minor League Matty," he never pitched in the majors. Although Baum became an official of the Hollywood team, he referred to modern players as "lemonaders" and said he thought they had things too easy. "There's not enough fight today," he told Bob Ray, a Los Angeles writer. "Why, I remember once when Ike Caveney hit a home run off me, smashing the ball into the poplar trees at Salt Lake, I ran around the bases with him, telling him what I thought of him." Spider did not bother to explain what he accomplished by that jaunt, but modern pitchers, lacking aggressiveness, would probably consider such a trip an expression of childish rage.

As for base-running, in 1953 the National League stole 342 bases, the American, 326, for a total of 668. In 1911, however, when Cobb was in his prime, the National stole 1,691 and the American, 1,703, for a total of

3,394. This would certainly bear out Cobb's contention that base-stealing is a lost art. But 1911 was the year in which A. G. Spalding published his history of the game, and Spalding was worried *at that time* about the decline of base-stealing. Spalding cited an article by Hugh Fullerton that said: "The cause of the degeneracy of the art of base-running is twofold; first, the hit-and-run play and sacrifice, and, second, the tendency towards stereotyped playing."

Athletes today are just as fast as their fathers. The record time for the one hundred-yard dash or any other sprint is faster, not slower than it was a generation ago. Conditioning methods and equipment have improved. If such runners as Jackie Robinson played baseball as it was played in Cobb's time, they would steal a few bases. But to attempt a steal under present conditions is poor strategy. Fans do not want to see the possibility of a big inning destroyed by some runner being thrown out. Every batter today is a potential hitter of a home run, just as in football every play is a potential touchdown. Fans like action. When they tire of the home run, their feeling will be reflected in attendance figures. The game that Cobb played is a different game, but it can be brought back whenever the spectators ask for it.

Arlie Latham lived to be ninety-three and was around baseball all his life. He was a major league player from 1880 through 1899, and after that he was an umpire and coach. During his last years he worked as an attendant at the press box at Yankee Stadium. Just a few months before he died in 1952, a friend said to him, "Arlie, who is the best ballplayer you have ever seen?" Without batting an eye, Latham replied, "Phil Rizzuto. I played the infield myself, but I've never seen an infielder like him."

Abner Powell, the inventor of the rain check, was another nonagenarian who thought the game had improved. "The play as a whole is better nowadays," he said to the New Orleans writer, Val Flanagan. "In the old days it was every man for himself. Today the team works as a machine."

So there are players of other generations who appreciate the game as it is played today. They may not like home runs in such abundance, particularly when parks have to be shortened to provide them, but they do not blame the player for adapting himself to the conditions of his work. They realize that when today's pitcher fails to finish his starts, it is because the deck is stacked against him, not because he is the physical inferior of the player of yesterday.

One of the most frequent complaints heard about today's player is that he has grown soft, that he is brittle (soft and brittle both?), and that he asks to be taken out of the lineup because of the slightest injury. He is always being contrasted with the old Orioles who played for Baltimore in the nineties, the legendary team of players who feasted on scrap-iron and nailed the umpires to trees. It is true that for vulgarity, profanity, senseless abuse and general dirtiness the modern player cannot hope to compete with that Baltimore club, but he can compete in physical condition, courage and intelligence. Gordon Cobbledick of the Cleveland has investigated the myth about those old Orioles, with results that are disastrous for the old-timer. He found that Wilbert Robinson, who was frequently alleged to have gone behind the bat despite a broken hand, averaged about sixty games a season, and only twice caught more than one hundred. John McGraw, of the same team, never played an entire season in his life, and in his prime he had years in which his games played totaled seventy-six, ninety-three, nineteen, ninety-eight, seventy-three and fifty-four.

The record for consecutive games played, a true test of brittleness if there ever was one, is held by Lou Gehrig, one of the despised moderns, who lasted through 2,130 games from 1925 to 1939. The National League record in this department is the property of another modern, Gus Suhr, of the Pirates, 882 games, from 1931 to 1937. Let us see how these records were developed.

John E. Clapp, a catcher, was in the National League when the circuit was founded, and he managed to appear in 212 consecutive games before an injured finger stopped him on June 25, 1879. Paul Hines, the Providence outfielder, then raised the mark to 230 before giving way to a lame arm on June 29, 1880. John Morrill of Boston extended the record to 302 straight, ending his string on May 20, 1881. Orator Jim O'Rourke managed to establish a new mark when he was halted at 319 on July 3, 1883, and Joe Hornung, also a Boston outfielder, appeared in 464 in a row until he quit on September 13, 1884.

The only one of the Baltimore Orioles who remained in the lineup day after day was Steve Brodie, an outfielder, who got into 727 successive box scores in the nineties. That feat never got into the record books because of a typographical error in the official averages that showed he played in only

120 games one year when he was actually in all 129 played by his team. Although Brodie's record was not known, it stood until Everett Scott, a shortstop, played in 1,308 straight games in the twentieth century. It was Scott's record that Gehrig surpassed. In other words, the most notable feats of endurance in baseball have been accomplished very recently, when the players were supposed to be soft.

Catching is the most gruelling job in the game, and if ever endurance is to be tested it is behind the bat. But the records for consecutive games at that position in both major leagues are held by moderns. Frank Hayes of the Browns, Athletics and Indians caught 312 consecutive games starting in 1943; and Ray Mueller of the Reds, 233 straight, starting the same season. The most games caught over an entire major league career total 1,918, and they were caught by Al Lopez of the Dodgers, Braves, Pirates an Indians from 1928 to 1947.

Old-time pitchers, who threw the dead ball in larger parks, often sneer at the modern hurler, who has his arm rubbed by a trainer and who uses such fancy clubhouse appointments as whirlpool baths. Naturally, the feats of pitching endurance that constitute records were performed when it was a pitcher's game. But even with the handicaps imposed by current conditions, Robin Roberts of the Phillies was able to complete thirty out of thirty-seven starts in 1952 and thirty-three out of forty-one in 1953. What he would have done under the conditions that Cy Young knew will never be determined.

One of the saddest sights in baseball is the manager who continually berates his team for lack of initiative and keeps talking about how things were in the good old days. There have been a few of them in recent years, but the game has gone past them, leaving them with their memories and little else. The successful manager knows that today the methods that John McGraw employed will not work, and that McGraw himself, if he were alive, would recognize the change in the quality of players and act accordingly. Baseball may be more of a business than it used to be, but if that is the case, the players want to succeed in business, and they no longer have to be tailed by detectives, shouted at like slaves and driven like oxen.

Joe McCarthy, who managed the Yankees to four consecutive pennants and world championships, was smart enough to recognize the changed conditions. He had played in the so-called good old days and one of his prized possessions is a loving cup inscribed as follows: "With best wishes to the fighting leader of a fighting team. Market Street Merchants' Association, Louisville, 1921." But after he had won his third straight flag for the Yanks in 1938, McCarthy said to the veteran writer, Fred Lieb:

"It has been said that I was tougher in my early years as a manager, especially in my early years in Louisville. Ballplayers were different, and I suppose I have changed. I guess I used to blow off steam a little oftener. It seems to me that the time when a manager used to talk to his players as though he were driving a bunch of mules is pretty well past. Present-day players no longer stand for it. If they do not openly resent it, such a bawling out leaves a mental sore spot. An older generation of players shook off those clubhouse oaths like water off the back of a duck. But you can't run a present-day club by using systems of the nineties any more than you could run an industrial plant by using 1895 methods with your hired help."

Everything is bound to change, and the time is not far distant when some player will look back at the road he has traveled and say, "This is not the same; the game isn't as good as it used to be. This is not the way it was when I broke in in 1954. Those were the good old days."

XXIII
The Hottest Stove of All

The endless pageant of games and players that has accompanied the flow of seasons, piling record upon record and memory upon memory, has warmed each winter for the follower of baseball, brightening his life with the glow of recollection. If winter, for the baseball fan, is a time to look ahead and visualize successes for his favorite team, it is also a time to look back at the bittersweet path, to review the triumphs and the heartbreak of the past. Baseball knows no season, really. But fortunately there is a lull in the action that permits the fan to take pause and consider what he has seen and read about.

There is no way of measuring the heat generated by each annual loading of the old, hot stove. No one has ever tried to show which was the greatest winter of all for the game's devotees. It may have been in St. Louis in the chill months that followed the hot victory of the first Cardinal pennant in 1926; or in Boston after the Miracle Braves climbed from the cellar and smacked down the Athletics four straight times in 1914; or perhaps in New York after Bobby Thomson's incredible home run brought victory to the Giants over the despised Dodgers and made the World's Series an anticlimax in 1951.

But for sheer excitement, controversy, gooseflesh thrills and variety of accomplishment the Hot Stove League has never provided anything to equal the year of 1884. Few are alive who remember it, and the parade has long gone past those who do. Baseball in that day was primitive, of course; the players and the cranks who followed the action were as crude as sculptor's clay. The game of 1884 was not so good a game as we have today, but those who watched and loved it were just as intent and much more partisan than today's spectators. More major league teams were fielded in 1884 than any other year, a total of thirty-four. In addition to the eight National League clubs, there were thirteen teams in the American Association and thirteen more in a bawdy, outlaw circuit known as the Union Association. Big league baseball that year reached out to such places as St. Paul, Minnesota, and Altoona, Pennsylvania, for the only time.

The most exciting story of that year involves the Providence Grays of the National League and their star pitcher, Charles (Old Hoss) Radbourne. There have been a lot of pitchers in a lot of years, but none ever worked so hard or accomplished so much in so short a time as the Old Hoss.

In the middle of June of that year Radbourne sat in disgrace on the bench, accused of throwing a game. Providence was so demoralized then that the management seriously considered disbanding the club. But when Radbourne was reinstated because of necessity, he began to pitch like no one had ever pitched before. The Grays passed Boston and took first place, and Radbourne kept pitching, day after day, until the pennant was assured. Final averages showed that he had worked in seventy-five games, winning sixty and losing twelve.

Providence started that season with two pitchers, Radbourne and Charlie Sweeney. They did not like each other and were constantly wrangling. At first the Old Hoss did most of the pitching, and Sweeney complained to his manager, Frank Bancroft, asking for more work. When given a chance, Sweeney was such a sensation that Radbourne was relegated to the bench. At Boston on the afternoon of June 7, Sweeney struck out nineteen batters in a nine-inning game, winning, 2 to 1. No pitcher had ever fanned that many before, and although seventy years have elapsed, no National League pitcher has ever duplicated the feat.

Some of the early accomplishments in baseball are difficult to verify, but there is no question at all about Sweeney's work that afternoon. Ezra Sutton was the only Boston batter who did not strike out. Jack Burdock fanned four times, Sam Wise and Joe Hornung three times, John Morrill, Jimmy Manning, Bill Crowley and Mike Hines twice, and Grasshopper Jim Whitney, the opposing pitcher, once. Whitney fanned ten men himself.

Sweeney's great work seemed to make Radbourne jealous, and he began to sulk. When called upon to pitch, he would throw the ball as hard as possible, and he was continually crossing his catcher, Barney Gilligan, and arguing about the signs. By this time Sweeney had a lame arm, or so he said, and Radbourne told Bancroft that if he had to do all the pitching himself, he wanted more money. The Old Hoss then became so quarrelsome and his work in games so careless that he was suspended, and Providence, boasting the two greatest pitchers in baseball, actually had no pitcher at all.

The Grays went up to Woonsocket, Rhode Island, for an exhibition game one day, and Sweeney showed up at the park drunk and in the company of a lady friend. After the game he refused to accompany the team home, saying he would follow on a later train. He got back to Providence the following day, and although still under the weather was permitted to pitch against the Phillies. He had them beat, 6 to 2, at the end of seven innings, and Bancroft thought he ought to change places with the right fielder, Joe Miller, and rest his arm for the following day's game, Radbourne still being under suspension. But when ordered to the outfield, Sweeney walked instead to the clubhouse and began putting on his street clothes. Bancroft raced after him, but Sweeney swore at him, finished dressing and walked off. The Grays never saw him again, as he joined St. Louis of the Union Association. Meanwhile, Providence had to finish the game with only eight players, a circumstance that complicated their defense. Miller pitched through the eighth without trouble, but in the ninth the Phillies punctured the sparse alignment against them, scored eight runs and won the game, 10 to 6.

"All hope of winning the pennant in this city has been abandoned," said a dispatch from Providence to the Boston *Globe*. "The Providence management, after extraordinary efforts to get a good team together, and after having given the players every opportunity to make a good record for themselves, allowing them full pay when disabled and providing surgical treatment when 'bunged up' seem to have been sold out, and by men who made their fame in the profession in this club. Radbourne was the first to show signs of disaffection, and is charged with throwing a game last week. Everything seems to indicate that Sweeney has received an offer of better terms from some other quarter; besides, when told that he would be let off without pay, he sneeringly replied that he did not care; he could make more money by not playing."

But the defection of Sweeney, which seems to have been planned, was just the tonic that Radbourne needed. Reinstated immediately because he was the only able pitcher on the club, the Old Hoss really went to work. Although he did not, as legend has it, pitch every inning for the remainder of the season, he did pitch thirty-six out of the next thirty-nine games, including twenty-two in a row. Eleven of his sixty victories were shutouts. Some mornings his arm was so sore he could barely raise it, but by late afternoon he was almost always able to mystify the opposition.

Sweeney did not do badly either, at least not right away. Although he did not report to St. Louis until August, he won twenty-four games in what remained of the season, losing only eight. But it was his last winning year. After a few more seasons he drifted out to California and was sentenced to prison for eight years on a manslaughter charge after a fatal saloon fight with a rough named Con McManus. He died in 1902, soon after his release.

Radbourne capped his great year by pitching and winning three games in as many days in the first World's Series ever played, defeating the Metropolitans, champions of the American Association, 6 to 0, 3 to 1, and 12 to 2, allowing ten hits in the three games. Some historians have written that the first World's Series took place in 1882 when the Chicago White Stockings, victors in the National League, met the Cincinnati Reds of the American Association. Each team had won once when that series was abandoned, and although it marked the first post-season meeting of champions, there was no title at stake. The Reds and White Stockings both had numerous postseason games scheduled, and the fact that each team had won its respective league race was incidental.

The real father of the World's Series was Jim Mutrie, manager of the Metropolitans. It was he who issued the original challenge for the event, and here are the terms of his proposal as reported by the Boston *Herald* on September 30, 1884:

> NEW YORK—As there is no longer any doubt that the Metropolitans will carry off the American Association championship pennant of '84, Manager Mutrie today issued a challenge to the Providence club, the champion league team of '84, to play them a series of five games for the championship of the United States and $1,000 a side, under the following conditions: two games to be played under the National League rules and two under the

American Association rules. The manner and place of the playing of the fifth game are to be decided thereafter. The $1,000 to go to the poor of the city represented by the club winning the greater number of games. Manager Mutrie thinks he can play a strong game against the Providence team, and, should the Mets succeed in winning the series, they will make an extensive tour through the South.

Frank Bancroft, manager of the Grays, at first turned down the Mutrie challenge, observing that he did not intend to add to the financial success of a rival league; but when public pressure was applied, he changed his mind. Radbourne then personally handled the challenge by the Mets, exhibiting the same near-perfect pitching that he had employed all year.

But Radbourne and Sweeney, with all their heroics, were not the only exciting pitchers of 1884. Hugh Daly, the one-armed twirler, spent the year with the Chicago Unions, and although he lost more games than he won, there were days on which he was superb. One of them was on July 7, when he duplicated Sweeney's feat of whiffing nineteen batters. The Boston Unions were his victims, and Daly beat them, 5 to 0, allowing only one hit, a sixth-inning triple by Cannonball Crane.

"A pitcher never had nine baseball players so completely at his mercy as did the one-armed Daly yesterday afternoon, when the thick coat of whitewash was administered to the local Union team," said the Boston *Herald*. "He was so skilful, and employed so many ins and outs and drops that when the ball did come over the base the home players would stand and look at it as if dazed while the umpire called a strike. But when some tremendous curve would shoot the ball way out to one side, the batsman would bang the air viciously and smile to think how nicely the wily pitcher had fooled him. Nineteen times did a Boston boy step to the plate and retire to the bench as the umpire shouted, 'Three strikes and out.' But for a missed third strike by Krieg, twenty men would have retired in this manner on the Boston side."

Another great pitcher that season was Gentle Jim Galvin, who worked for Buffalo of the National League. In Detroit on August 2 Galvin beat the Wolverines, 2 to 0, and yielded only one hit, a single by Charlie Bennett. After a day's rest, he pitched a no-hitter against the same team, winning, 18 to 0. The only runner to reach base got there in the ninth when Dan Brouthers, the big Buffalo first baseman, dropped a thrown ball. In the third game of the set Galvin allowed three hits, two by Ned Hanlon and one by Bennett, but earned his third shutout in five days, giving up only four safeties in the three games.

Smiling Mickey Welch was another superlative pitcher. Welch was employed by the New York Maroons, soon to be known as the Giants. Against Cleveland at the Polo Grounds on August 28 he struck out the first nine batters, coasting to a 10 to 2 victory. This unprecedented feat went unnoticed for years, and was discovered by Harry Simmons, now secretary of the International League. When the Maroons won their first twelve games that season, their followers began to sniff a pennant, but first Providence and then Boston and Buffalo passed them. Welch finished with a record of thirty-eight and twenty-two.

But the year of 1884 was important not only because of the events of the playing field but also because of happenings in the front offices of the game. It was a time of expansion far in excess of anything previously known. More than three hundred players made their first appearances in major league scores that year, three times as many recruits as come along in a season today. Newspapers that had previously ignored baseball began to cover it in earnest, and the enthusiasm that originated in the three major leagues radiated down through the numerous minor circuits that started to shoot up.

The Union Association, though losing its fight for recognition, was an attempt by outsiders to cut into the profits of the game. Henry V. Lucas, a wealthy young man from St. Louis, was the originator of the league, and only faulty organization prevented him from succeeding. The circuit was formed at a meeting in Pittsburgh on September 12, 1883, and the open warfare that was to come resulted from a resolution that was adopted, as follows: "Resolved, while we recognize the validity of all contracts made by the League and Association clubs, we cannot recognize any agreement whereby any number of ballplayers may be reserved by any club beyond the term of the contract with said club."

That was the first attempt to fight the reserve clause, a battle that has continued, from time to time, until this day. When the Unions began to invade major league cities, the newspapers started to take sides and whipped up interest in baseball everywhere. Hardly a day passed without some sensational rumor about a star jumping from one club to another, and until it was definitely decided that the Unions would not operate in 1885, the turmoil continued after the playing schedules had been completed.

Lucas lost a fortune in the Union venture, so much so that he had to go to work as a passenger agent for a railroad. By the time the Brotherhood League was organized in 1890, bringing on another costly war, he was merely a spectator.

The fates were not always kind to the pioneers of the game, and that was particularly true in the case of Jim Mutrie, the manager of the Metropolitans whose challenge brought about the first World's Series.

One day during the 1920's, Charlie Stoneham, owner of the Giants, was sitting in his box at the Polo Grounds.

"Charlie," said a friend of his. "Have you noticed that old man who works on the turnstile down near the pass gate?"

"I think I know the one you mean," Stoneham replied.

"Do you know who he is?"

"No."

"That's Jim Mutrie, the first owner the Giants ever had."

It is to the credit of Charlie Stoneham that Jim Mutrie, after that, did no more gate tending. The Giants provided him with a pension that made his last days a little easier.

XXIV
Raking the Embers

Every ballplayer dreads the day he knows eventually must arrive. No matter how great he has been, there always comes the time when his body can no longer respond, when his legs fail and his reflexes slow. Fans may think of baseball as a game that is fun to play, and as a child it is, but to the aging professional each succeeding season engenders more physical punishment than the one before. Spectators are inclined to be amused when a player complains of hardships: they see no hardships in Pullman travel, double shrimp cocktails and mash notes. For them the horribly named twi-night doubleheader is a time to buy hot dogs and swill beer.

But baseball *is* hard work, doubly hard on the boiled skin of a diamond on a Sunday afternoon in August in such stifling places as Washington and St. Louis; and it is not made easier by the gallery that is ever ready to jeer. The thick-skinned veterans, hardened to their craft, can overlook the catcalls of the mob, but there is no way to overlook the bruised muscles that do not heal or the arm that is chronically sore. The batting eye is the last to go—Rogers Hornsby, at fifty-seven, could hit line drives.

The ballplayer has to retire at an age when men in most occupations are just beginning to enjoy the years of greatest earning power. The player is forced to give up the occupation in which he spends years to attain proficiency and start all over again in some business that is foreign and often distasteful to him. For baseball gets into the blood.

Where do they go, these men who once played baseball for a living? What becomes of them in later life? What other occupations can they follow?

Very often they go back to the little towns that spawned them, and for a while bask in the celebrity that is properly theirs. But they sometimes discover that their neighbors, with whom they grew up, have not necessarily been cheering them on through the years. Friends with less talent or no talent often resent them. When the players learn this, they are greatly disillusioned, and some have psychological difficulties as a result.

Most players today can make this adjustment and pursue less exciting careers that bring a moderate satisfaction. More than ever before players plan for the future, and a few have educated themselves with a definite objective in mind.

The Phillies, in 1953, organized their former players into an alumni group. Bob Carpenter, the president of the team, sent to each a season pass and the first of a regular series of news letters, so that the Phillies of yesterday might keep abreast of their old club's progress. The response by the players was a spontaneous burst of gratitude and surprise.

Russell Miller, a pitcher for the team in 1927 and 1928, seemed to be speaking for them all when he wrote:

"Thanks for your fine gesture. I have often wondered why baseball was so cold; cutting off possibly valuable connections with former players who, however insignificant, might some day be able to do them a good turn.

"Baseball has its sentiments, and every player who ever was fortunate enough to play with a major league team is proud of that achievement and has fond memories of the acquaintances and associations, and the achievements, however mediocre.

"I wasn't much of a player or very valuable property, and I guess we were rather a lousy team in 1927 and 1928, but I'll never forget the gang I played with and against.

"I still follow the records and movements of the few old-timers whom I played with or against. I have often wondered why club owners completely abandon the great majority of their former players. I personally know that the players never forget each other.

"For many years after quitting I kept up my interest by working with youngsters, my own two and others, hoping to benefit the game in some way."

One remarkable aspect of the Phillies' survey of former players is the wide range of their present occupations. Here are a few of the jobs that they hold:

Adding machine dealer	Hardware merchant
Analyst in textile machinery	Heat treater
Anhydrous ammonia worker	Industrial relations chief
Antique dealer	Inspector
Architect	Insulation service worker
Athletic director	Insurance agent
Attorney	Internal Revenue chief
Automobile salesman	Investigator
Beer salesman	Justice of the Peace
Biscuit salesman	Landscaping contractor
Citrus grower	Liquor store owner
Clerk	Loftsman
Coach	Lumber dealer
Coal company executive	Machinist
County Agricultural Agent	Minor league executive
Detective	Plumbing contractor
Dispatcher	Printer
Dry cleaning plant owner	Promotion director
Electrician	Radio dealer
Estate analyst	Railroader
Farmer	Railway express agent
Fireman	Real Estate dealer
Furniture salesman	Recreation director
Game warden	Recreation parlor owner
Gas company manager	Refinery operator
Golf professional	Restaurant owner
Guard	Roofing contractor
Scout, baseball	Theatre manager
Service station operator	Truck driver
Sporting goods buyer	Umpire
Sporting goods dealer	Welder
Sports writer	Welfare worker
Steelworker	Wholesaler
Telephone company worker	Yardmaster
Textile worker	Zinc worker

The ability to play baseball prepares men for few of these occupations. The game cannot begin to absorb its players, even the major leaguers, as minor league managers, or as scouts, coaches and umpires. Opportunities are few in such allied fields as college coaching and the sporting-goods industry. But despite the disadvantage of a late start and little preparation, these men have found a variety of occupations that range alphabetically, as the list shows, from adding machine dealer to zinc worker.

At present time a cancer foundation has undertaken an enormous study to try to determine whether there is any connection between cancer of the tongue and the practice of chewing tobacco. Because, in the old days, so many players chewed, the foundation is gathering death data on every major league player. When the director of the project first wrote to the Commissioner of Baseball, he was astonished to learn that the game kept no records of its former players, and that help from that source would be out of the question. Fortunately, however, private individuals who try to keep such records were able to supply the data that was needed.

The Phillies and the Reds are the only big league clubs who have ever even attempted to determine the whereabouts of their former players, but that at least is a start, and the day may yet come when all sixteen teams will acquaint themselves with their own personnel.

The deaths of former major leaguers are discovered at the rate of about one a week, and it is probable that these men now live longer than they once did, but no accurate statistics on that subject are yet possible. It is known that the men who entered the National League between the years of 1876 and 1883 died at an average age of sixty-two. The big killers in those days were tuberculosis and typhoid fever. Those two plagues have now been largely conquered, and today heart disease is by far the greatest cause of death with cancer in second place.

Anyone who will bother to read carefully the newspapers of a half century and more ago will be struck by the criminal indifference to suffering that was commonplace. Former players, like people in all walks of life, died on the street like insects, or struggled miserably to live under conditions of indescribable squalor. There were individual philanthropies, but the theory that the government should concern itself with the welfare of citizens was yet to be practiced. The result was that the great majority of players joined the ranks of the unemployed. A fortunate few became bartenders, policemen and firemen or assumed some petty post in ward politics. The garbage of

Utica, New York, was for years collected by one of the greatest hitters of the eighties, at the same time that the garbage of Lynn, Massachusetts, was sorted daily by a once famous catcher. But such jobs went to those who were favored by fortune, and the others became lookouts for handbook operators, bouncers in low bistros, or else took up street begging to get enough money for liquor. No one asked for whom the bell tolled in those days.

Exaggerated? Well, consider what has happened to some of the men who played for one particular team, the Cincinnati Reds. The cause of death of 180 Redleg alumni has been determined, and although forty-three were carried off by heart trouble, sixteen by pneumonia, fifteen by tuberculosis and twelve by cancer, eleven were fatally injured in traffic accidents, nine committed suicide, six were murdered, one was hanged, four died of paresis, one of acute alcoholism, one killed by a pitched ball, one killed in battle, one burned in a chemical plant, one killed in a shipyard accident, one in an airplane crash, one in a hunting accident, one in a factory accident, one fell from a trestle and one was blown up in a copper mine explosion.

It is strange and striking how many players die violently. Suicides, murders and accidental deaths occur among players at a much greater rate than among the population at large. Bill Bryson and Howard Kluender have also investigated this subject. They quoted government statistics showing that the violent death rate per nine thousand population (the approximate number of men who have played major league ball) is: suicide, 2.3; homicide, .48; and accident, 6.6. Among players, Bryson and Kluender found, the rates are: suicide, 17; homicide, 13; accident, 47. It should be remembered, however, that athletes often take up occupations that involve physical peril. They become policemen, firemen and construction workers, and are subjected to the risks of being shot, being hit by falling weights or falling themselves.

This does still not explain the high incidence of suicide, which is probably accounted for by the psychological readjustment necessary when a player retires from the diamond. The ones who are not able to adjust themselves to a less spectacular life simply crack up.

In an earlier chapter the case of Henry Kessler, the player who set fire to a hotel at Franklin, Pennsylvania, was cited. Kessler committed his act of arson in December, 1884, and it is a little late in the game to search for a motive. But there is a clue in the New York *Clipper*. Several years before his retirement, Kess and a fellow player from Brooklyn, Jake Knowdell, drifted out to Colorado and became attached to a team known as the Leadville Blues. One night they awoke in their room at the Hotel Windsor in Leadville, smelling smoke and hearing the crackling of flames. They roused other sleepers and escorted several of them to safety, and were cited as heroes, first by the local press and then by the *Clipper*.

Later, too old to play baseball and unfit for any other occupation, Kessler certainly must have brooded over his fate, recalling the days when he was prominent in his profession. Frequently in his cups, he must have often thought of his heroic role in the fire at Leadville. Perhaps his twisted mind told him that the only way he could recapture the glory of that high moment was to create another such fire. If such an explanation is acceptable to psychiatrists it might also help explain the high rate of violence that awaits so many former players.

Baseball is at last getting around to honoring its dead. The shrine at Cooperstown is a splendid tribute to the game's greatest players, but recognition should also be extended to the lesser heroes. That too seems to be coming.

Warren Giles, now the president of the National League, performed a highly public-spirited act while serving as president of the Reds by giving recognition to a forgotten hero of his team, Charlie Gould.

Gould was the only native Cincinnatian on the Red Stockings of 1869, and later he served as the club's first manager in the National League. Released because his players were not good enough to make a strong showing, he served as the team's groundskeeper for one season, caught on as a clerk in the city's police department, and eventually became a street-car conductor on a route that, ironically enough, passed the ball park where he had once doffed his hat to cheers. But in the shuffle of city life he was soon lost sight of, and when he died of apoplexy in 1917, there were few to remember and fewer to mourn.

Giles heard about Gould's fate in 1950 and learned the location of his nameless grave. He arranged for the erection of a suitable monument, and when the season opened the entire team took part in memorial services, and Gould's grandchildren were brought on to help dedicate the shaft of granite.

The better-educated players of the present time are more highly equipped to cope with the realities of life after their careers are spent, but all of them are nevertheless sentimental enough to treasure their memories of the diamond.

They love, as fans do, the warmth of baseball conversation around the old hot stove, but mostly they look forward to the coming of another season. For despite his hundreds of visits to ball parks the veteran player or fan knows nothing that can equal the thrill of opening day, with its circus atmosphere of high excitement, the pushing throng at the turnstile, the smell of mustard, the cry of the vendors and the neat geometry of the friendly and familiar field.

Index

McGinnity, "Iron Man," 67
McGraw, John (Muggsy), 16–17, 21,
    26–27, 33, 37, 49, 67, 90, 96,
    113, 118–119, 123, 164,
    186–187
  Mrs., 164
McJunkin, Fred, 157
McKean, James, 152
McKechnie, Bill, 18, 71
McLean, Billy, 125
McMasters, Jack, 114
McMillin, A. N. (Bo), 140
McMullen, Hugh, 36
McNichol, Bob, 130
McVey, Calvin, 145
Meacham, Louis, 51
Meany, Tom, 3, 69
Medwick, Ducky, 11
Meine, Henry William (Heinie), 17
Merkle, Fred, 131
Merrill, H. G., 28
Metkovich, George (Catfish), 16
Meusel, Bob, 36
Meusel, Emil, 36
Meyers, John, 85
Michaels, Cass, 3
Milan, Clyde, 31
Milan, Horace, 31
Miller, Clyde, 105
Miller, Edmund (Bing), 18
Miller, George, 53
Miller, Joe, 191
Miller, Russell, 197
Mitchell, Bobby, 53
Mitchell, Virne Beatrice (Jackie),
    157–159
Mize, Johnny, 176, 179
Mizell, "Vinegar Bend," 13
Moore, D. C. (Dee), 5

Moore, Eddie, 79
Moore, Joe Gregg, 6
Moore, Wilcy, 137
Mooty, J. T. (Jake), 5
Morgan, Tom, 64
Moriarty, George, 129
Morrill, John, 186, 190
Morrison, Johnny (Jughandle), 75,
    133
Morrissey, John, 152
Moses, Wally, 21
Moss, Malcolm, 58
Moss, Woodson, 58–59
Muckenfuss, Benjamin Stewart, 22
Mueller, Don, 59
Mueller, Leroy, 59
Mueller, Ray, 187
Mueller, Walter, 59
Mullane, Tony, 34, 155, 162
Murnane, Tim, 87, 102
Murphy, Charlie, 131
Murphy, Johnny (Grandma), 16, 141
Murray, William J., 98
Musial, Stan, 72, 181
Mutrie, Jim, 166, 192, 195

Nava, Vincent, 25
Naymick, Mike, 45
Nelson, Lynn (Line Drive), 16
Neun, Johnny, 103
Niarhos, Gus, 23
Nichols, Al, 151, 153
Nichting, Ray, 72
Northey, Ronnie, 36
Nushida, Kenso, 23
Nuxhall, Joe, 71

Oakes, "Rebel," 13
Oana, Henry (Prince), 23